Volume 1

A first look at the brief account of the lives of some of the 313 Companions of the Promised Messiah (peace be upon him)

By Bashir Ahmad Hayat

Fountains of Life

First edition published in July 2011

ISBN: 978-0-85525-997-6

CONTENTS

بسم اللہ الرحمن الرحیم

نَحْمَدُهٗ وَنُصَلِّی عَلٰی رَسُوْلِهِ الْکَرِیْمِ وَعَلٰی عَبْدِهِ الْمَسِیْحِ الْمَوْعُوْدِ

خدا کے فضل اور رحم کے ساتھ

ھوالنّــاصر

لندن

07 / 07 / 10

مکرم رفیق احمد حیات صاحب

السلام علیکم ورحمۃ اللہ وبرکاتہ

آپ کا خط ملا جس میں آپ نے یہ لکھ کر کہ آپ اپنے والد مکرم بشیر احمد حیات صاحب کے اکٹھے کئے ہوئے صحابہ اور بزرگان سلسلہ کے حالاتِ زندگی شائع کرنا چاہتے ہیں مجھ سے بھی کچھ لکھنے کی خواہش کا اظہار کیا ہے۔ انہوں نے ماشاء اللہ یہ بہت مفید اور بابرکت کام کیا ہے۔ جماعت کے ابتدائی لوگوں نے جن مشکل حالات میں بیعتیں کیں اور اخلاص و وفا کے اعلیٰ معیار قائم کئے بعد میں آنے والوں کو ان کے حالات سے ضرور آگاہ کرنا چاہئے۔ وہ نیکی اور تقویٰ اور دینی فہم کے اعتبار سے بہت بلند مرتبہ رکھتے تھے اور تقویٰ اور اخلاص ہی بیعت کا خلاصہ ہے۔

صحابہ تو وہ لوگ ہیں جنہوں نے قربانیاں دیں اور جماعت کو آگے پھیلانے میں حضرت مسیح موعود علیہ السلام سے تربیت پاکر نہایت اہم کردار ادا کیا۔ اس لئے ان کا ذکرِ خیر چلتے رہنا چاہئے۔ اسی طرح جماعت کے جو دوسرے خدمت گزار ہیں ان کا بھی نیک ذکر ہمیشہ جاری رہنا چاہئے تاکہ آئندہ نسلوں کو تحریک پیدا ہوتی رہے کہ ہم نے بھی ان کے نقشِ قدم پر چلتے ہوئے نیکی کے کام کرنے ہیں اور جماعت کی ترقی کے لئے کوشاں رہنا ہے۔

اللہ تعالیٰ آپ کے مرحوم والد کی نیک کاوش کو قبول فرمائے اور آپ کو اس کی تکمیل کی توفیق دے۔ آمین

والسلام

خاکسار

[signature]

خلیفۃ المسیح الخامس

نقل دفتر P.S لندن

Respected Rafiq Ahmad Hayat sahib,

Assalamoalaikum warahamatullahe wabarakathu

Your letter expressing a wish that I write something regarding the life stories of companions and elders of the movement, as collated by your respected father Bashir Ahmad Hayat sahib, which you want to publish, has been received. MashaAllah, this is a very helpful and blessed task undertaken by him. Those who join [the Community] later should certainly be informed about the circumstances of the earlier people of the Community who took Bai'ats in difficult conditions and set excellent standards of loyalty and sincerity. They had a very high status as regards piety, Taqwa (righteousness) and religious insight. Indeed, Taqwa and sincerity alone are the summation of Bai'at.

The companions were the people who gave sacrifices and having received Tarbiyyat from the Promised Messiah (on whom be peace), played an extremely important role in broadening the Community further. This is why their acclamation should carry on. Likewise, citation of others who serve the Community should also always continue so that the next generations are inspired to follow them in doing pious works and in endeavouring for the progress of the Community.

May Allah the Exalted accept the virtuous effort of your late father and enable you to accomplish it. Ameen.

Wassalam

Humbly

Khalifatul Masih V

Messages of support and approval from Hadhrat Khalifatul Masih IV

London
9.5.92

Mr Bashir Ahmad Khan Rafiq
Additional Wakilul Tasneef

السلام علیکم ورحمۃ اللہ وبرکاتہ

During a question and answer session Mr Bashir Hayat proposed that a book should be published in English on a brief introduction of various dignitaries of the Jama'at and heads of families who initiated the message of Ahmadiyyat in their families. I responded that the proposal was good and in the absence of sufficient staff I instructed him to personally undertake this work. Therefore during this period he reviewed some books and contacted several individuals and managed to deduce summarised narrations regarding two hundred persons and has presented this material in three volumes. But before the publication of this material the Jama'at needs to take a few necessary steps.

Firstly whether or not the dignitaries who have been mentioned or their families are wiling to co-operate with the Jama'at regarding the following two issues:

1. How much will they contribute wholeheartedly to cover the expenses of its printing and publication?

2. The relevant material should be sent to the dignitaries or the present heads of the families of these famous personalities and some intellectual, intelligent and pious members of the families may be asked to review and make sure that no important and faith inspiring aspect of their life has been ignored. Furthermore they should inform us about different parts of the world where their family members have settled including the bounties of Allah with which the family has been blessed by Allah. The present accounts do not reflect these points and it is the duty of the progeny of these dignitaries to prepare an account of such points without any

exaggeration. These points should not exceptionally highlight a particular individual rather it should include data and general discussions of Allah's blessings which were bestowed upon their family.

The people to whom this draft is being sent should, provided they are unable to respond to our request due to lack of time or for any other reason, propose alternative names of people who could be contacted to do this job in a better way. If possible members of the family can themselves make a committee to complete this job together. The worldwide Ahmadis will benefit by reading this book and Allah will reward not only the dignitaries mentioned in the book but all their (co-operative) children who will help in the completion of this task. It is hoped that people will derive maximum benefit from these precious drafts compiled by Mr Bashir Hayat who has worked with a lot of sincerity, hard work and dedication.

You can draft a letter to the members of these families mentioning my instructions which should have a follow up. Mr Bashir Hayat will offer his services to you and should proceed with this task under your supervision. (I am sending you three volumes of the draft).

Wassalam

Mirza Tahir Ahmad
Khalifatul Masih IV

cc: Mr Bashir Hayat

London
26.11.1370 Hijri

Nazir Sahib Isha'at Rabwah

السلام علیکم ورحمۃ اللہ وبرکاتہ

On my instructions Mr Bashir Ahmad Hayat of London is compiling in English language the memoirs regarding the life histories of various heads of Ahmadi Families and dignitaries of the Jama'at. He will be visiting Pakistan for a while. You should render full co-operation and guidance to him regarding this project. Jazakallah.

Wasalam

Mirza Tahir Ahmad
Khalifatul Masih IV

Bashir Hayat Sahib asking one of his many question during a Question and Answer session with Hadhrat Khalifatul Masih Iv(ru)

Private Secretary
to
Hazrat Khalifatul Masih IV

3rd May 1992

Mr Bashir Ahmad Hayat,

السلام علیکم ورحمة اللہ وبرکاتہ

Your letter dated 30th April 1992 was received by Huzur Aqdas. Huzur Anwar has instructed about the book you have complied on the life histories of the heads of different Ahmadi families and dignitaries of the Jama'at that because it has a mention about those distinguished personalities who spread the life-giving message of Ahmadiyyat to their families hence the book can be named accordingly as "Fountains of Life" which in Urdu will be translated as "Sarchashma Hayat". In the Preface the reason for naming this book as "Fountains of Life" can be explained. As regards the publication of this in Review of Religions Huzur Anwar has granted permission to go ahead with the publication.

May Allah make this book useful and beneficial.

Wasalam

Naseer Ahmad Qamar

Publication Office
London Mosque
cc: PS Office

About the Author

Mr Bashir Ahmad Hayat (Late)

The late Bashir Ahmad Hayat, the compiler of this work, was born in Sialkot, India (now Pakistan) on 28th November 1920. His father, Mr Muhammad Umar Hayat, accepted Ahmadiyyat during the Khilafat of Hadhrat Fazle Umar, Khalifatul Masih II(ra). Mr. Umar Hayat served in the Indian Army during the First World War. He then moved to Kenya, in the early 1920s and was one of the first Ahmadis who took the message of Ahmadiyyat to that part of the world. He died in 1968. Bashir Hayat Sahib's mother, Mrs. Karam Bibi, also a very pious Ahmadi woman, had passed away in 1946. Both were buried in Kisumu, Kenya. Mr. Muhammad Umar Hayat, his wife, Mrs. Karam Bibi and his son Bashir Ahmad Hayat's names are also included in the First List (Daftar Awwal) of the five thousand contributors to the Tahrik Jadid Fund.

After completing his primary education in Sialkot, Mr. Bashir Ahmad Hayat moved to Qadian, India. There he completed his matriculation examination in 1938. He then went on to study at Murray College, Sialkot from 1939 to 1942. By 1944 he had established a successful business in Kisumu.

Mr Bashir Ahmad Hayat was also the first Financial Secretary of the Kisumu Jama'at, which was formed under the Presidency of Qazi Abdus-Salam Bhatti Sahib. The Late Sheikh Mubarak Ahmad Sahib also visited the Jama'at and a strong Tabligh (Preaching) campaign was launched in the Nyanza Province of Kenya. An aggressive opposition was launched by non-Ahmadis but by the grace of Allah and with the efforts of the Jama'at and Missionaries like Choudhry Inayat Ullah Sahib, Maulana Muhammad Munawar Sahib, Sheikh Amri Abedi Sahib, Maulana Abdul Karim Sharma Sahib and other active and sincere members, the Ahmadiyya Community was established around Kisumu. In Kisumu, through Bashir Hayat Sahib's efforts, a local resident, Mr Fazal Ahmad Odder also accepted Ahmadiyyat.

Bashir Hayat Sahib took a keen interest in the general affairs of primary schools in Nairobi. He served on various school committees of the Education Department of City Council of Nairobi. He held different offices in the Nairobi Jama'at including Zaeem Ansarullah. For several years, he was the Muhasib (Accountant) for Jama'at Ahmadiyya, Nairobi, Kenya.

Bashir Hayat Sahib moved to Nairobi in 1950 where he took up employment with Kenya Shell Limited in their Finance Department until 1968 when he moved with his family to settle in London. In 1969, he gained employment at New Scotland Yard and remained in this Civil post till his retirement in 1985.

Bashir Hayat Sahib also held various offices within the UK Ahmadiyya Jama'at. He worked with such respected people as Hadhrat Sir Chaudhry Muhammad Zafrulla Khan Sahib, Bashir Ahmad Rafiq Khan Sahib, Sheikh Mubarak Ahmad Sahib and many others. He held the office of Secretary of the Nusrat Jehan Scheme, UK in early 1970s. He was also appointed Secretary Talim and Tarbiyyat and Zaeem Ansarullah for Wimbledon Park Jama'at, London.

Bashir Hayat Sahib was married to Safia Begun Hayat, daughter of Maulawi Qamar-ud-Din Sahib of Rabwah, Pakistan. His wife, Safia Hayat Sahiba was born at Qadian, India on 9th April l927. After her marriage in 1948, she accompanied her husband to Kenya where she took an active part in the Lajna Imaillah of Nairobi. She moved to London in 1968 where she worked for over ten years as Sadr (In-charge) Halqa (Nigran) Southfields Branch of Lajna Imaillah. Along with the official tasks of the Jama'at, she devoted much attention to teaching young children in the recitation of the Holy Qur'an. Following the arrival of Hadhrat Khalifatul Masih IV(ru) in 1984, Bashir Hayat Sahib became a popular personality throughout the world for his participation in 'Majlis-e-Irfan' (Question and Answer) sessions of Hadhrat Khalifatul Masih IV(ru) which were broadcast regularly on MTA (Muslim Television Ahmadiyya). He

also complied a book entitled *Basic Knowledge About Islam*.

Mr. Bashir Hayat sahib and his wife Mrs Safia Begum Hayat both joined the Nizam-e-Wasiyyat. They have four sons, one daughter and many grandchildren. His children are, Mr Rafiq Ahmad Hayat (present Amir of the Ahmadiyya Jama'at UK), Mr Laiq Ahmad Hayat, Mrs. Bushra Malik, Mr Zaheer Ahmad Hayat and Mr. Nasir Ahmad Hayat.

Bashir Ahmad Hayat Sahib passed away on 8th March 2003 after a short illness. He was preparing to participate in one of the Majlis-e-Irfan to be held in the evening on Friday 7th March 2003. He suddenly fell ill and passed away the following morning at the hospital – Inna Lillahe Wa Inna Ilehe Rajioon. It is sad that this book could not come into print during his lifetime. We hope, however that the excellent work he carried out with such a zeal and devotion will make a very faith-inspiring reading.

Hadhrat Khalifatul Masih IV(ru) proposed the name of the book Fountains of Life when he was shown the first draft of the book. Hadhrat Khalifatul Masih IV(ru) himself guided Bashir Hayat Sahib and Hashim Saeed Sahib on several occasions during the compilation of the book. Hashim Saeed Sahib assisted Bashir Ahmad Hayat Sahib in compiling this work into book form.

On the gravestone of Bashir Ahmad Hayat, the following inscription has been inscribed:

Bashir Ahmad Hayat
(son of the late Umar hayat)
Born on 20th november 1920

Died peacefully at the age of 82 years on 8th March 2003.
Surely to Allah we belong and to Him shall we return.
Hadhrat Khalifatul Masih IV rehmahullah led his funeral prayer
on 12th March 2003 in the compound of the Fazl mosque and observed"
"A good pious man has departed from this world.
Our Hayat Sahib used to adorn the question/answer sessions
held after Maghrib prayers. 'Wherefore shall we see such scenes'.
As you lower his coffin in the grave bid him my Assalamo Alaikum.
He was a very dear person; I loved him & he loved me."
May Allah overwhelm him with Mercy"

(Wasiyat No: 6186)

Fountains of Life

Volume 1

A first look at the brief account of the lives of some of the 313 Companions of the Promised Messiah (peace be upon him)

By Bashir Ahmad Hayat

Introduction by Rafiq Hayat – Amir UK and eldest son of the author of this book

When my father proposed the idea of this book to Hadhrat Khalifatul Masih IV(ru) during a Majlis-e-Irfan session in September 1990, I do not think he was aware of the enormity of the task that he faced in its compilation. But even if he did from the outset, this was a project that he passionately believed should be recorded, preserved and relayed to generations to come. His endeavour never to give up is a testament to his dedication and one that I feel extremely proud of. But this fascination and desire stems from an extremely important period of the history of the Ahmadiyya Community.

At the time when these Companions pledged their allegiance to the Promised Messiah(as), the hostility they faced was immense. But how fortunate were those people who Allah had given guidance to be among those were able to take bai'at at the hands of Hadhrat Mirza Ghulam Ahmad(as). These Companions were ready and did sacrifice all they had to part of the blessed community. 313 Companions is indeed a small number to have taken bai'at but today the numbers are in millions in every part of the world and growing. The institution of Khilafat has maintained and guided this Community and it through Allah's sheer grace and mercy we expanded as indicated by God Almighty to the Promised Messiah(as) that ' I shall spread thy message to all corners of the world'. Let us not forget this was a message relayed in the early part of the last century.

Whilst the Companions did endure difficult times after accepting Ahmadiyyat, their legacy has been left in their progeny who today work tirelessly in all areas to spread the message. I encourage all readers to read the entire book.

There were 313 companions of the Promised Messiah(as) and this book, at this moment in time deals with just under 120. We hope it will encourage families of other Companions to forward details to me so that we may add to further revisions of this book. The next revision will hopefully include photos and we welcome suggestions from readers as to further improvements that can be implemented.

My father always sought to expand his mind and understanding on issues in both the religious and secular worlds. It was because of this, he became a regular fixture in all of Khalifatul Masih IV's(ru) Question and Answer sessions. His intrigue, sense of humour and gentle demeanour won the respect and friendship of Hudhur(ru). Hudhur(ru) would always be sure to make time for my father, who usually had a pocket full of questions ready to ask. In his last question and answer session my father was unable to attend, but his questions were prepared and presented by others on his behalf.

After leading the janaza prayer of my father, Hadhrat Khalifatul Masih IV(ru) went over to my father and said with great sadness: 'This will be the last time I see this face.' Hudhur(ru) then instructed us to send his heartfelt Salam to Bashir Hayat sahib before the burial.

Following the janaza prayer, my family and I went to meet Khalifatul Masih IV(ru). and he gave us words of comfort and recollected many fond memories he shared with my father. After our meeting, Hudhur(ru) sent me a letter with a message he wanted written on my father's grave stone which read:

> 'He was a very dear person; I loved him & he loved me.'

This beautifully worded sentiment still stands as a true symbol of their unique and undying friendship.

My father spent a great deal of time collating not just these reports on the Companions of the Promised Messiah(as) but also started work on another book – that of short biographies of other prominent Jama'at members who have sinced passed away. We hope to reproduce this book before the end of the year and hope just like this one, it will be a source of inspiration and enlightement. .

The Fountains of Life, Vol. 1, will be available to read on-line and until Volume 2 is published in book format, on-going content of this book will appear on-line. We therefore invite readers to submit accounts of prominent Jama'at members as well as providing any new information to existing accounts and especially welcome the submission of photos. The website, which will be regularly updated is:

www.fountainsoflife.co.uk

I wish to thank all those people who have contributed to the production of this book. There are too many to list here but they include people who have helped fund the publication, assisted in translation from Urdu to English and helped source original material and facts. May Allah bless them all.

Readers should also note that the account of the Life of the Holy Prophet Muhammad(saw) and lives of the Khulafa-e-Rashideen, the Promised Messiah(as) and the Khalifas of Ahmadiyyat are only given in brief detail. To do them any justice, complete books can be written about each of them and indeed just the life of the Holy Prophet(saw) can easily extend to hundreds of pages. On the fountains of life website, there are links to further reading in this regard.

Rafiq Ahmad Hayat
National Amir, UK

INTRODUCTION AND ACKNOWLEDGEMENTS

During the Majlis-e-Irfan session on 22nd September 1990 at Islamabad (Tilford), a humble suggestion was made by Bashir Hayat Sahib to Hadhrat Khalifatul Masih IV(ru) regarding the compilation of a reference book for our writers, missionaries and other members of the Jama'at in general, containing the brief introduction of Islam, Ahmadiyya Movement in Islam, profile of the Promised Messiah(as), a brief account of the Khalifas and largely the prominent Companions of the Promised Messiah(as). It was also suggested the life sketch of missionaries and other prominent members of the Jama'at Ahmadiyya as well as prominent Ahmadi Ladies, who rendered notable services for the cause of Ahmadiyyat, should also be included in this book.

Hudhur very kindly appreciated the need for such a book and appointed Bashir Hayat Sahib as the Secretary and authorised him to form a working committee to assist in the compiling of this book. Hudhur was to be kept informed of its progress.

The initial task took a very long time to come to reality. With the help of many sincere and helpful friends, Bashir Hayat Sahib was able to present the very early draft of this book to Hudhur at the end of May 1991. Hudhur expressed his pleasure and gave some further instructions for its completion.

The work continued rather slowly from then onwards. Bashir Hayat Sahib collected material from various sources, much of it was translated and then typed. Each chapter sometimes took months to complete. Several drafts were prepared and amended. Finally, the manuscript took the shape of a book towards the end of 1999. Work to review and retype the chapters continued and now by the grace of Allah, this compilation has been completed and is presented here in the form of a long awaited book.

This compilation in no way is claimed to be comprehensive and complete. There is always room for improve-ment. What is presented here is just a first attempt. It is hoped that this book will produce an urge to learn more about the pious people mentioned in the book. At the same time, the feedback from the learned readers will make the next edition of this book better.

The compilation of material was not without difficulties, there were many problems. Firstly, there was no proper library available to gather research material. Material that was available was mostly in Urdu, which was then translated into English by a team.

On Bashir Hayat Sahib's request, Hudhur named this compilation book, *Fountains of Life.* Hudhur suggested this name because the book contains the life account of those pious persons who were the source of delivering the life-giving message of Ahmadiyyat to their families and friends.

Many useful life accounts are taken (with little alterations where necessary) with thanks from the book, *In the Company of the Promised Messiah* by Ch. Ali Mohammad B.A., B.T. Appropriate references have been added in the book at relevant places.

Mr Bashir Hayat wrote as part of the initial introduction:

"Special thanks are made to the following people: Mr B.A. Rafiq, (former Imam of the London Mosque and Director of Ahmadiyya Muslim Publications) who rendered valuable service in raising the funds for the book and also in its preparation, and Miss Amatul Majeed Choudhary for going through the entire manuscript of the book. Also to Mr Hashim Saeed of London who looked after most aspects of the work including its publication into a book form. He worked tirelessly for many years for many years on this book. Without his great efforts this book would not have been produced. I am much grateful to him for it. I pray may Allah give him good health.

Several other distinguished members of the community assisted me in producing the material, preparing the manuscript, typing, reviewing and even proof reading. I list here their names and request you to pray for all of them.

1. Mr. Hashim Saeed
2. Mr. Bashir Ahmad Rafiq
3. Mr. Mohammad Akram Khan Ghauri
4. Mr. Bashir-u-Din Sami
5. Mr. Iqbal Ahmad
6. Mr. Muhammad Rafiq Chaudhry
7. Mr. Ally Akbar
8. Dr. Navid-ul-Haq Khan
9. Mr. Milk Hamid-ud-Din Nasir
10. Mr. Nusratullah Nasir Chowdhry
11. Mr. Maulana Abdul Majid Tahir
12. Mr. Choudhry Sardar Ahmad
13. Mr. Major (Retd.) Abdur Rahmam Mughal
14. Mr. Mian Muzaffar Ahmad Mansoor
15. Mr. Raja Masood Ahmad
16. Dr. Naseer Ahmad Mubuashar
17. Mr. Syed Abdul Haye
18. Mr. Maulawi Muhammad Siddique MA
19. Mr. Syed Naeem Ahmad Shah
20. Mr. Ahad Bhunnu
21. Mr. Bashir Anmad Akhtar
22. Mrs. Safia Begum Hayat
23. Mrs. Shakira Hayat
24 Mrs. Nuzhat Hayat
25. Mrs. Tayyeba Hayat
26. Meliha Hayat
27. Shaukia Mir
28. Tanveer Khokhar

This book is on no account exhaustive. There is much room for additions and improvements. This is my first attempt; any suggestions towards the betterment of this book will be welcomed and appreciated.

I also humbly request all those who will be benefit from this humble effort to please pray to Allah that He may enable us to serve the cause of Islam, the country and humanity as a whole throughout our lives. Amen."

Bashir Ahmad Hayat, 23 Nov, 2001

> ***Note:*** *This Introduction was written by Late Bashir Ahmad Hayat Sahib at a time when it was thought that the book is ready for publication. However, a further review was necessary and the publication was delayed*

FOUNTAINS OF LIFE

Hadhrat Khalifatul Masih IV(ru) proposed the name of the book *Fountains of Life* when he was shown the first draft of the book. Hadhrat Khalifatul Masih IV(ru) himself guided Bashir Hayat Sahib and Hashim Saeed Sahib on several occasions during the compilation of the book. Hashim Saeed Sahib assisted Bashir Ahmad Hayat Sahib in compiling this work into a book form.

This book is a compilation of just over 120 Companions of the Promised Messiah(as) and is unique in many aspects. Firstly, a single person has not written this book. Many have contributed by writing (mostly in Urdu), collating, translating, typing and reviewing the material contained in it. The one single individual who devotedly and constantly worked on it tirelessly for many years was the late Bashir Hayat Sahib himself. He was constantly on the move, meeting people and asking them to provide the material about any Companion of the Promised Messiah(as) especially from within their own family. He would follow the trail meticulously until he obtained the correct material, reviewed it himself and got it translated, if needed. This dedication is unique and unparalleled.

Secondly, this compilation consists of different styles of writing, numerous narrations of events, different feelings and emotions expressed for people mentioned therein, different naming of the terms and of course, different spellings of the same word. For example, the Founder of the Ahmadiyya Community has been written as The Promised Messiah, Masih-Maud, Hudhur, Hadhrat Sahib, Imam Mahdi, Masih and Mahdi, Spiritual Master etc., each with its own expression of unique love and affection from the writer. To keep this emotional flavour as expressed, little effort has been done to change the words into a uniform terminology, except for clarity.

Thirdly, no effort has been made to shorten or expand the details contained in or the length of each chapter except where it was felt that some details are not greatly influential and need removing or where a few more words are necessary to add for clarification. Indeed, a complete book can be written on some of the Companions of the Promised Messiah(as) but this was not the intention of this book. In each chapter, the reader will find one or more special personal aspect from the life of a particular Companion of the Promised Messiah(as). In many cases, complete books exist about their lives, but this compilation mentions only specific and special events or characteristics of the Companions. This also makes the compilation unique. No efforts have been made to adjust the length of a short version of a well-known Companion of the Promised Messiah(as) and a longer version of a relatively unknown Companion except where necessary.

As mentioned before, there is indeed room for improvement in this compilation. No claim is made for complete authenticity of each and every fact or event mentioned therein as more than 60 people have written these chapters. These improvements are two fold; First, readers are requested to inform Mr. Rafiq Hayat Sahib (National Amir Sahib, UK) who is the eldest son of Late Bashir Hayat Sahib, of any obvious mistakes in the text so that these can be rectified in the next edition of the book. Secondly, any Companion of the Promised Messiah(as) whose life sketch was sent and has not appeared in the book.

It is intended that life sketches of some female pioneers in Islam and Ahmadiyyat (including Sahabiat of the Promised Messiah(as)) which were collected by respected late Bashir Hayat Sahib, will also be included in the next edition and on the on-line version.

Muhammad – The Holy Prophet of Islam

(Peace and blessings of Allah be upon him)

The article below has been reproduced, with minor edits from www.alislam.org website: www.alislam.org/books/message/life.html

---

This comprehensive message was conveyed in verbal revelation to the Holy Prophet of Islam(saw) over a period of approximately twenty-two years (610-632), and every aspect of it was illustrated by the Holy Prophet(saw) in his own life. He has been described in the Holy Qur'an as an excellent exemplar (33:22). Also, he was commanded to announce:

> *If you love Allah, then follow me, Allah will then love you and forgive you your faults. Allah is Most Forgiving, Ever Merciful.* (3:32)

This necessitated that his life should be lived in the light of day and that a full account of it should become available. It was also necessary that his life should be multi-faceted, in the sense that he should be called upon to fill a diversity of roles, and that he should fill them to perfection. He was born in Makkah in AD 570 and lived through the first third of the seventh century. A full and detailed account of his life has come down to us and is open to study and research by seekers after truth. All this could not have been contrived by the Holy Prophet(saw) on his own. At every stage and every step of his life, the hand of God was clearly visible as Protector, Guide and Helper.

The Holy Prophet(saw) was born an orphan, his father having died a few months before his birth. His mother died when he was about six years old, and his grandfather, who was his loving and devoted guardian, died when he was eight years old. He was then passed into the care of his uncle, Abu Talib, brother of his father. Even at this early stage the Divine design is retrospectively perceptible that God Himself was his true Guardian. This is confirmed beyond question or cavil by the fact that though his childhood, boyhood and youth had been spent in the corrupt and debased society of Makkah, he arrived at his full maturity without the least suspicion of the slightest stain on his character. In later years, he was wont to say that before he received the Divine Call, he had little understanding of moral and spiritual values, yet Divine wisdom fully safeguarded him against every kind of lapse. He never paid homage to an idol, never ate of anything presented as offering to an idol, never touched liquor, nor gambled, nor took part in any of the frivolous activities of his fellow youths.

At one period of his youth, Muhammad(saw) was employed, like other young men of his age, in tending the sheep and goats of Makkah upon the neighbouring hills and valleys. On one occasion, when he was engaged in his duty in company with a lad of Quraish, he asked him to look after his flock also, so that he could go into Makkah and divert himself there as other youths were wont to divert themselves at night. But no sooner had he reached the precincts of the city than a marriage feast engaged his attention, and he soon fell asleep. On another similar occasion, he again fell asleep on his way to the city till morning. Thus he escaped temptation and no more sought after such diversions.

All the authorities agreed in ascribing to the youth of Muhammad(saw) a modesty of deportment and purity of manners rare among the people of Makkah. It was quite in keeping with his character that he should have shrunk from the coarse and licentious practices of his youthful compatriots. Endowed with a refined mind and delicate taste, reserved and meditative, he lived much within himself, and the ponderings of his heart supplied occupation for leisure hours spent by others of a lower stamp in rude sports and profligacy. The fair character and honourable bearing of the unobtrusive youth won the approbation of his fellow citizens; and by common consent, he received the title Al Ameen, meaning 'The Faithful'. After the Divine Call came to him, and his message was treated with ridicule and suspicion, he was urged by God to challenge his opponents in the words: "I have spent a whole lifetime among you before this; will you not then understand?" (10:17). Not even his bitterest enemy could point to a single incident in his previous life to which exception could have been taken.

When he arrived at the age of maturity, his uncle recommended him to Khadija, a wealthy, highly respected widow among Quraish, who, like most of her contemporaries, had a substantial interest in the trade caravans that travelled from Makkah to Yemen in the south, and to Syria in the north, so that she might employ him as her agent in a caravan that was about to set out for Syria. She readily agreed and Muhammad(saw) acquitted himself so well in the discharge of his duties that she was deeply impressed by his honesty, integrity, business acumen and his pleasing and attractive personality.

She had been twice married and had children from both marriages. Though approaching her fortieth year, she had, after the death of her second husband, received a number of proposals of marriage, which she had turned down. Now she made up her mind to sound Muhammad(saw), whether he would be willing to consider a proposal of marriage. She sent one of her maids to him on this errand. Muhammad(saw) was surprised and took counsel with his uncle, who expressed himself favourable and the match was arranged. Muhammad(saw) was twenty-five years of age and thus fifteen years Khadija's junior.

The marriage, despite the disparity in age and affluence, proved a very happy one. Khadija bore Muhammad(saw) several children; of these, the sons died in infancy, but the daughters grew to womanhood and in due course married. The descendants of only one daughter, Fatima, (who was married to the Prophet's cousin, Ali, son of his uncle, Abu Talib), have survived. All those who today claim direct descent from the Holy Prophet(saw) are descended through Fatima and her two sons, Hasan and Husain.

Muhammad was a loving and affectionate husband, showing tender regard and consideration for Khadija. When at home, he occupied himself in helping with the household tasks and taking care of his wife and children. He persuaded Khadija to give away the greater part of her wealth in charity to help the poor and the needy. It speaks highly of her character that she voluntarily agreed to a life of simplicity and benevolence in the company of her husband. She was so devoted to him and had come to admire him so deeply that when, fifteen years after their marriage, he received the Divine Call, she responded to it immediately, and was a constant source of comfort and support to him throughout the remaining ten years of their life together.

As time passed, Muhammad(saw) spent more and more time in contemplation and meditation. He possessed a sensitive mind and a grave and serene disposition. He felt keenly the distress of every fellow being and reacted very quickly to it, affording such relief and assistance as were within his power. On one occasion, he observed an old slave labouring hard to fulfil his task of drawing water in a heavy bucket for tending his master's garden. Muhammad(saw) went to his assistance and drew up a quantity of water, which gave relief to the old man for a short while, so that he could rest and gather his failing strength. Muhammad(saw) spoke cheering and comforting words to him, and on parting from him, said kindly: "Whenever you feel you are in need of help, you may call on Muhammad." Many such incidents are on record.

What affected his mind most deeply and painfully, however, was the moral and spiritual decline into which his people had fallen, and from which he could see no way of rescuing them, save through Divine guidance and help. For the purpose of communing with himself and imploring the light and guidance of the Supreme Being concerning the problems that troubled his mind and soul, he formed the habit of retiring, for several days at a time, to one of the hills a few miles out of Makkah. There he occupied himself in prayer and contemplation. Taking with him a modest supply of dates and water, he would spend his days and nights in self-examination, in reflecting on the problems that troubled him, and in prayer and supplication to God. There is no record of the struggle that went on in his soul during this period of retreat. In the nature of things, it is not granted to any of us to probe into the depths of another's soul, to appraise accurately and completely its travail and its ecstasies. This is a holy secret between each individual and his Maker.

Those years were, however, years of preparation, when Muhammad's(saw) soul was being deepened and proved and made ready for the heavy responsibility that the Divine will had decreed should be placed on him.

Concerning Moses(as), it is said in the Qur'an:

> *I wrapped thee with love from Me, and this I did that thou mightst be reared before My eye... We proved thee in various ways... then thou camest up to the standard, 0 Moses, and I chose Thee for Myself.* (20:40-42)

As with Moses(as), so with Muhammad(saw). He is reminded of this in the Qur'an:

> *Did He not find thee an orphan and take* thee *shelter?*
> *And he found thee wandering in search for* Him *and guided thee* unto Himself.
> *And He found thee in want and enriched* thee.
> (93:7-9)

The Commencement of Revelation

Muhammad(saw) was forty years old when the Divine Call came to him in his retreat in Hira, to which he was in the habit of repairing for prayer and contemplation. He beheld a gracious Presence, who asked him to recite. Muhammad answered that he knew not how to recite. The. Presence insisted:

> *Recite in the name of thy Lord Who created; created man from a clot of blood. Recite! Thy Lord is the Most Beneficent, Who taught man by the pen, taught him what he knew not.* (96:2-6)

Muhammad(saw) repeated the words as commanded. The Presence then vanished. Overpowered by the experience, Muhammad(saw) immediately made his way home, all atremble. He told Khadija what had happened, and expressed fearful apprehension whether a frail human being like himself would prove equal to the heavy responsibility that the incident portended God was about to lay upon him. "Surely, God will not suffer thee to fail," was Khadija's comforting response. "Thou art kind and considerate towards thy kin. Thou helpest the poor and forlorn and bearest their burdens. Thou strivest to restore the high moral qualities that thy people have lost. Thou honorest the guest and goest to the assistance of those in distress."

At Khadija's suggestion, Muhammad(saw) accompanied her to her aged cousin, Waraqa, who was a Christian hermit, and related the experience to him. Waraqa assured him, "The Angel that descended on Moses hath descended on thee. I wish I would be alive to give thee my support when thy people turn thee out." "Will they turn me out?" Muhammad(saw) exclaimed in surprise. "Never has that come to any which has come to thee," Waraqa replied, "but that his people have turned against him."

Possibly Waraq's reference to Moses(as) was prompted by the prophecy:

> 'I will raise them up a prophet from among their brethren like unto thee, and I will put My words in his mouth; and he shall speak unto them all that I shall command him. And it shall come to pass that whosoever will not hearken unto My words which he shall speak in My name, I will require it of him.'
> (Deut. 18:18-19)

It is striking that the very first revelation that came to the Holy Prophet(saw) commanded him: "Recite in the name of thy Lord". Also, every chapter of the Qur'an opens with: "In the name of God, Most Gracious, Ever Merciful."

For a while there was no further experience of the same kind; but after an interval the Holy Prophet(saw) began to receive revelation at brief intervals. He has described the experience vividly in these words: "Revelation comes to me in different ways. Sometimes the words strike directly at my heart, like the ringing of a bell, this is physically hard on me. Sometimes I hear the words as if spoken from behind a veil. At other times I see a Presence that speaks the words to me." This is confirmed by the Qur'an (42:52-52).

Four persons believed in the Holy Prophet(saw) from the very outset: his wife, Khadija; his young cousin, Ali(ra), son of his uncle, Abu Talib, a lad only eleven years of age; his freed man, Zaid, and his closest friend, Abu Bakr(ra). These four joined the Holy Prophet(saw) and undertook to help him spread the Divine Light. When this became known to the Makkahns, they laughed in derision. But they did not laugh long. Verse by verse, the revelation proceeded, until some wondered, and one by one began to be drawn to it. Soon mockery gave way to active concern. The Makkahns began to feel that the message Muhammad proclaimed, of the Oneness of God, threatened their whole way of life and their very means of subsistence. If the worship of idols was abandoned, they reasoned, Makkah would cease to be a resort for pilgrims, and lose its position as a leading town, and would see its main industry wither. Even the trade caravans might be diverted from Makkah. It was, therefore, resolved to suppress this threat to their established way of life and to their prosperity.

The new doctrine made a strong appeal to the weak and the oppressed. The slaves, who suffered extreme hardship and indignity, began to hope that the Holy Prophet's(saw) message might bring deliverance to them. Women, who were in some respects esteemed lower than animals, began to look up, and felt that the time was nigh when they might gain a position of dignity and honor beside their fathers, husbands, and sons. Young men were inspired with visions of a noble and dignified existence. The early converts came from the ranks of such as these.

As the little band grew in number, the Makkahns embarked upon a course of persecution which grew more cruel and savage as time passed, but their efforts failed to arrest the progress of the new doctrine of the Unity of God, the dignity and equality of man, and the lofty and noble goal of human existence.

Opposition and Persecution

Quraish, becoming more and more apprehensive of the inroads being made by the new doctrine, sent a delegation to Abu Talib(ra), the Holy Prophet's(saw) uncle, to whom they explained that though his nephew's denunciation of idol worship was intolerable to them, they had so far refrained from taking any extreme measure against him out of respect for Abu Talib(ra). Would he not persuade his nephew to give up preaching the new doctrine, perhaps on pain of being disowned? They made it plain that if Abu Talib(ra) did not adopt this course, they would be compelled to disown him.

Abu Talib(ra) spoke to his nephew, conveying to him what the delegation had said, but he replied firmly that while he lamented his uncle's dilemma, he was under Divine orders which he could not disobey. "Do not give up your people, uncle", said the Holy Prophet(saw). "I do not ask you to stand by me. You may disown me as they have suggested. As for me, the One and Only God is my Witness when I say that if they were to place the sun on my right and the moon on my left, I would not desist from preaching the truth that God commands. I must go on doing so until the end."

Abu Talib plunged into deep thought. He was not ready to declare his faith in the Holy Prophet(saw)'s message, but he was very fond of him and must have felt a surge of pride at his firm and noble resolve to carry out his mission as commanded by God. Finally, he raised his head, and said: "Son of my brother, go thy way; do thy duty as thou seest it; my people may disown me, but I shall stand by thee."

The tempo of persecution continued to mount and the Holy Prophet(saw) advised those of his followers who could do so to leave Makkah and migrate across the Red Sea to Abyssinia, where they would find conditions more bearable under the rule of the Christian Emperor. A small band under the leadership of a cousin of the Prophet departed for Abyssinia. A delegation of Quraish followed them, demanding of the Emperor that the fugitives be delivered to them. The Emperor heard both sides and rejected the demand of the Makkahns.

About this time, the persecuted and harassed Muslims of Makkah received some support and encouragement from the adherence of Umar, and Hamza, uncle of the Holy Prophet(saw) to Islam. But these conversions did not bring about any change in the attitude of the Makkahns. Umar(ra) was treated in the same manner as the rest of the Muslims. Indeed, the persecution grew more bitter and intense.

Aiming to starve them out, a complete boycott of the Muslims together with all members of the Prophet's family was instituted. They were blockaded within a narrow defile belonging to Abu Talib. All contact with them for any purpose whatever was forbidden. This imposed great hardship, particularly on children and old people. This terrible situation continued for nearly three years, when some leading Makkahns reacted against the savagery and inhumanity of their fellow citizens, and let it be known that they would invite the Holy Prophet(saw) and his companions to come out of their place of confinement and go about their business as before.

Thus was the blockade lifted. But the privation and hardship endured during the blockade had gravely affected the health of both Khadija and Abu Talib. Khadija died within a few days, and Abu Talib's end came a month thereafter. The death of his faithful and beloved wife left the Prophet bereft of his principal source of earthly comfort and consolation, and the death of his uncle exposed him to greater ill-treatment and persecution. In dozens of ways, his opponents made it almost impossible for him to leave his house to carry his message to any section of the people of Makkah or to those who might be on a visit there.

In this situation, the Holy Prophet(saw) decided to carry his message to Taif, a town about sixty miles south-east of Makkah, which was also a resort of pilgrimage and was more pleasantly situated than Makkah itself. On his journey to Taif, he was accompanied by Zaid, his freed man.

In Taif, the leading townsmen received the Prophet and let him have his say freely, but paid little heed to his message. After a while, they began to show signs of apprehension lest his presence in Taif might embroil them with the Makkahns, with whom they had trade relations, and whose friendship they valued. So they left him to be dealt with by street urchins and the riff-raff of the town. The Prophet and his companion were finally turned out by mocking and jeering crowds who pelted them with stones. Both were wounded and bleeding as they left Taif behind them.

The Holy Prophet(saw) was now in a ver difficult situation. He had left Makkah and he had been rejected by Taif. Under Makkahn custom, he could not go back there unless his re-entry was sponsored by some leading Makkahn. There was nowhere else to go. He prayed earnestly for light, guidance, and help, and then set out with Zaid on the return journey to Makkah.

The Holy Prophet(saw) stopped on the way at Nakhla, and sent word to Mut'am bin Adi, a leading Makkahn, asking whether he would sponsor his reentry into Makkah. Mut'am agreed, and the Prophet and Zaid thus returned to Makkah. But the situation in Makkah was as hostile and difficult as it had been when he had left it. His prayers and the revelation that came to him steadily, containing assurances of Divine help and final triumph, were his only source of consolation and strength. The latest revelations began to hint at the necessity for him to leave Makkah.

It was the town of his birth, where he had spent the whole of his life, and married, where his children had been born, and where the Divine call had come to him. Despite the bitter and cruel persecution that he and his followers continued to suffer, its people were dear to him and he knew that the parting, whenever it came, would be hard for him to bear. His life however, was completely dedicated to his mission and he was ready to carry out in good spirit whatever might be God's pleasure concerning him. The painful prospect of having to leave Makkah was, however, softened by the Divine assurance that God would surely bring him back to it (28:86).

Invitation from Madinah

In the eyes of the worldly, the Holy Prophet(saw) had arrived at a dead end. The chances of his success and of the acceptance of his message were nil. But he was steadfast, and was confident that God would open a way. It had been his custom to make contact with parties from other parts of the country who visited Makkah on the occasion of the annual pilgrimage, and to try to interest them in his mission and message. On one such occasion, he met a party of six pilgrims from Madinah, then known as Yathrib, who were encamped in a valley outside Makkah. At that time, Madinah was inhabited by two Arab and three principal Jewish tribes. The Arab tribes, Aus and Khazraj, were pagan idol worshippers, but had to some degree become familiar with the Jewish traditions. They had heard from their Jewish fellow townsmen that they were expecting the advent of a Prophet which had been foretold in their Scriptures (Deut. 18:18).

The men whom the Holy Prophet(saw) encountered on this occasion belonged to the Khazraj tribe. When he told them that God had appointed him His Messenger, and had charged him with a message for mankind, they gave him a ready and eager hearing. They were convinced of his truth and declared their faith in him and in his message, agreeing to convey it to their fellow townsmen upon their return to Madinah.

The next year, twelve of them, representing both Aus and Kharaj, who were persuaded of the truth of the Prophet, came on pilgrimage and had a secret meeting with him in which they formally pledged their allegiance to him. They also requested him to send someone to Madinah who might instruct them in the doctrine and teachings of Islam and help them to carry the Prophet's message to their brethren. The Prophet chose Mus'ab bin Umair for this purpose and dispatched him to Madinah.

When the next season of the pilgrimage came, a large and representative delegation from Madinah, seventy men and two women, met the Holy Prophet(saw) and assured him that not only were their people in Madinah ready to receive and give shelter to their brethren in faith from Makkah, but that they were eager and would be greatly honoured to receive the Holy Prophet(saw) himself if he decided to go to Madinah. On this occasion, the Holy Prophet(saw) was accompanied by his uncle, Abbas, who though he had not yet accepted Islam, was fond of the Holy Prophet(saw) and was anxious for his safety. He warned the Madinah delegation that they were undertaking a heavy responsibility in inviting the Holy Prophet(saw) to Madinah. The leader of the delegation replied that they had carefully considered all the implications involved in their invitation, and they would guard the Holy Prophet(saw) with their lives. The Prophet decided that the Muslims of Makkah would migrate to Madinah, and that for himself he would await God's command.

The Migration

Under the Holy Prophet(saw)'s direction, the Muslims in Makkah began to proceed to Madinah quietly and without creating any stir. After a short period, the only adult male Muslims left in Makkah, besides the Prophet, were Abu Bakr and Ali, and a handful of slaves, who had no choice in the matter. Quraish took alarm that the Prophet might soon move beyond their reach, and they resolved to put a violent end to him on a particular night. At this point, the Prophet received God's command to leave Makkah, and he did so in company with Abu Bakr.

When it was discovered that the Prophet had left Makkah, the Quraish organised a party to pursue him and Abu Bakr. Guided by a tracker, the party arrived outside the cave in which the two fugitives had taken shelter. The tracker assured them that the fugitives had not gone any further. He was ridiculed, as there was nowhere for anyone to go except inside the cave, and this possibility they ruled out. Who would take the risk of serious bodily harm, and possibly death, from the vipers and reptiles that abounded inside and around the cave? Abu Bakr heard the voices of Quraish in altercation and was much afraid that if their hiding place was discovered, serious harm might befall the Prophet. When he mentioned his fear, the Prophet replied: Have no fear. We are not only two, there is a third with us, i.e., God (9:40).

The pursuers returned to Makkah, foiled in their immediate objective, but firm in their purpose. They announced that anyone who brought back the Holy Prophet(saw), alive or dead, would receive a reward of one hundred camels. This was widely proclaimed in all directions.

The Holy Prophet(saw) and Abu Bakr(ra) spent two nights in the cave and on the third left for Madinah accompanied by a trusted servant of Abu Bakr(ra) and a guide. Ten days after leaving Makkah, the party arrived within sight of Madinah and were joyfully welcomed by the Muslims from Madinah and those from Makkah who had preceded them. The Holy Prophet(saw) decided to stop for a few days in Quba, a suburb of Madinah, and then proceed to Madinah. On arrival in Madinah, his first act was to purchase the site where his camel had stopped, for the purpose of building a mosque thereon. He then accepted the offer of a Muslim whose house was nearest to the selected site to put him up temporarily, while the mosque and his own quarters next to it were being built.

With the arrival of the Holy Prophet(saw) in Madinah, Islam began to spread rapidly among the two Arab tribes of the town. But, as often happens in a mass movement, not all who declared their adherences to the faith were inspired by sincerity and high ideals. It was, however, generally felt that the Holy Prophet(saw) was the most appropriate person, in the conditions and circumstances of

Madinah, to take the responsibility of administering the affairs of Madinah. Under his direction, a covenant was drawn up which was subscribed to both by Arabs and Jews. A common citizenship of Madinah was established and conditions were prescribed for the regulation of the affairs of the town as well as for organizing its internal order and external security. It was agreed that the internal affairs of each section would be regulated according to its laws and customs, but that if the security of Madinah was threatened from outside, all sections would co-operate with each other in its defense. No section would enter into any separate treaty relations with any outside tribe, nor would any section be compelled to join in any fighting that might take place outside Madinah. The final determination of disputes would be referred to the Prophet and his decision would be accepted and carried out.

Thus, the already heavy responsibilities of the Holy Prophet(saw) were augmented by the problems related to the administration of the affair of Madinah. Abdullah bin Ubayy, Chief of Khazraj, was deeply chagrined at the loss of a crown, which, before the arrival of the Prophet, he had thought was assured for him. He became the leader of the disaffected party in Madinah who became known as the hypocrites. The Jews on their part were not well disposed towards the Prophet. They were, it is true, awaiting the advent of a Prophet foretold in their scriptures (Deut. 18:18), but they felt that to accept an Arab as fulfilment of that Prophecy would raise the prestige of the Arabs above that of the Jews in the religious and spiritual spheres and this, as Jehovah's chosen people, they were not prepared to tolerate. While not daring to oppose the Prophet openly, they let no opportunity pass of intriguing and conspiring against him and the Muslims, both inside Madinah and outside.To the internal problems of Madinah and the dangers and hazards confronting the Muslims, and most of all the Prophet himself, a formidable threat was soon added from Makkah.

When the Makkahns learned that the Holy Prophet(saw) had arrived safely at Madinah, they resolved to adopt coercive measures to secure his expulsion from Madinah. They addressed a letter to Abdullah bin Ubayy, warning him and the people of Madinah that if they did not expel Holy Prophet(saw) from the city, or, failing that, did not take up against him and the Muslims, jointly with the Makkahns, the Makkahns would invade Madinah with a mighty force and put to the sword all its male adults and enslave all its women. On receipt of this ultimatum, Abdullah held a secret council of his supporters proposed that, in view of the

Makkahn threat, the only course open to them was to force the Holy Prophet(saw) and his followers to leave When news of this reached the Holy Prophet(saw), he went to Abdullah and tried to dissuade him from embarking on such a course pointing out that any such adventure could lead only to is own ruin. For the time being, Abdullah forbore, but he never abandoned the hope that an opportunity might arise when he could take measures to rid Madinah of the Holy Prophet(saw) and the Muslims, and secure his own recognition as the chief and ruler of Madinah. Thus the stage was set for open warfare between the Makkahns and the Muslims in Madinah.

All the great qualities of the Holy Prophet(saw) were now challenged and came into play. Though God's promise of succour for, and ultimate triumph of, Islam was wholly true and completely to be depended upon, God required that every effort be put forth in support of the cause. Therein lies the secret of the strength of Islam as a faith. The fullest confidence in, and reliance upon, God's grace and help, and the putting forth of the utmost effort that man is capable of, both these in combination, as taught by God Himself, help to achieve the goal. All success in every beneficent endeavor comes from God, but it follows upon sincere and steadfast effort combined with perfect trust and humble supplication to God.

The Battle of Badr

Space would not permit of even the briefest reference to all the precautions that the Holy Prophet(saw) took, and all the measures that he adopted, for the building up of the Muslim community, for the security of Madinah, and for the ultimate triumph of the faith. By way of illustration, however, a brief account might be set out of the first battle fought out in Islam. About a year after the Emigration, intelligence began to reach the Holy Prophet(saw) that the Makkahns were preparing a strong force to advance upon Madinah. Their pretext was that one of their large caravans returning from arms Syria was likely to be attacked by the Muslims at a point near Madinah, and that an adequate force had to proceed north to secure its safe passage. They may have been genuinely apprehensive concerning the caravan, in view of their declared objective of putting and an end to the Holy Prophet(saw) and the Muslims by use of force. It was a large caravan, carrying valuable merchandise and was accompanied by a sizeable armed guard. By the time the Makkahn army set out on its march north, however, news arrived that the caravan had passed safely through the danger zone. Nevertheless, the Makkahn army continued its march in the direction of Madinah.

On the side of the Muslims, permission to take up arms in defense having been accorded in Divine revelation (22:40-42), the Holy Prophet(saw) assembled a force of just over three hundred Muslims from Makkah and Madinah, and marched out with them. This heterogeneous body – it scarcely deserved the designation 'force' – was united only by the common bond of faith and the determination to die in defense of it. It included some of the older Makkahn Muslims who were good fighters, but the greater number were young men who had little, if any, combat experience. Their devotion to the faith and their zeal in its support were their only qualifications. Ill-armed, in poor physical condition, with but two horses, and.a few camels, they presented a pitiful contrast to the Makkahn army, which consisted of a thousand tried warriors, well-armed, and well-mounted.

After a march of three days, the Muslims arrived at Badr and took up their position near a well. The ground underfoot was sandy and the few experienced fighters in the group were apprehensive that this would be a serious handicap during battle, as the sand would not permit easy and rapid movement. The Makkahn army on its arrival took up a position opposite on firm clay soil.

Night set in and the Holy Prophet(saw) spent the greater part of it in earnest prayer and supplication. He had firm faith in every Divine promise, but he also realised fully the complete supremacy of the Divine Being and the many weaknesses that beset mortals. He prayed for success; he prayed for strength; he prayed for steadfastness for himself and those with him. Part of his prayer during that fateful night has come down to us. It reveals the core of his anxiety: "Lord, if Thou wilt suffer this little band to perish, Thy Holy Name will no more be glorified on earth and there will be none left to worship Thy Majesty in true sincerity."

The morning approached. There had been a shower of rain which firmed the sand underfoot while turning the clay into slippery mud, and the Muslims were comforted and encouraged. They beheld, in hope and fear, the dawn of the day which was to decide the issue of the most fateful contest ever waged in the history of man between the forces of truth and righteousness, and those of falsehood and ignorance. The Holy Prophet(saw) drew up his men in battle array and, leaving them with his instructions, retired again to supplicate the Divine. He was prostrate before his Lord in agony when the general fighting began. Abu Bakr(ra) approached him and put a gentle hand on his shoulder, saying: Messenger of Allah, thou hast prayed enough. The Holy Prophet(saw) raised himself and announced that God had just given him to understand that the time had arrived for the fulfilment of the prophecy revealed sometime earlier at Makkah:

The hosts shall soon be routed and will turn their backs in flight.
Aye, the Hour is their appointed time; and the Hour will be most calamitous and most bitter. (54:46-47)

The Muslims had their backs to the rising sun, while it shone on the faces of Quraish. For a short while the advantage appeared to be with Quraish on account of the superiority of their numbers and equipment. The Holy Prophet(saw) took up a handful of gravel and sand and threw it in the direction of the enemy. Immediately a fierce gust of wind began to blow gravel and sand into the faces of Quraish, which almost blinded them, and made their movements erratic and ineffective.

The issue now was no longer in doubt. The flower of chivalry of Quraish was soon left upon the field, dead and dying. Seventy, all leading men of Quraish, including Abu Jahl, were killed and an equal number taken prisoner, including the Prophet's uncle, Abbas, and one of his sons-in-law. Of the Muslims, fourteen, six Emigrants and eight Ansar, became martyrs but none was taken prisoner. The Prophet, while giving thanks to God for the great deliverance which He had vouchsafed, was deeply grieved that so many of Quraish had perished in pursuit of their vain purpose.

There was much debate as to the fate of the prisoners. According to Arab custom, they could have been dispatched immediately; but the Prophet determined that those who could offer suitable ransom would be released on payment of ransom, and those who could not offer ransom would be released as an act of grace. The ransom of such prisoners as were literate was fixed at teaching ten Muslim boys to read and write.

When the news of the catastrophe reached Makkah, there was mourning in every house. But all customary lamentations and other expressions and exhibitions of grief were forbidden by the Elders till Quraish had time to reorganise their forces and to avenge the disastrous defeat. The profits gained by the caravan that had arrived safely in Makkah were not distributed, but were reserved for the purpose of equipping another force against the Muslims.

There is no other instance in human history of such a clear and decisive Divine Sign in support of truth against falsehood. The grave disparity in all respects between the opposing forces predicated the certain and utter ruin of the weaker side. Except for the succour and grace of God, there can be no feasible explanation of the disaster that overtook Quraish. The unequal struggle would continue for another four years, but there is no doubt that the spine of the vaunted might of Quraish was effectively broken in the field of Badr.

Opposition Continues

A year later, at Uhud, the disparity in numbers and equipment was even more striking than at Badr, yet in the beginning of the battle the Muslims put the enemy to flight; but owing to a grave default on the part of a small group, the triumph was converted into near disaster for the Muslims. Even so, Quraish failed to take advantage of the situation which had placed Madinah at their mercy and returned to Makkah without the achievement of their ultimate purpose.

Viewing with grave alarm the increasing strength of the Holy Prophet(saw) and the Muslims, and the slow but steady progress of Islam, Quraish now had recourse to calling in aid the large number of tribes whom their hostile propaganda had converted into bitter enemies of Islam. A mighty host, numbering between eighteen and twenty thousand, now advanced against Madinah with the determined purpose of putting an end, finally, to what they conceived to be a grave threat to their way of life and to all that which had value in their eyes.

On arrival near Madinah they discovered that their advance on the city was barred by a wide trench, which was manned by the Muslims at various places on its inner side. Chagrined, but not discouraged, they laid siege to Madinah. The siege continued for nearly three weeks and imposed unendurable suffering and hardship upon the inhabitants of the city. There was little fighting, except whenever a party of Quraish made an attempt to cross the trench. Each such attempt was gallantly foiled by the Muslims. Yet the Muslims were reduced to such a state of weakness and helplessness, that from the purely human point of view, they could not imagine that any chance of their deliverance might still be available. To add to the anxiety and concern of the Holy Prophet, he received intimation that the only remaining Jewish tribe in Madinah had yielded to the solicitations of Quraish and had agreed to attack the Muslims in the rear while the confederate army mounted a joint attack all along the trench in front. The Muslims would thus be crushed between the upper millstone of the confederate forces and the nether millstone of Banu Quraidah, the Jewish tribe, who had treacherously, contrary to their covenant, gone over to the enemy.

The situation was one of utter hopelessness and despair for the Muslims, but for their firm faith in God and His promise of security. About the middle of the night, a fierce storm began to blow, which threw the entire camp of the confederates into utter confusion. They were so terrified that they felt that there was no security for them except in flight. By the break of dawn, not one of them was left within visible distance of the trench. This was the end of the armed aggression of

Quraish against the Muslims.

These were, however, only the highlights of the struggle which had throughout the years continued to erupt in every shape and form, including treachery, deceit and ambush. All such attempts were frustrated by the foresight and wisdom of the Holy Prophet(saw) who spared no effort in safeguarding the security of those who had been entrusted into his care. Yet that was not his only, or even his main, purpose. This type of struggle was not of his seeking, but had been forced upon him against his will. Through all this, he continued to pursue his main purpose which was the propagation of the Unity of the Divine and the training of his people in the beneficent values of Islam which pervade every aspect of human life.

In the sixth year after his Emigration from Makkah to Madinah, a truce was arranged with Quraish at Hudaibiyya, for a period of ten years, the terms of which, even in the eyes of the Muslims, were utterly unequal and were even humiliating for them. But the Holy Prophet(saw) knew better and it soon became clear that the truce had opened wide avenues for the spread and progress of Islam. Within less than two years, Quraish committed a glaring breach of the terms of the truce, by a party of them attacking and ravaging a tribe in alliance with the Muslims.

On the entreaty of the oppressed tribe, the Holy Prophet(saw)marched against Makkah at the head of ten thousand devoted Muslims. Quraish realised that no way of deliverance was left to them. They threw themselves upon the mercy of the Holy Prophet(saw).

All the scorn and ridicule poured on him by the Makkahns in his early years; their implacable hatred and enmity; the long years of bitter, cruel, and sustained persecution; all the fighting, the hardship and suffering; the loss of dear and devoted Companions – all, all was in the moment of triumph laid aside, banished from the mind and forgiven in the name of the Lord on High, the Gracious, the Merciful, the Creator and Master of all. The gates of love and mercy were opened wide. Bitter enemies of the morning became warm friends by midday. Some hearts were still sullen; the humiliation, though softened by magnanimity, was hard to endure, but even these could not long withstand the healing effect of the balm so generously and so beneficently applied by the Holy Prophet(saw). History furnishes no parallel instance of such complete forgiveness, such utter beneficence, on so large a scale.

Makkah had fallen, but this did not bring peace. Within less than a month, while the Holy Prophet(saw) was still in Makkah, he had to go forth to face a huge army of hostile tribes at Hunain. The battle, even before it was fairly joined, took an adverse course, and the Muslim forces were thrown into utter confusion. They were, however, soon rallied and the fighting that ensued ended in complete victory for them. A very large number of prisoners was taken and enormous booty fell into the hands of the Muslims. Eventually, the prisoners were all freed without ransom and out of the spoils munificent largesse's were bestowed upon the Makkahns, some of whom had not even embraced Islam.

Taif still stood out, and though the Jewish stronghold at Khaibar which had long been the centre of intrigue against the Muslims had been subdued earlier, danger still threatened from the north. There were persistent rumours, subsequently discovered as originating in malice, that a large force was gathering on the border of Syria with hostile intent. In the face of great difficulties, the Prophet assembled a force and marched to the border of Syria. Arrived there, he dispatched parties in different directions to report on the situation. These returned and reported that they had not observed any concentrations anywhere. Being reassured, the Holy Prophet(saw) decided to return to Madinah, stopping only for a few days to conclude peace treaties with some tribes on the border. There was no fighting. Delegations now poured in from all parts of Arabia offering submission and announcing acceptance of Islam.

Pilgrimage to Makkah

In the eleventh year of the Hijra, the Prophet decided to go on pilgrimage to Makkah. On the day of pilgrimage, there was assembled in the valley of Arafat a concourse of a hundred thousand devout pilgrims. Muhammad, the chosen of Allah; rejected by Quarish; persecuted; boycotted; hounded out of Taif; forced out of Makkah with a price of one hundred camels proclaimed for his person, dead or alive; pursued by the hatred of Quraish even in Madinah; challenged by force, besieged, plotted against; faithful, loyal, steadfast, humble, obedient servant of Allah; His Messenger par excellence was now surrounded by an ocean of faithful, devoted hearts, all proclaiming the glory of Allah, celebrating His praise, affirming His Unity, supplicating Him for forgiveness, mercy, compassion; and invoking His blessings on Muhammad.

The Holy Prophet(saw) proceeded on his camel, Qaswa, to the Mount of Mercy, and standing on the back of Qaswa, made his address of farewell. After the recitation of the Shahadah, he said that he did not know whether he would be able to meet them again on the occasion of the pilgrimage, and he asked them to lend an attentive ear to what he had to say. He went on to admonish them to order their lives in accordance with the commandments of God; to take particular care that no trespass was committed against any person in respect of his life, property, or honour; to treat women with due regard and consideration, fully observing their rights, which corresponded to the rights that men had. He expressed solicitude for the welfare of the prisoners of war, some of whom they still had among them, saying that they must be accorded the same treatment as was due to the members of their families.

He stressed that all human beings were equal, whatever their individual status, and that no one could claim any privilege or superiority against any other. He ended by asking them to hold fast to the Unity of God, and to the principal articles of faith. He then inquired whether he had conveyed God's message to them and had discharged his trust. There was a deafening and repeated response that he had. He asked those present to convey what he had said to those who were not present on the occasion.

At the end of his address, he received the revelation:

> *...This day have I perfected your religion for you and completed My favour upon you and have chosen for you Islam as religion...*
> (5:4)

This was a clear indication that his mission having been fulfilled, he should now prepare for his return to his Lord.

It was time for prayer and the Holy Prophet[saw] led the combined noon and afternoon Prayer services. Thereafter he again mounted Qaswa and returning to the vicinity of the Mount of Mercy, among the boulders, he stood on the back of Qaswa, facing in the direction of the Ka'aba, and raising his arms, became absorbed in entreaty and supplication in the attitude of one who, sore troubled and distressed, begged for mercy. He continued thus till sunset.

The pilgrimage over, the Prophet returned to Madinah and occupied every available moment with expounding and teaching the principles of Islam and the philosophy that lay behind them, and with urging the Muslims to order their lives accordingly. One day he announced that he had received the revelation:

> *When the help of Allah comes and the victory,*
> *And thou seest men entering the religion of Allah in troops,*
> *Glorify they Lord, with* His *praise, and seek forgiveness of him. Surely He is Oft-returning* with compassion.
> (110:2-4)

Hearing this, Abu Bakr[ra] was overcome by emotion and exclaimed: Were it possible, we would ransom thee with our fathers, our mothers and ourselves; upon which the Prophet observed: If it were permissible to love a human being with the heart's full devotion, I would have so loved Abu Bakr(ra); but such love is only for God. He went on to add that all doors that opened into the courtyard of the mosque should be closed, except the door of Abu Bakr(ra).

Soon the Holy Prophet(saw) fell ill. For some days, despite his illness, he continued to lead the Prayers, but when he became too weak to do so, he directed that Abu Bakr(ra) should lead the Prayers in his place.

The Holy Prophet(saw) passes away

The end approached. The Holy Prophet(saw) expressed great anxiety lest after his death his followers might be tempted to have recourse to practices which might assign to him a position above that of a human being, as had been done in the case of some previous Prophets by their followers. He impressed repeatedly upon those who visited him that he was but a human being to whom God had vouchsafed revelation for the guidance of mankind. He breathed his last with the words: "To the Companionship On High, to the Companionship On High."

The Holy Prophet(saw)'s death struck the Muslims as a fearful calamity, and they were crushed with grief. 'Umar(ra) drew his sword and said he would cut off the head of any who dared to assert that the Holy Prophet(saw) was dead; he could not die. Abu Bakr(ra) arrived. Entering the chamber where the Holy Prophet(saw)'s body lay, he kissed it on the forehead and said: God will not inflict two deaths upon thee. He then came out and asked Umar to desist while he addressed the people briefly. He recited from the Holy Qur'an:

> *And Muhammad is only a Messenger. verily,* all *messengers have passed away before him. If then he die or be slain, will you turn back on your heels...?* (3:145)

He added: Harken, he who worshipped Muhammad should know that Muhammad is dead, but he who worships God should remember that God is Ever-Living and does not die.

Thus ended a life that has stood unmatched in every respect in human history.

Conclusion

"Philosopher, orator, apostle, legislator, warrior, conqueror, of ideas, restorer of rational dogmas; the founder of twenty terrestrial empires and of one spiritual empire, that is Muhammad. As regards all standards by which human greatness may be measured, we may ask, is there any man greater than he?" *(Lamartine, History of Turkey, p.276)*

> 'If the object of religion be the inculcation of morals, the diminution of evil, the promotion of human happiness, the

expansion of the human intellect; if the performance of good works will avail on the Great Day when mankind shall be summoned to its final reckoning, it is neither irrelevant nor unreasonable to admit that Muhammad was indeed an Apostle of God.'
(S. P. Scott, History of Moorish Empire in Europe, p.126).

The Holy Prophet(saw) left an enduring impress upon a large mass of mankind. He indeed proved an excellent exemplar, as God had described him in the Qur'an (33:22). God proclaimed:

Allah sends down His blessings on the Prophet, and His angels constantly invoke blessings on him; do you, 0 believers, also invoke Allah's blessings on him and offer him the salutation of peace. (33:57)

In obedience to this Divine command, all through the centuries, Muslims have constantly prayed for, and invoked Allah's blessings upon, the Prophet. There are, today, more than 800 million Muslims in different parts of the world, and the number is daily increasing. An average Muslim invokes God's blessings on the Prophet at least forty times during the course of each day, and many of them do it much oftener. Every time the Prophet is referred to in conversation by name or by his Prophetic office, Allah's blessings are invoked upon him and Allah's peace is called down upon him. Thus every moment of the night and day, millions of hearts supplicate the Almighty for His blessings on His Prophet(saw).

One who devoted his life so utterly to the service of God and His creatures, as did the Holy Prophet(saw), is deserving of the deepest gratitude on the part of the whole of mankind. By constantly invoking the blessings of God upon him, those who do so seek to repay a fraction of the great debt that humanity owes him.

His greatest follower and most devoted servant in modern times, the Promised Messiah(as), has summed up the proof of the truth of the Holy Prophet(saw), and the perfection of the faith that he taught in two Persian verses which may be rendered as follows:

Unlettered, yet matchless in respect of his inner learning and wisdom. What brighter proof can there be of his truth?

My eye has roamed far afield and has not observed any spring purer than the faith that he inculcated.

KHULAFA-E-RASHIDEEN
(The Rightly Guided Successors)

The article below was written by Majeed A Mian and has been reproduced from www.alislam.org website

---

The four Khulafa of the Holy Prophet, peace and blessings be upon him, are known as the Khulafa-e-Rashideen, or the rightly guided successors. The following article is a brief account of the lives and achievements of those Khulafa, may Allah be pleased with them.

HADHRAT ABU BAKR SIDDIQ(ra)

The personal name of Hadhrat Abu Bakr(ra) was Abdullah, but in respect of his fatherhood he was known as Abu Bakr. His father was known as Abu Qahaafah and his mother as Ummul-Khair Salma. His lineage can be traced back to the Holy Prophet(saw), in the sixth generation before him.

He was born to a sub tribe of Quraish, in 572 AD in Makkah and was raised there. When he came of age, he became a cloth merchant. He was a close friend of the Holy Prophet(saw). He was the first among men to confirm truth of the claim of the Holy Prophet(saw), and thus he earned the title Siddeeq. Throughout his life, he remained fully devoted to the service of Islam.

He held fast to the company of the Holy Prophet(saw), and remained by his side whether it was peace or war. The Holy Prophet(saw), sought his wise counsel in almost every matter when advice was needed. He was in the company of the Holy Prophet(saw), during his migratory journey (Hijra) from Makkah to Madinah. He was the only companion of the Holy Prophet(saw), in the Cave Thaur, where they both took refuge during this journey. The Holy Qur'an mentions this in chapter 9 verse 40 (Al-Taubah).

He always tried to surpass others in financial sacrifices. Once, for the Battle of Mauta, the Holy Prophet(saw), was in urgent need of financial contribution. Hadhrat Umar(ra), presented half of all his belongings, while Hadhrat Abu Bakr(ra), brought all that he had in his house, to the Holy Prophet(saw).

The Holy Prophet(saw), married his daughter, Hadhrat Ayesha, may Allah be pleased with her. Also, following the Hajjatul-Widaa or the Last Pilgrimage, when the Holy Prophet(saw), fell ill seriously, he instructed Hadhrat Abu Bakr(ra), to lead the daily prayers. He was one of the ten blessed ones to whom the Holy

Prophet(saw), had given the glad tidings that they had been rewarded the Paradise.

After the sad demise of the Holy Prophet(saw), Hadhrat Abu Bakr(ra), was elected as the first Khalifa. He had to deal with an extremely difficult situation developed due to the sudden demise of the Holy Prophet(saw).

The first problem was that some of the tribes renounced Islam, simply because their tribal chiefs did not feel necessary to remain loyal to the successor of the Holy Prophet(saw). Not only that but they started preparing to attack Madinah to end the newly established institution of Khilafat. Hadhrat Abu Bakr(ra), after knowing their intentions, sent troops and succeeded in suppressing their rebellion.

The second major problem faced by Hadhrat Abu Bakr(ra, was that many people refused to pay the Zakat, which was essential for fulfilling the needs of the Islamic state and care for the poor. Hadhrat Abu Bakr(ra), vowed to collect Zakat from everyone and took all necessary measures to achieve this goal.

The most dangerous of all the problems was that a number of ambitious persons pretending to be prophets, started planning a rebellion against the Islamic state. Masailma and Aswad Ansi, raised large armies and captured some of the Muslim territory. Hadhrat Abu Bakr(ra), was prompt to fight back these rebellious false prophets. Despite meagre resources, Allah granted him victory against the mischief mongers.

After successfully dealing with the internal disorders, Hadhrat Abu Bakr(ra), turned to the external enemies threatening the security of the Islamic state. The Muslim army, under the command of Khalid Bin Waleed(ra), crushed a rebellion in Bahrain. Then the Persians was defeated, who had supported the rebels of Bahrain. The Muslim army also defeated the Roman army in the battles of Ajnadan and Yarmuk, and thus the whole of Syria fell under the control of the Islamic state.

Another great achievement of his Khilafat was the collection of the Holy Qur'an at one place. Although the writing and arrangement of the Holy Qur'an was done under the supervision of the Holy Prophet(saw), himself, yet it was written on various pieces of skin, leaves and slate. Hadhrat Abu Bakr(ra), collected all these pieces of writings in one place, and re-organized the Hufaaz, or those who committed it to memory, in a systematic way, for the preservation of the Qur'an.

Hadhrat Abu Bakr(ra), passed away on August 23, 634 AD, after remaining ill for fifteen days. He remained Khalifa for a little over two years. During his Khilafat, Hadhrat Abu Bakr(ra), successfully secured the integrity of the Islamic state against all the internal disorders and the external enemies. Also, he successfully united the Muslims under the system of Khilafat.

Hadhrat Abu Bakr(ra), loved the Holy Prophet(saw) so dearly that even after the demise of the Holy Prophet(saw), Hadhrat Abu Bakr(ra) took extreme care to carry out his wishes. During the last days of his life, the Holy Prophet(saw) had raised an army to be sent against the Romans who had made some incursions into the Northern borders. This army was still in Madinah when the Holy Prophet(saw), passed away. As Hadhrat Abu Bakr(ra), became the Khalifa, the law and order situation within and outside Madinah became very delicate. In view of this grave danger, many Companions of the Holy Prophet(saw), advised him not to send the army against the Romans. But Hadhrat Abu Bakr(ra), replied forcefully, "What authority has the Son of Abu Qahaafa, to stop that which was started by the Holy Prophet(ra)."

HADHRAT UMAR FAROOQ(ra)

His personal name was Umar, Farooq was his title, and Ibn-ul-Khattaab, his family name. He was born in 581 AD in Makkah, and belonged to a noble family of the Quraish. He was a renowned businessman and used to lead trade delegations to Syria and Iraq.

When the Holy Prophet(saw), announced his claim to prophet hood, he became a fierce opponent of Islam. So much so, that one day he took up his sword and left his house with the intention to kill the Holy Prophet(saw). On his way, someone told him to first deal with his own sister and brother-in-law, who had already accepted Islam. He went straight to them and knocked at their door, he could hear the Holy Qur'an being recited in the house. This made him furious and he started beating his brother-in-law, and wounded his sister who tried to protect her husband. His wounded sister said in a resolute voice, "Umar! You may beat us as much as you like, but we are not going to give up our faith." This made him calm down, and he asked them to recite a portion of the Holy Qur'an for him. He was so moved by the Qur'anic verses that his eyes filled with tears. He went straight to the Holy Prophet(saw), and accepted Islam at his hands. As he was a strong, fearless and influential man of Makkah, he proved to be a source of strength for the Muslims. This miraculous change in Hadhrat Umar(ra), was in fact the result of the Holy Prophet's(saw) prayers for him.

Hadhrat Umar(ra) sacrificed his wealth and dedicated his life for the cause of Islam. He was an intelligent and God-fearing person. He participated in almost all the battles along with the Holy Prophet(saw), who used to consult him in many important matters. He was one of the ten blessed ones to whom the Holy Prophet(saw) had given the glad tidings that they had been rewarded the Paradise.

Hadhrat Umar Bin Khattab(ra) was the second successor of the Holy Prophet(saw). During the ten years of his Khilafat, the Islamic state expanded and progressed extensively. Peace and prosperity prevailed everywhere in the state. During the period of his Khilafat, the Muslims had to fight a number of battles against Iran, Iraq, Syria and Egypt. As a result of this, vast areas of these countries came under the Muslim rule. When the city of Jerusalem in Palestine was conquered by the Muslims in 17 Hijri, Hadhrat Umar(ra) himself visited the city on the request of the Romans, and signed a treaty between the Muslims and the people of Jerusalem.

Apart from the conquest of vast areas, Hadhrat Umar(ra) paid full attention to the welfare of his people. He was able to establish a splendid system of administration for the Islamic state and his Khilafat marked a golden period in the history of Islam. Some of his main achievements in this field are:

- Establishment of Majlis Shura, a consultative body of advisors to the Khalifa.
- Division of the whole Islamic state into provinces to facilitate administration.
- Establishment of a finance department, and building of schools and mosques in different parts of the state.
- Introduction of Islamic Calendar of Hijra.

Hadhrat Umar(ra) was a pious, kind and farsighted man. He possessed the fine qualities of bravery, honesty and simplicity. He was so anxious about the welfare of his people that he used to go around in disguise, in the city of Madinah at night, to see for himself if anyone was in need of help. Once, during his patrol at night, he observed a woman cooking something in a pot while her children were crying around her. He found out from the woman that her children were hungry for two days and the pot was put on fire just to console them. Hadhrat Umar(ra) immediately went to the treasury, and brought all the necessary food items to the woman. On his way, one of his servants offered to carry the load but he stopped him saying: "On the Day of Judgment you will not carry my load." The woman, who had not seen Hadhrat Umar(ra) before, was so pleased that she prayed aloud for him saying, "May Allah make you the Khalifa in place of Umar." On hearing this, Hadhrat Umar(ra) started crying and without saying a word left the place.

In the year 644 AD, Hadhrat Umar(ra) was stabbed by a Persian slave, while he was offering his prayers in the mosque. This proved fatal and he passed away at the age of sixty-three. He was a truly great Khalifa whose period of Khilafat was undoubtedly a golden period in the history of Islam.

HADHRAT UTHMAN GHANI(ra)

Hadhrat Uthman Ghani(ra) was elected the third Khalifa by the council appointed by Hadhrat Umar(ra) shortly before his death. He belonged to the well-known family, Banu Umayya of the Quraish. His lineage can be traced back to the Holy Prophet(saw) in the fifth generation before him. His generosity for the poor was so well known that he earned the title Ghani.

Hadhrat Uthman(ra) embraced Islam through the preaching of his close friend, Hadhrat Abu Bakr,(ra) He was the fourth person to embrace Islam, but he faced much hardships as his uncle started persecuting him. He migrated twice, first to Abyssinia and then to Madinah.

The Holy Prophet(saw) held him in great esteem, and married his daughter, Ruqayyah to him. On her death, he married his second daughter, Umme Kulthoom to him. Thus Hadhrat Uthman(ra) was called Zun-Noorain, meaning the one with two lights.

He spent a lot of his wealth for the cause of Islam. Once, he purchased an expensive well of good quality drinking water from a Jew for the benefit of the Muslims. To meet the expenses of the battle of Tabook, he offered 10,000 dinars, 1,000 camels and seventy horses loaded with necessary goods. He was one of the ten blessed ones to whom the Holy Prophet, peace and blessings be upon him, had given the glad tidings that they had been rewarded the Paradise.

During the Khilafat of Hadhrat Uthman(ra) the Islamic Empire expanded still further. A rebellion in Iran was crushed. In the north, the Romans were once again defeated by the Muslim forces led by Hadhrat Ameer Muawiah. Then the Romans came by the sea to invade Egypt, but were once again repelled by the Muslim forces. As a result of these battles, the whole of Iran, Asia Minor and Egypt came under the Muslim control. It was during his Khilafat that a navy and an Islamic fleet were established.

During the first six years of his Khilafat, the Islamic Empire not only expanded, but also its people enjoyed peace and prosperity. Standard copies of the Holy Qur'an were prepared from the ones compiled by Hadhrat Abu Bakr(ra) and sent to all the provinces of the state. This was certainly his most important deed. The Holy Qur'an, as we see it today, was compiled during his Khilafat and under his direct supervision. The last six years of his Khilafat, however, passed in chaos and conflicts due to the conspiracies of certain groups including that of Abdullah Bin Sabah, a Jew who had become a Muslim with an intention to weaken the Islamic state.

As a result of this, some people from various groups started laying unjustified charges against Hadhrat Uthman(ra) whose sincere explanations seemed to go unheeded. Also, due to his extremely kind and gentle character, these rebellious people increased in their mischief. In this dangerous situation, Hadhrat Uthman(ra) showed great tolerance and utmost patience to avoid the bloodshed of innocent Muslims.

Towards the end of his Khilafat, various groups who wanted to depose Hadhrat Uthman(ra) entered Madinah. He refused to fight them, as he did not want to shed the blood of fellow Muslims. His house was surrounded by the rebels who demanded that he step down, but Hadhrat Uthman(ra) refused to step down from the God-given position of Khilafat because of his just and firm belief that a Khalifa was made by God and not by people.

Hadhrat Uthman(ra) was then martyred on June 17, 656 AD, at the age of eighty-two, while he was reciting the Holy Qur'an. He certainly sacrificed his life for the integrity of Khilafat and in the best interest of Islam.

HADHRAT ALI BIN ABI TALIB(ra)

Hadhrat Ali(ra) was the son of the Holy Prophet's(saw) uncle, Abu Talib. He was born in Makkah about twenty years after the birth of the Holy Prophet(saw). His father, Abu Talib and mother, Fatima were two persons who took care of the Holy Prophet(saw) in his early childhood.

When Hadhrat Ali(ra) was born, the Holy Prophet(saw) himself became his guardian, as his father's financial position was very weak.

Hadhrat Ali(ra) stayed in the bed of the Holy Prophet(saw) the night when the Holy Prophet(saw) left Makkah for Madinah. The Makkahn leaders had planned to arrest and kill the Holy Prophet(saw). Next morning, they were enraged when they found Hadhrat Ali(ra) instead of the Holy Prophet(saw).

The Makkahn leaders could not get any information from Hadhrat Ali(ra) about the whereabouts of the Holy Prophet(ra) in spite of their threatening attitude. Thus all their plans to kill the Holy Prophet(saw) were frustrated.

Hadhrat Ali(ra) was a brave and skilled warrior. He participated in almost all the battles along with the Holy Prophet(saw). He was an intelligent, very learned, and a pious companion of the Holy Prophet(saw). The Holy Prophet(saw) once said, "I am the city of knowledge and Ali is its gate." Hadhrat Ali(ra) was married to Hadhrat Fatima, may Allah be pleased with her, who was the favourite daughter of the Holy Prophet(saw). He was one of the ten blessed ones to whom the Holy Prophet(ra) had given the glad tidings that they had been rewarded the Paradise.

Hadhrat Ali(ra) was chosen to be the fourth Khalifa on June 23, 656 AD, six days after the death of Hadhrat Uthman(ra). In those days, there was no law and order in the city of Madinah. Therefore, Hadhrat Ali(ra) moved the capital from Madinah to Kufa in Iraq.

After his election, he faced the popular demand of Muslims including the influential companions of the Holy Prophet(ra) like Hadhrat Talha, and Hadhrat Zubair, may Allah be pleased with them both, to immediately punish the murderers of Hadhrat Uthman(ra).

Hadhrat Ali(ra) announced that his top priority was to restore law and order in the state and only then he would be able to bring the assassins of Hadhrat Uthman(ra) to justice. But Hadhrat Talha and Hadhrat Zubair did not agree with Hadhrat Ali(ra) and started raising an army. Hadhrat Ayesha, may Allah be pleased with her, who was not aware of the real situation, also joined Hadhrat Talha and Hadhrat Zubair, in effort to punish the assassins. The three led a small army towards Basra.

Hadhrat Ali(ra) tried his best to avoid the fighting and bloodshed, but all his efforts failed. Unfortunately, a battle took place between his forces and the forces of Hadhrat Ayesha, may Allah be pleased with her. Hadhrat Talha, may Allah be pleased with him, and Hadhrat Zubair, may Allah be pleased with him, left their forces even before the battle, and were killed by some other opponents. Hadhrat Ayesha's forces were defeated, but Hadhrat Ali(ra) gave her due respect and took care of her safety.

This battle was called the battle of Jamal (camel), because Hadhrat Ayesha rode a camel during the battle. Later, Hadhrat Ayesha, may Allah be pleased with her, was regretful throughout her life to have fought against Hadhrat Ali(ra).

After the battle of Jamal, Hadhrat Ali(ra) urged Ameer Muawia, who had not yet taken the ba'at of Hadhrat Ali(ra) to submit him in the best interest of Islam. But Ameer Muawia refused to submit on the pretext that the blood of Hadhrat Uthman(ra) who also belonged to the family of Umayyah, must be avenged first.

Ameer Muawiah, with the help of Amr Bin Aas, started raising an army. Hadhrat Ali(ra) had no alternative but to advance towards Syria to fight Ameer Muawiah. In July, 567 AD, the two armies met in a battle at Saffain.

There were heavy casualties on both sides, but the battle ended in an accord that the matter be decided by an arbitration committee. This consisted of Abu Musa al-Ashari representing Hadhrat Ali(ra), and Amr Bin Aas representing Ameer Muawiah. Unfortunately, this arbitration ended in failure because Amr Bin deviated from the decision agreed upon with Abu Musa al-Ashari(ra).

A large group of people, who were basically against the proposal of arbitration, separated from Hadhrat Ali(ra) and chose an independent

Ameer for themselves. This group was called Khawaarij, meaning, 'the outsiders.' At first, Hadhrat Ali(ra) tried to persuade them to submit to him, but failed. This led to a fierce battle in which most of the Khawaarij were killed.

After their crushing defeat, the Khawaarij planned to assassinate Hadhrat Ali(ra) Hadhrat Ameer Muawiah, and Amr Bin Aas. The latter two escaped from the attempts on their lives. Hadhrat Ali(ra) was fatally wounded by his attacker, while going to the mosque for Fajr prayers. Two days later, this courageous and pious Khalifa passed away. Undoubtedly, Hadhrat Ali(ra) sacrificed his life for the integrity of Khilafat.

References

The following materials were used in preparing the above article:

- *A Book of Religious Knowledge*, compiled by Sheikh Abdul Hadi, and published by Ahmadiyya Muslim Jama'at, Canada.
- *Hadhrat Abu Bakr Siddiq (Urdu)*, Published by Lajna Imaillah, Qadian.
- *Hadhrat Umar Farooq (Urdu)*, Published by Lajna Imaillah, Qadian.
- *Hadhrat Uthman Ghani (Urdu)*, Published by Lajna Imaillah, Qadian.
- *Hadhrat Ali (Urdu)*, Published by Lajna Imaillah, Qadian.
- *Encyclopaedia Britannica*
- http://www.alislam.org/library/links/00000078.html

Ahmadiyyat, the Renaissance of Islam

Heavenly Sign
The Holy Prophet[saw] is reported to have said:

> For our Mahdi there shall be two signs which have never happened for anyone else since the creation of the heavens and the earth; At his advent there shall occur an eclipse of the moon in the first of its appointed nights and an eclipse of the sun on the middle one of its appointed dates and both will occur in the month of Ramadan.
> *(Dar Qutni, p.88)*

The eclipse of the moon actually occurred on Thursday evening the 13th of Ramadan, 1311 A.H. (March 21, 1894) and that of the sun occurred on Friday morning the 28th of the same Ramadan (April 6, 1894). The eclipse of the sun occurred as predicted on the middle date which was the 28th confirming the prophecy.

Early Life
Hadhrat Mirza Ghulam Ahmad[as] was born on 13th February 1835 in Qadian (India). From childhood, Mirza Ghulam Ahmad[as] engaged himself in spiritual and religious matters and extensively studied the Holy Qur'an, Hadith (sayings and traditions of the Holy Prophet[saw] and Fiqa (Jurisprudence). It was the Promised Messiah's firm belief that all religions were true at their source, and he always sought to uphold the dignity of religion and to demonstrate its relevance to everyone.

The Promised Messiah's[as] education amounted to elementary knowledge of Urdu, Persian and Arabic. By the time he was 18, he became a keen reader and spent most of his time in reading books from his father's library or in studying the Holy Qur'an. During his early youth, he became aware of the hostile attacks by non-Muslims on the teachings of Islam and was much perturbed to watch them unchallenged. He resolved to make a response to this onslaught by writing articles in papers and periodicals refuting the criticisms made against Islam and advancing arguments proving the superiority of its teachings.

In accordance with his father's wishes, he enlisted himself in 1863 for Government service and worked for 5 years as a reader in a Law Court at Sialkot. Back at Qadian in 1869, he received one of his first revelations: *'He (God) will bless thee abundantly; so much so that Kings shall seek blessings from thy garments'.*

When his father, Mirza Ghulam Qadir passed away, Hadhrat Mirza Ghulam Ahmad[as] was concerned about his future. Thereupon he received a revelation in Arabic:

"Is not Allah sufficient for His servant?"

The Promised Messiah(as) said after receiving this revelation:

"This was the first day on which I experienced a sign of divine mercy through revelation concerning which I cannot imagine that it would ever cease to have effect during my lifetime. I had the words of the revelation carved on a semi-precious stone and set in a ring which I have with me securely."

The Promised Messiah(as) continued to receive divine revelation of assurances of security, progress, support and success, grand prophecies and Divine signs.

Following the death of his father, Mirza Ghulam Murtaza in 1876, he devoted all his time and energies to the divine assignment of serving Islam and reviving the true faith, an indication of which he had received in a vision some years earlier. He began to write his famous book *Braheen-e-Ahmadiyya*. This book refuted the allegations levied at Islam and furnished powerful arguments to display the countless beauties of Islam. The first two volumes of this magnificent book were published in 1880. The third part followed in 1882 and the fourth in 1884.

In 1886, under Divine direction, he retired in seclusion for 40 days at Hoshiarpur for meditation and prayers. During this period, he received numerous revelations including the prophecy of the birth of an illustrious son, a blessed progeny for him and a large and ever increasing following of devoted servants of Islam. The same year he claimed to have been appointed the Reformer of the Age. In 1889, he was commanded by Allah to raise a party of his sincere followers and initiate them through formal Bai'at. The first initiation took place on 23rd March 1889 at Ludhiana, which heralded the birth of Ahmadiyyat in Islam.

In 1891, Hadhrat Mirza Ghulam Ahmad(as) claimed that he was the Mahdi and Messiah of the latter days as foretold by the Holy Prophet of Islam(saw). He declared that he had been raised in the spirit of Jesus(as) to be the

Messiah of Islam.

In 1896, he wrote his famous essay entitled *The Philosophy of the Teachings of Islam* which has since attracted many a convert to Islam by its lucid style and persuasive presentation. In 1905, he wrote *Al Wassiyat*, informing, his friends and followers that the time for his departure from this world was imminent and he urged his followers to welcome and submit to the second manifestation of Khilafat after him and continue their crusade for the victory of Islam.

The Promised Messiah(as) travelled extensively across the subcontinent of India preaching the true meaning of Islam and defending accusations and criticism levelled against Islam and the Holy Prophet Muhammad(saw). He gathered thousands of followers within his lifetime, engaged in numerous debates and dialogues with the Muslim, Christian and Hindu priesthood and leadership, proclaimed Islam as the religion of mankind and promoted the spread of Islam through peaceful propagation. The Promised Messiah(as) said:

"I proclaim to all Muslims, Christians, Hindus and Aryas that I have no enemy in the world. I love mankind with the love a compassionate mother has for her children; even more so. I am only the enemy of the false doctrines which kill truth. Human sympathy is my duty. My principle is to discard falsehood. I reject paganism, wrong-doing, mis-conduct, injustice and immorality." *(The Promised Messiah(as) from his book, Ruhani Khazain, Vol.12: Tsiiajum Muneer, p.28)*

The Promised Messiah(as) has said on prophet hood.

"Many people are misled by the use of the word prophet in my claim and imagine as if I have claimed a prophet hood which was bestowed upon the prophets in earlier times, but they are mistaken in so thinking. I have made no such claim. The Divine wisdom has bestowed this grace upon me that I have raised to the station of prophethood through the blessings of the grace of the Holy Prophet, so that the perfection of the spiritual grace of the Holy Prophet, peace and blessings of Allah be upon him, might be established."
(Haqeeqatul Wahi, p.150)

Hadhrat Mirza Ghulam Ahmad(as), devoted the whole of his life to the service of Islam. He died in Lahore on 26th May 1908.

Some photos of the Promised Messiah(as) with some of the Companions

Some photos of the Promised Messiah(as) with some of the Companions

Khalifas of Ahmadiyyat - Brief Summaries

HADHRAT MAULAWI NUR-UD-DIN – Khalifatul Masih I
(May Allah be pleased with him)

The Promised Messiah(as) stated:

Among my many pious friends, there is one far-sighted, gifted with vast knowledge, soft spoken, polite, steadfast in faith, God-fearing, trusting, a savant, pious, scholar, devout, saintly spiritual, towering Muhaddith (scholar of Hadith), outstanding Hakeem, Haji-ul-Haramain, Hafiz-i- Qur'an, and an offspring of Farooq. His name is Maulawi Nur-ud-Din Bhervi. In sincerity, devotion, dedication, loyalty and love, he is foremost among my followers.

Early Life

Born 1841, Hadhrat Maulawi Nur-ud-Din(ra) was the 34th in direct male lineal descent from Hadhrat 'Umar(ra), the second successor to the Holy Prophet Muhammad(saw).

Hadhrat Maulawi Nur-ud-Din(ra) mastered Punjabi, Urdu, Persian and Arabic in his youth and memorised the entire text of the Holy Qur'an thus becoming a Hafiz-ul-Qur'an.

He demonstrated a very keen intellect, a very just appreciation of spiritual values and a highly developed faculty of expression both in speech and in writing. He became headmaster of a school at the age of 21.

Hadhrat Maulawi Nur-ud-Din(ra) travelled in search of a spiritual preceptor and in quest of religious knowledge developing into an eminent divine in his own right. He was a reputed physician and was appointed Chief Physician to the Maharaja of the State of Jammu and Kashmir and served in that capacity for 15 years.

Foremost Disciple

His search for a spiritual preceptor came to an end when he met the Promised Messiah(as) readily accepting him without the least hesitation. He migrated to Qadian shortly afterwards devoting himself to the service of the Promised Messiah(as). In 1889, when the first pledge of allegiance took place, Hadhrat Maulawi Nur-ud-Din(ra) had the honour of being the first to take the pledge (Bai'at) at the hands of the Promised Messiah(as).

In 1906, the Promised Messiah(as) established the Sadr Anjuman Ahmadiyya (Central Ahmadiyya Association) charged with the administration of the affairs of the Movement and appointed Hadhrat Maulawi Nur-ud-Din(ra) as its first President.

On the demise of the Promised Messiah(as), he was unanimously elected as Khalifatul Masih I on 27th May 1908.

Community Cohesion

Hadhrat Maulawi Nur-ud-Din(ra) established the Baitul Maal or Treasury charged with the responsibility of collecting all funds and donations. He established the Madrasah Ahmadiyya, a Theological Seminary and also laid the foundations of Talim-ul-Islam High School.

The *Al-Fazl* newspaper which was to become the official organ of the Movement was started during his tenure. He also established the Nur Hospital making generous personal donations towards its construction.

Hadhrat Maulawi Nur-ud-Din(ra) sent the first missionary to England in 1913 to lay the foundations of the first foreign mission outside of the Indian subcontinent.

Milestones of His Khilafat

Hadhrat Maulawi Nur-ud-Din(ra) secured the immediate unity and solidarity of the community and nurtured the seed of the community planted by the Promised Messiah(as) much to the chagrin of his opponents. He continued all projects which were pending or contemplated at the time of the demise of the Promised Messiah(as).

By his example, he infused into the members of the community an all-consuming love for the Holy Qur'an and was perpetually engaged in expounding the inexhaustible treasures of wisdom comprised in it.

By his precept, Hadhrat Maulawi Nur-ud-Din(ra) instilled into the members of the community the spirit of Tawakkul – absolute trust in and reliance upon Allah. Through his special relationship with his Lord, he demonstrated the efficacy of prayers. Initiated numerous humanitarian projects in his boundless care for, and sympathy towards, the poor, needy and marginalised.

In short, his life, time, property, and energies were wholly dedicated to the service of Islam. The money he earned by treating patients was largely donated to the community or used for looking after the orphans, the destitute and the poor. An old-age home Dar al-Shuyukh and an orphanage Dar-al-Yatama were established in Qadian under his directive.

Books

Hadhrat Maulawi Nur-ud-Din(ra) wrote a number of books including the notable ones of *Fasl-ul-Kitab* and *Tasdiq Barahin-e-Ahmadiyya*. He also oversaw the translation of the Holy Qur'an into English.

> "His greatest service to the cause of Islam and humanity was the courageous and valiant defence, justification and exposition of the institution of Khilafat which was vital for the spiritual survival and progress, not only of Islam and the Muslims, but of the whole of humanity. His love for the Holy Qur'an was proverbial, his devotion to the Holy Prophet(saw) was exemplary and his obedience to the Promised Messiah(as) was perfect and matchless. May Allah reward him richly and without measure for his devoted service. Amen."
> (Hadhrat Maulawi Nur-ud-Din(ra) by Muhammad Zafrulla Khan)

His Demise

After leading the community for 6 years, Hadhrat Khalifatul Masih I(ra) passed away at 2:15 pm on Friday March 13th, 1914, in Qadian. May his soul rest in peace. Inna lillahe wa inna ilehay rajeoon (*To Allah we belong to Allah shall we return)*.

Hadhrat Maulana Nur-ud-Din was a true devotee of Islam, the Holy Qur'an, the Holy Prophet of Islam(saw) and the Promised Messiah(as). He was a personification of many treasured qualities, above all a Siddiq (the most truthful and devoted). He served Islam to the last breath of his life. He was laid to rest in the Bahishti Maqbara on March 14 at 6:15pm, next to the tomb of his holy master and benefactor, the Promised Messiah(as).

For further reading on the life of Hadhrat Khalifatul Masih I(ra), please visit:
www.fountainsoflife.co.uk

HADHRAT MIRZA BASHIR-UD-DIN MAHMUD AHMAD – Khalifatul Masih II

(May Allah be pleased with him)

Prophecies

The Holy Prophet Muhammad(saw) had given the tidings of the advent of a spiritual, pious and Promised son of Mahdi at a time when Islam would be at a stage of decline and depression. He had prophesied he would come with a mission to revive and strengthen the Islamic theology and, through him, Islam, would resurge on the surface of the Earth. The Holy Prophet(saw) described this Holy Spiritual son as the Musleh (Reformer) and the Promised one.

One of the prophecies revealed to the Promised Messiah(as) by God Almighty was:

> "Rejoice therefore, that a handsome and pure boy will be bestowed on thee. Thou wilt receive an intelligent youth who will be of thy seed and will be of thy progeny...He has been invested with a holy spirit, and he will be free from all impurity. He is the light of Allah. Blessed is he who comes from heaven ... He is the Word of Allah, for Allah's mercy and honour have equipped him with the Word of Majesty."

The prophecy was fulfilled in the person of Hadhrat Mirza Bashir-ud-Din Mahmud Ahmad, son of the Promised Messiah(as) who was born in 1889. At the demise of Khalifatul Masih I(ra), he became the second successor of the Promised Messiah(as) at the age of 25. Therefore, he was also known as Hadhrat Musleh Ma'uod, the Promised Reformer.

Khilafat Years of Hadhrat Khalifatul Masih II(RA)

Hadhrat Mirza Bashir-ud-Din Mahmud Ahmad said about the Holy Prophet(saw).

> "Ignorant men blame us that by believing in the Promised Messiah(as) as a Prophet we insulted the Holy Prophet of Islam(saw). What do they know about the state of one's heart? How could they fathom the great love, deep affection and high reverence we have for the Holy Prophet(saw). And what do they understand, how did the love of the Holy Prophet(saw) penetrate in my heart. He is my life,

my heart, my desire. In his slavery is my honour and his shoe-bearing, is more valuable to me than the Imperial throne. The control of seven continents is nothing in comparison to sweeping in his house. He is the beloved of the Lord – why should I then not love him? He is the intimate of God so why should I not search for his intimacy?"

With the growth of the community, the second Khalifa began to send missionaries to various parts of the world to spread the message of Ahmadiyyat. Missionaries were first sent to Mauritius, USA and Nigeria. Soon new missions were established across the Middle East, West and East Africa, the Caribbean, Europe and Asia.

The community itself was to face opposition and persecution and Hadhrat Khalifatul Masih II(ra) provided leadership to guide the community safely through these trials. The radical Muslims often attacked the Ahmadiyya Muslim community with violence and aggression. The second Khalifa set the tone for the community by insisting that the response would be non-violent and dignified.

In 1924, Hadhrat Khalifatul Masih II(ra) attended the 'Conference of World Religions' in Wembley. His renowned speech on Ahmadiyyat and Islam was read out by Sir Muhammad Zafrulla Khan.

On 19th October 1924, Hadhrat Khalifatul Masih II(ra) laid the foundation stone of the Fazl Mosque (London's first mosque) with over 200 people of various nationalities and religious beliefs present at the ceremony. Hadhrat Khalifatul Masih II(ra) said he hoped "that this mosque would help to remove all friction and strife and establish peace, amity and goodwill among men ..."

In 1934, he established Tahrik Jadid ('New Appeal') to fund new missions and Mosques and the translation of Islamic literature into many languages. During his Khilafat, missions were established in 46 new countries.

Under his, the Holy Qur'an was translated into many new languages including Dutch, Danish and German. Hadhrat Khalifatul Masih II(ra) also wrote the commentary of the Holy Qur'an.

Mr Muhammad Ali Jinnah, a prominent Muslim politician had settled in the UK but under the instructions of the second Khalifa, the Imam of the London Mosque persuaded Jinnah to return to India and resume the leadership of Muslims in India. Hadhrat Khalifatul Masih II(ra) gave moral, constitutional, and financial support to Mr Jinnah in carving out a homeland for the Muslims now called Pakistan.

Hadhrat Mirza Bashir-ud-Din(ra) also encouraged inter-faith dialogue and Religious Founders Days were established in which people of all faiths celebrated their religious leaders. This has continued to this day.

Administrative Structure of the Community

In 1919, he established various departments to run the administration of the community.

In 1922, Hadhrat Khalifatul Masih II(ra) established the system of Majlis Shura to provide a consultative forum to debate the future direction of the community – this is the second most important institution in the community after Khilafat. He later also established five auxiliary organisations of the community. These included:

- Lajna (1922) – (the religious upbringing and administration of ladies)
- Majlis Khuddamul Ahmadiyya (1938) – (similar organisation for males)
- Majlis Ansarullah (1940) – (males over the age of 40).

The partition of India in 1947 required the community to move from Qadian to Lahore. His leadership kept the community intact and stable during this traumatic era. Soon after, land was purchased to create the future world headquarters of the movement and the town of Rabwah was created.

In 1957, he created a department called Waqf Jadid ('New Dedication') to provide missionaries for the rural areas and to help cope with international growth.

Books

Hadhrat Khalifatul Masih II(ra) wrote close to 200 books including Introduction to the Study of the Holy Qur'an and Invitation to Ahmadiyyat.

His Demise

Hadhrat Khalifatul Masih II(ra) 76, breathed his last on the 8th November, 1965 in Rabwah. He had led the community for almost 52 years.

---

or further reading on the life of Hadhrat Khalifatul Masih II(ra), please visit:
www.fountainsoflife.co.uk

HADHRAT MIRZA NASIR AHMAD – Khalifatul Masih III
(May Allah have mercy on him)

Hadhrat Mirza Nasir Ahmad – Khalifatul Masih III on the Holy Prophet (peace and blessings of Allah be upon him).

> "The paths, treading on which he [the Holy Prophet(saw)] found his Lord and was bestowed the bounties of both worlds, still bear the marks of his footsteps. Follow those footsteps, for if you do that, you shall win the love of God, and you shall hear His dear voice assuring you: 'If you will be Mine, the universe will be yours.'"

Prophecies

In Talmud (Hebrew Scripture), there is a passage which indicates that on the death of the Messiah, his spiritual Kingdom will pass to his son and grandson. Again, in the book *Haqiqatul Wahi*, the Promised Messiah(as) thanks God for his four sons and the birth of a grandson at a future date. The much awaited prophecy was fulfilled when Hadhrat Mirza Bashir-ud-Din Mahmood Ahmad(ra) was granted a son on 16th November, 1909. He was named Nasir Ahmad. The grandson spoken of in the prophecy is none other than Hadhrat Hafiz Mirza Nasir Ahmad(ru).

Early Life

Hadhrat Mirza Nasir Ahmad's early education was both religious and secular. He had memorised the entire Holy Qur'an by the age of 13.

Hadhrat Mirza Nasir Ahmad(ru) qualified as Maulawi Fadhil (theological and oriental studies) in July 1929. In 1934 he obtained his BA Degree from Lahore and later his Honours Degree from Oxford University, England. He also achieved a Master of Arts from Oxford University.

Appointments Prior to Khilafat

Hadhrat Mirza Nasir Ahmad(ru) was appointed lecturer at Jamia Ahmadiyya (The Ahmadiyya Theosophical College), becoming its Principal in 1939.

He has also served as President of the auxiliary organisations of Khuddamul Ahmadiyya and Majlis Ansarullah.

From 1944 to 1965 Hadhrat Mirza Nasir Ahmad(ru) was principal of Ta'limul-Islam College. In May 1955, he became Executive Director of Sadr Anjuman Ahmadiyya a post he held up until he was elected the third Khalifa.

Administrative Structure of the Community

On 8th November 1965 Hadhrat Mirza

Nasir Ahmad(ru) was elected as third Khalifa by a majority vote.

In 1965, he established the Fadl-i-'Umar Foundation to further the projects started by the Second Khalifa.

In 1966, Hadhrat Mirza Nasir Ahmad(ru) established the Waqfe Arzi scheme to promote the learning and teaching of the Holy Qur'an.

Historical Tour of Africa

In 1970, Hadhrat Khalifatul Masih III(ru) was the first Khalifa to tour West Africa. He conceived the 'Nusrat Jehan project' which established a substantial number of schools, colleges, clinics and hospitals in Africa. The scheme was so successful that it was extended from the initial 3-year programme to become a permanent endowment.

In August 1976, Hadhrat Khalifatul Masih III(ru) became the first Khalifa to visit the United States of America and Canada. The third Khalifa travelled abroad extensively extolling the teachings of Islam to all people and was admired by everyone who met him.

Standing Firm Against Persecution & Oppression

In 1974, riots erupted against the Ahmadiyya Muslim community throughout Pakistan. Hadhrat Khalifatul Masih III(ru) led a team of scholars to explain the teachings of the Promised Messiah(as) to the National Assembly of Pakistan. Despite convincing arguments, they were discarded and an amendment to the Constitution on 7th September, 1974 was passed which declared Ahmadis as non-Muslims.

Jesus(as) Conference In London

A conference titled 'Deliverance of Jesus from the Cross', was held in London in June 1978. Hadhrat Mirza Nasir Ahmad(ru) presented arguments to prove that Jesus(as) survived the ordeal of crucifixion and travelled to Kashmir where he lies buried.

Love For All, Hatred For None

When Hadhrat Khalifatul Masih III(ru) visited Spain in 1980, he laid the foundation stone of the first mosque in Pedroabad on 9th October. It was at this occasion that he announced the Ahmadiyya motto: 'Love for All, Hatred for None'.

Books

The third Khalifa wrote a number of books including *A Message of Peace – A Word of Warning* and *23 Great Objectives of Building the House of Allah*.

His Demise

Hadhrat Khalifatul Masih III(ra) passed away on 9th of June 1982 at Islamabad at the age of 73. He led the community for 17 years.

For further reading on the life of Hadhrat Khalifatul Masih III(ru), please visit:
www.fountainsoflife.co.uk

HADHRAT MIRZA TAHIR AHMAD – Khalifatul Masih IV
(May Allah have mercy on him)

A Man of God

Hadhrat Mirza Tahir Ahmad(ru) grew up righteous and virtuous under the guidance of his father – the second Khalifa and devout mother. Once, during his childhood, he was asked: "Which reward would you cherish most for doing good work? "Allah – Only Allah" was the 10 year old's spontaneous answer. The gift of spiritual awareness was apparent long before his tenure as Hadhrat Khalifatul Masih IV(ru) – the head of the worldwide Ahmadiyya Muslim community.

Early Life of Hadhrat Khalifatul Masih IV(ru)

Hadhrat Mirza Tahir Ahmad(ru) was born in Qadian on 18th December, 1928. He was the grandson of the Promised Messiah(as) and the son of the second Khalifa(ra).

Hadhrat Mirza Tahir Ahmad(ru) obtained his academic and religious degrees from Punjab University in Lahore and Jamia Ahmadiyya in Rabwah. In 1955, he joined the School of Oriental and African Studies in London.

Hadhrat Mirza Tahir Ahmad(ru) travelled around Europe where he became more accustomed with its culture and customs. On this, he said: "...From childhood, I knew both German and English ways. I knew how they looked at things. And, of course, from reading so many English books I was familiar with English life and English humour."

On his return to Pakistan in 1957, he devoted himself to the service of the Ahmadiyya community where held a number of important positions.

Defining Moments of His Career

Hadhrat Mirza Tahir Ahmad(ru) was elected Khalifa on 10th June 1982. Nineteen years of his Khilafat were spent in England.

In April 1984, General Zia-ul-Haq, the then President of Pakistan, proclaimed an ordinance that severely restricted the religious and civil liberties of Ahmadi Muslims. The provisions of this ordinance made it impossible for Hadhrat Khalifatul Masih IV(ru) to function as head of his community. Three days after the promulgation, he left Pakistan for England and never returned to Pakistan.

Milestones of the Fourth Khalifa

The first project launched by Hadhrat Khalifatul Masih IV(ru) was the construction of houses for the poor, widows and orphans in Rabwah, Pakistan and Qadian.

On 10th September, 1982, Hadhrat Khalifatul Masih IV(ru) inaugurated the first mosque to be built in Spain in 700 years.

Under his Khilafat, the Ahmadiyya Muslim a celebrated its centenary in 1989.

'Humanity First', now an international charitable organisation, was established at the behest of Hadhrat Mirza Tahir Ahmad(ru) in 1992, with the charter of helping the needy in calamity stricken areas.

Mosques

During his Khilafat, 5200 mosques were built around the world. On 19th October, 1999 Hadhrat Khalifatul Masih IV(ru) laid the foundation of one of the largest mosques in Europe – Baitul Futuh.

Under his Khilafat, the Holy Qur'an has been translated into more than 60 major languages and one of his greatest achievements was the comprehensive translation of the Holy Qur'an into Urdu.

"I shall cause thy message to reach the corners of the earth" was one of the revelations revealed to the Promised Messiah(as). The fulfilment of this can be credited to Hadhrat Mirza Tahir Ahmad's creation of a global television network called MTA (Muslim Television Ahmadiyya) which today broadcasts all over the world.

Question & Answer sessions:

These historical and timeless sessions were held regularly throughout by Hadhrat Khalifatul Masih IV's and illustrated his remarkable prowess at answering questions on a large breadth of subjects. These are regularly broadcast on MTA.

'Islam's Response to Contemporary Issues' lecture

Hadhrat Mirza Tahir Ahmad's(ru) Delivered an historical lecture on 'Islam's Response to Contemporary Issues at the Queen Elizabeth Conference Centre, London, 1989. A short piece from this lecture is as follows:

> "The right of every human being that his religious sensibilities and sentiments shall not be violated and offended must be recognised... The Qur'anic declaration that all religions are the same at their sources should not be treated lightly. It comprises a world of wisdom, which should be examined and explored by all religions. ...Schemes for the

mutual benefit of mankind must be promoted and encouraged. For instance, philanthropic projects could be undertaken jointly between Christians and Muslims and Hindus and Jews, etc."
(Hadhrat Mirza Tahir Ahmad. From his book and lecture titled *Islam's Response to Contemporary Issues*).

MTA
It was Hadhrat Khalifatul Masih IV's vision for a global channel to promote peace through education that led to the creation of MTA's global satellite network. Many countries also now have their own production studios and all mainly run entirely by volunteers from all walks of life.

Other Important Projects
A passionate believer in the efficacy of homeopathic medicine, Hadhrat Khalifatul Masih IV(ru) imparted his knowledge and skills on the subject through MTA programmes and a book.

Waqf-e-Nau scheme: On April 3rd, 1987, Hadhrat Khalifatul Masih IV(ru) asked community members to dedicate their children to the service of Islam in a scheme called Waqf-e-Nau. Thousands of children worldwide are now part of this program.

On 21st February, 2003, Hadhrat Khalifatul Masih IV(ru) launched the Maryam Shaadi Fund to help poor families affray the cost of their daughters' marriages. This was to be the last major undertaking of his life.

Books
His numerous works were written in English and Urdu. The English books include *Islam's Response to Contemporary Issues* and his magnum opus titled *Revelation, Rationality, Knowledge and Truth*.

Demise
Hadhrat Khalifatul Masih IV(ru) passed away on April 19th, 2003 at his home in London. He was 74 years of age and led the community for 21 years.

For further reading on the life of Hadhrat Khalifatul Masih IV(ru), please visit:
www.fountainsoflife.co.uk

HADHRAT MIRZA MASROOR AHMAD – Khalifatul Masih V
(May Allah Assist him)

Prophecy concerning the fifth Khalifa as recorded in *Tadhkirah*, a book of the Promised Messiah's revelations.

Inni Ma'aka ya Masroor
(I am with you O Masroor!)

Today the Ahmadiyya Muslim community stands at one with its fifth Khalifa, Hadhrat Mirza Masroor Ahmad whose life has been a reflection of dedication, steadfastness, prayer and success. His bond with God leads him to urge his community never to forget the Almighty and never to despair. His focus on prayer is evident for all to see and the fruits of the success of such prayer bear testament to his faith. His sympathy for mankind drives him and his community to serve humanity in the same spirit that the early Muslims served the poor and the needy. His sense of sacrifice mirrors the spirit of sacrifice integral to Islam. Indeed his very life and mission reflect a pure spirit that is ever wary of its responsibilities and ever vigilant for the honour of Islam, its Prophet(saw) and the prophet of the latter days.

Early Life and Before Khilafat

Hadhrat Mirza Masroor Ahmad was born on the 15th September, 1950 in Rabwah, Pakistan. He is the great grandson of the Promised Messiah(as).

At 17 years of age, he became a Moosi – an initiative started by the Promised Messiah(as), where at least one-tenth of lifetime earnings and property are dedicated to the community for progress. Since becoming Khalifa, he has successfully encouraged Ahmadis around the world to also partake of this blessed commitment especially at a young age.

Hadhrat Mirza Masroor Ahmad graduated in 1976 with a Master's of Science Degree in Agricultural Economics.

In 1977, Hadhrat Mirza Masroor Ahmad devoted his life to serve the community and as directed by the third Khalifa, proceeded to Ghana under the 'Nusrat-Jahan' Scheme which supports a large number of hospitals and schools in West Africa. He also served as Principal of two schools at different periods.

Whilst in Ghana, Hadhrat Mirza Masroor Ahmad carried out research on wheat production – the result of which was the first successful experiment of planting, growing and nurturing wheat as an economic crop in Ghana.

His other posts prior to becoming the fifth Khalifa included Naib Sadr (Vice President) Majlis Khuddam-ul-Ahmadiyya Pakistan, Sadr (President), Chairman of the Nasir Foundation, President of Taza'een Rabwah Committee (Committee for the Beautification of Rabwah), Department In-Charge of Financial Affairs, Nazir Ta'lim (Director of Education) and Nazir A'ala (Principal Director) and local Amir (the Executive Head). He remained in this office until his election as Khalifa.

Hadhrat Mirza Masroor Ahmad also expanded the Gulshan-e-Ahmad Nursery and made a personal effort to make Rabwah lush and green.

Imprisonment for Religious Belief

In 1999, Hadhrat Mirza Masroor Ahmad was falsely charged with blasphemy and wrongly accused of defaming verses of the Holy Qur'an. He was arrested and imprisoned for eleven days in Rabwah, Pakistan until it was proven that the charges brought against him were entirely unfounded.

Prayer and Practice of Islam's Teachings

On 22nd April 2003, in the Fazl Mosque in London, Hadhrat Mirza Masroor Ahmad was elected as the fifth Khalifa and has since urged the community to focus on prayer – a sentiment that was apparent from the moment of his election when his admonishment to the community was for "Prayer, Prayer and more Prayer."

Hadhrat Mirza Masroor Ahmad is particularly dedicated to removing misconceptions about Islam and extolling Islam's pure virtues and as a religion of peace.

On 3rd October 2003, Hadhrat Khalifatul Masih V inaugurated the Baitul Futuh Mosque – an event covered by the world's media.

The respect and dignity shown to the Khalifa by prominent people including world leaders, kings and VIPs is testament to his standing as a great spiritual leader.

In 2008, during the Khilafat centenary, he delivered historical addresses to MPs, VIP's and other dignitaries at the House of Commons and at the Queen Elizabeth II Conference Centre in Westminster.

Since his election as Khalifa, Hadhrat Mirza Masroor Ahmad has travelled abroad extensively and has delivered a number of inspiring speeches to audiences from all cultures and backgrounds. Presented below are just some extracts of various speeches that illustrate some of his aspirations, hopes and wishes for a more peaceful society for all.

"There is no religion in the world – be it Islam, or Christianity, or Hinduism or for that matter any other faith – that advocates the destruction of peace. Each person likes peace and hates disorder. Every heart is inclined towards good deeds and every good-natured person wants that peace should be established in the world."

"Remember that a very great good work is to be loyal to your nation and to love it. In fact, according to one Hadith, to love one's country is a part of faith."

"Terrorism of any kind has no place in religion. Islam is no exception, for it is a faith that professes peace and respect for all. Indeed, the Holy Qur'an likens anyone who takes the life of innocent people, as one who has committed a crime against all of humanity"

Lord Avebury, a distinguished Parliamentarian, founder and former Chair of the All Party Parliamentary Human Rights Group, speaking to a packed audience about the fifth Khalifa at the peace conference said:

"His Holiness eloquently and persistently returns to these themes of peace and tolerance love and understanding among the followers of different faiths...

...We desperately need the moral leadership and guidance that we can look for to His Holiness to provide...

...I have heard in many of his sermons, emphasis on what is called the Rahmaniyyat of the Gracious God. This is the Divine quality of kindness, compassion and benevolence spoken of by the Holy Prophet and his own [Hudhur's] predecessor, the Promised Messiah...

In asking His Holiness to address us we thank the Ahmadiyya Muslim community for their presence here in the UK and throughout the world, and we humbly and respectfully thank Hudhur the example that he provides not just for his own community but for the whole of the human race."

Hadhrat Mirza Masroor Ahmad has written a number of books including *Conditions of Bai'at* and *Responsibilities of an Ahmadi*.

For further reading on the life of Hadhrat Khalifatul Masih V, please visit:
www.fountainsoflife.co.uk

Companions from the blessed family of the Promised Messiah(as)

Companions from the blessed family of the Promised Messiah(as)

A brief sketch of Hadhrat Khalifatul Masih II(ra), Mirza Bashir-ud-Din Mahmood Ahmad has already been given in the previous chapter. Here are the other Companions from the family. The life sketch of lady members of the family and other pioneer women companions will published in the revised volume of this compilation.

QAMAR-UL-ANBIYA HADHRAT MIRZA BASHIR AHMAD

Hadhrat Mirza Bashir-ud-Din Ahmad(ra) was the second son of the Promised Messiah(as). He was born on 20th April 1893. The revelation that the Promised Messiah(as) received before his birth was: 'The moon of the prophets is going to come and you will succeed in your work. God Almighty will make thee very happy and grant thee very strong arguments and He will grant thee a son. The grace of God shall also be granted to thee and My Divine Light is very near.' (*Aeenah Kamalat-e-Islam*, pp.266-7, printed February 1893.)

Hadhrat Mirza Bashir-ud-Din Ahmad(ra) learned to read the Holy Qur'an at home. Hadhrat Mian Bashir-ud-Din Ahmad passed his Entrance Examination from the Talim-ul-Islam High School, Qadian and his intermediate with Honours from the Government College Lahore. He obtained his B.A and M.A degrees as a private candidate.

He was married to Sarwar Sultana Begum, daughter of Maulawi Ghulam Hassan Khan of Peshawar.

Hadhrat Mirza Bashir Ahmad served the Jama'at in various capacities which include the following.

1. Teacher of mathematics in the Ta'lim-ul Islam High School, Qadian.
2. Editor of T*he Review of Religions*.
3. Officer-in-Charge Madressah Ahmadiyya and the T.I High School.
4. Naazir Umoor-e-Ammah.
5. Naazir Ta'leem-o-Tarbiyat.
6. Officer Jalsa Salana.
7. Assistant to Hadhrat Maulawi Sher Ali in translating the Holy Qur'an into English.
8. Supervised the collection and publication of *Tadhkira*, a book

containing the revelations of the Promised Messiah(as) in 1935.

9. He was the first President of Khilafat Jubilee Committee.
10. He was appointed Naazir-e-A'ala
11. On 31st August 1947 he was appointed the Ameer of Qadian and all other branches in India.
12. Hadhrat Khalifatul-Masih II(ra) appointed a board of seven members to supervise the work of the Sadr Anjamun-e-Ahmadiyya, the Tahrik-e-Jadeed and Waqf-e-Jadeed. Hadhrat Mirza Bashir Ahmad was appointed its president.

After the partition of India whenever Hadhrat Khalifatul- Masih II(ra) travelled out of Rabwah he would appoint Hadhrat Mirza Bashir Ahmad as local Ameer for Rabwah.

Hadhrat Mirza Bashir Ahmad(ra) is the author of the following books:

Seerat-i-Khaatam-an-Nabiyyeen, Seerat-ul-Mahdi, Tableegh-e-Hidaayat, Silsilah Ahmadiyya, Our God, Kalima-tul-Fasl, Al-Hujja-tul-Balighah, Khatm-e-Nabuwwat kee Haqeeqat, Chalees Jawahar pare (Forty-Piece of Diamond), Seerat-e-Tayyebah, Durr-e-Manthoor, Dur-e-Maknoon, Tarbiyati Mazameen.

Hadhrat Mian Bashir Ahmad(ra) was granted very blessed qualities and attributes by Allah the Almighty. In particular he used to look after the poor people of the Ahmadiyya Community as well as widows, orphans and deserving students.

Hadhrat Mirza Bashir Ahmad(ra) passed away on 2nd September 1963. He is buried in Bahishti Maqbra, Rabwah, Pakistan.

HADHRAT MIRZA SHARIF AHMAD SAHIB

Hadhrat Mirza Sharif Ahmad, the third son of the Promised Messiah(as) was born at Qadian in 1895. Before his birth, the Promised Messiah(as) received the following revelations:

"Allah will decree his life span. No enemy will succeed in terminating his life. He will die a natural death."

"Now you take our place – I am going," said Promised Messiah(as) in a vision to him. It is quite likely and his life history does confirm that he was to resemble the Promised Messiah(as) closely in some of his attributes. He was known, for example, in likeness of his father in appearance and humility of character.

"Allah will prolong his life beyond expectations".
This revelation miraculously testifies to its truth in that Sahibzada Sahib passed through many critical moments because of his health which were oft-returning and at times very grave, but his life span was prolonged by the grace of Allah.

"He will act as QAZI" [a judge].
Another revelation of the Promised Messiah(as). He was appointed officially as Judge at Ahmadiyya Headquarters together with Sheikh Bashir Ahmad. Justice Sheikh Bashir Ahmad states that he was eminently just, and possessed clear thinking for decision-making.

"Here, Came The King"
This is another divine revelation. He truly acted like a king and was humble at heart. Allah the Almighty had given him such a heart that even the worldly king was not given such a kingdom of heart. In every financial position, he always helped the poor and was very sensitive towards their feelings. He often went out of his way in finding out the problems and difficulties of his sub-ordinates, co-workers, neigh-bours or the general public in the community and would assist them.

Hadhrat Mirza Sharif Ahmad(ra) was well known for his humble nature, simple life-style and wise counsel. He was appointed director of a special department to protect and defend Qadian in the wake of a severe opposition mounted by Ahrars of India against Ahmadis.

Hadhrat Mirza Sharif Ahmad(ra) rendered services as a captain in the Territorial Regiment in British India at Ambala. He commanded Ahmadiyya

Territorial Force and maintained an excellent record of army discipline. He was very particular in reading out the Promised Messiah's[(as)] books to his family members after Fajr prayer and used to give dars from Hadith *Bukhari* at Mubarak Mosque, Rabwah.

Hadhrat Mirza Sharif Ahmad[(ra)] personally taught the Holy Qur'an to children of his family and relatives with particular emphasis on correct pronunciation. He also spent six months studying at Al-Azhar University in Cairo, Egypt.

Hadhrat Mirza Sharif Ahmad[(ra)] acted as Nazir Education, Nazir Islah-o-Irshad and Nazir special duty at Headquarters Qadian and Rabwah. He played a very important role in quelling the opposition that sprung up at the time of the last days of first Khalifa.

Hadhrat Mirza Sharif Ahmad[(ra)] passed away on 26th December1961 on the first day of Annual gathering of the Ahmadiyya Jama'at at Rabwah, Pakistan. He was buried in Bahishti Maqbara. May Allah be pleased with him and shower His abundant blessings on him. (Ameen).

HADHRAT ABDUL SATTAR SHAH SAHIB(RA)

Dr. Syed Abdul Sattar Shah Sahib (may Allah be pleased with him) was born in the village Kallar Syedan of District Rawalpindi. He belonged to a noble family of 'Sadaat'. His father Syed Gul Hassan Shah was a very pious person.

Dr. Syed Abdul Sattar Shah(ra) embraced Ahmadiyyat in 1901 and migrated to Qadian in 1920. Many of his narrations are recorded in the book *Seeratul-Mahdi*. One of these says that once Dr. Sattar Shah Sahib went to pay a visit to the Promised Messiah(as) and sat on a mat on the floor in the presence of Hudhur. When Hudhur saw him sitting on the floor, he insisted that Dr. Shah Sahib should sit on the bed rather than on the mat and added that as he was a Syed so he should be respected. Dr Shah Sahib said: 'Since then I became sure that I had really descended from a "Sadaat" family'.

Hadhrat Maulawi Sher Ali(ra), who was given the title of 'an angel' by the Promised Messiah(as), while paying tribute on the sad demise of Dr Sattar Shah Sahib said that he was a very pious person, beneficent and a blessed soul very rarely seen in this world. Hadhrat Abdul Sattar Shah Sahib(ra) died on 23th June at the age of 75 years.

■ HADHRAT MIRZA AZIZ AHMAD M.A.(RA)

Hadhrat Mirza Aziz Ahmad, son of (Hadhrat) Mirza Sultan Ahmad, was born on 3rd October 1890 at Qadian. He was the first grandson of the Promised Messiah(as) and joined the fold of Ahmadiyyat around 1905 whilst he was a student of the 9th class Talimul Islam High School, Qadian.

Mirza Aziz Ahmad Sahib passed his Entrance (Matriculation) Examination in 1906 and went on to join the Aligarh College where he graduated in 1910. He then joined the Government College, Lahore and obtained his Master's Degree in Economics after which he joined the Punjab Civil Service.

The Promised Messiah(as) had a vision on 20th October 1899, in which he saw a boy of slender built with a rosy complexion whose name was Aziz and the word 'Sultan' formed part of his father's name. This vision came true when Mirza Aziz Ahmad, son of Mirza Sultan Ahmad was brought to the Promised Messiah(as) in the Mubarak Mosque by Sheikh Yaqub Ali Irfani. He took initiation there and joined the Ahmadiyya Movement. The following day, Mirza Aziz Ahmad Sahib was invited to a feast along with other members of the family at the house of the Promised Messiah(as) who was very pleased with his own grandson's initiation and the fulfillment of his vision.

Mirza Aziz Sahib had also the privilege of being a member travelling to Peshawar as part of the marriage party of Sahibzada Mirza Bashir Ahmad(ra) on 10th May 1906. On the death of his first wife, Mirza Aziz Sahib married Nasirah Begum, the eldest daughter of Hadhrat Mir Muhammad Ishaq in March 1930.

After his retirement from government service, Mirza Aziz Sahib placed his services at the disposal of Hadhrat Khalifatul Masih II(ra). He was appointed Chief Secretary to Hadhrat Khalifatul Masih II(ra) in 1949 in which capacity he served the Community for many years.

Mirza Aziz Ahmad Sahib possessed all the good qualities of head and heart and the study of the Holy Qur'an gave him an insight into the realm of spirituality. He was a loving husband, kind father, faithful friend and a noble man. He was well known for his jovial talk, pleasing manners and sympathetic attitude. He died after a brief illness, on 23rd January 1973 and was buried in the special enclosure (Qita'a Khas) of the Bahishti Maqbara, Rabwah.

Companions of the Promised Messiah(as)

1. Mian Abdul Aziz Mughal (1875-1944)

Mian Abdul Aziz Mughal was born in 1875. He was a young student when his Arabic teacher in the Aitcheson High School Lahore showed a small pamphlet to his students. It was from Hadhrat Mirza Ghulam Ahmad of Qadian. The pamphlet clearly expressed in so many words that he (Mirza Ghulam Ahmad of Qadian) was the Mahdi and the Messiah whose advent had been foretold in all religious scriptures.

Abdul Aziz Mughal, a young student of eighth grade, listened intently as his teacher read out slowly the contents of the pamphlet to the class. He noted down a few details on a piece of paper and at the termination of the class went home straight to his maternal grandfather – Mian Qaim-Din. He meekly described to him the details of the pamphlet and requested him to take him to Qadian. An intense desire had arisen in his heart to see the man at Qadian who claimed to be the Promised Messiah and Mahdi. Baba Qaim-Din as he was known to the youngsters of the family, was somewhat hesitant in the beginning but later he relented when he saw tears rolling down the cheeks of his fifteen year old grandson.

They reached Qadian next day on a murky afternoon of Dec 1891. It was raining heavily and the atmosphere was cold and dark. Baba Qaim-Din was sick and extremely annoyed at his grandson's escapade, but the Promised Messiah(as) was kind enough to grant an audience to young Abdul Aziz who took the covenant of Bait the same evening.

From belief to practice in case of Mian Abdul Aziz was indeed a short step. Mian Abdul Aziz became an entirely changed person. His studies and later on his zeal as a businessman all became subservient to one intense desire; to serve the faith for all times and in all circumstances. He sat at the feet of his Master for a period of eighteen years and observed keenly the Promised Messiah's daily routine; the clothes he wore; the food he ate; the books he wrote and the way he talked and conversed with his own people and the hosts of strangers who poured into Qadian daily from all parts of the world.

Like Hadhrat Abu-Hurairah, a companion of the Holy Prophet(saw), Mian Mughal remembered a large number of the 'Rawayaat' of the Promised Messiah(as) and had them recorded during his lifetime. These 'Rawayaat' are held in the records of Fazle-Umar Library Rabwah.

He personally witnessed scores of signs and miracles of the Promised

Messiah[(as)]. Mian Mughal Sahib was a pious person. Once he told a non-Ahmadi friend that he had seen The Holy Prophet[(saw)] so many times in dreams and awakenings that he could be mistaken in recognising his own father in darkness or from a distance but never so in the case of the Holy Prophet[(saw)]. For days on end Mian Mughal would leave his house early morning for 'Tabligh' and would return home very late at night. His zeal for Tabligh was unending and according to an estimate he had converted at least 700 non-Ahmadis into the Ahmadiyyat. His prayers were mostly answered instantly or shortly afterwards. He died in April 1944 at Lahore.

Hadhrat Khalifatul Masih II[(ra)] was staying in Lahore in those days. He went to the house of Mian Abdul Aziz Mughal and on seeing the face of Mian Mughal Sahib, Hadhrat Khalifatul Masih II[(ra)] said: "The people of this kind do not come to this world very often".

It should be mentioned here that the Mian family of Lahore accepted Ahmadiyyat during the "Great Mubahala" between the Promised Messiah[(as)] and Maulawi Abdul Haq Ghaznawi held in 1892 at Idgah-Amritsar in which the Maulawis left the Mubahala ground utterly defeated.

(Written by Major (Rtd.) Abdur Rahman Mughal)

(2) Muhammad Abul Hassan Bazdar Baluch (d.1938)

Maulawi Abul Hassan, son of Maulawi Abdul Qadir, belonged to a Baluch clan of Dere Ghazi Khan. In his early youth he went from place to place to seek theological knowledge till he reached Delhi and had his lessons in Hadith from Maulawi Muhammad Ishaque of Rampur, a pupil of Maulawi Nazir Hussain of Delhi. In 1884 when Hadhrat Mirza Ghulam Ahmad of Qadian went to Delhi for his marriage, Maulawi Abul Hassan was constructing a house close to Hadhrat Mir Nasir Nawab's residence.

It was through the reading of the books of the Promised Messiah(as) that thoroughly convinced him of his truth. He hastened to write a letter of allegiance to the Promised Messiah(as) instead he personally paid a visit to Qadian in l900 and entered the fold of Ahmadiyyat at his blessed hands. It was a day of Eid. Maulawi Sahib doubly enjoyed the Eid because he joined the blessed company of the Mahdi whose advent had been expected by Muslim divines for centuries.

Maulawi Sahib took upon himself as a duty to preach the message of the Promised Messiah(as) to the people in his native district. He met with severe opposition from his own people on either side of the river Indus but he was firm as a rock and finally succeeded in establishing Ahmadiyya communities at Kot Qaisarani, Basti Rindan, Basti Mandarani and Basti Buzdar.

He preached to his nearest relations and was extremely successful in his efforts. Maulawi Muhammad Khan, a relative of his, went to Qadian and passed his Maulawi Fazil (highest proficiency in Arabic) from there. The Ahmadiyya communities of Dera Ghazi Khan are visible proof of his sincere and strenuous efforts of the propagation of Ahmadiyyat, the true Islam. He breathed his last on October 29, l938.

May his soul rest in perpetual peace. Ameen

(3) Hadhrat Maulawi Abdul Kareem Sialkoti (1858-1905)

Hadhrat Maulawi Abdul Karim Sahib was born in 1858 at Sialkot. He was named Kareem Bukhsh, which was later changed by the Promised Messiah(as) to Abdul Kareem.

Abdul Kareem Sahib received his initial instructions of the Holy Qur'an and Hadith and read a few books in Persian at the local mosque. He also read and studied Arabic and Persian and became very fluent and accomplished in his efforts. He was employed by the American Mission School in Sialkot to teach Persian and subsequently joined the Board Middle School.

Abdul Kareen Sahib soon left this post and began a series of public addresses aimed at the general improvement of Muslims. The site of these lectures used to be the market place in Sialkot called Raja Bazaar.

Hadhrat Maulawi Sahib was blessed with a very prominent and pleasant voice and his lectures were well received and proved to be very effective. His recitation of the Holy Qur'an had such a pleasant and harmonious rhythm that even Hindus and Sikhs were, at times, deeply touched when they listened to it. At some occasions, the atmosphere would become so charged with a sense of spirituality that it would seem that the angels themselves had come to sing the hymns of the Almighty.

The fame of Hadhrat Maulawi Sahib's lectures spread far and wide and people used to come from far-off places to listen to him. He soon became a very accomplished orator. His fluency in Arabic, Persian and English was acknowledged by many well-known scholars in these languages. The local Christian Missionaries became very worried by his growing fame and tried continously to get him to work for them, but all their efforts were in vain.

For some time, Hadhrat Maulawi Sahib had been closely associated with Hadhrat Maulawi Nur-ud-Din Sahib(ra). On one occasion, Maulawi Abdul Kareem Sahib had stayed with Hadhrat Maulawi Nur-ud-Din Sahib(ra) in Kashmir for a period of six months. It was this close friendship of Hadhrat Maulawi Sahib that eventually led him into the fold of Ahmadiyyat.

Hadhrat Maulawi Sahib first met the Promised Messiah(as) in March 1888. In September 1898, he moved permanently to Qadian. He lived in the part of the house of the Promised Messiah(as) which was attached to the upper terrace of the Masjid Mubarak. Below this were situated the living quarters of the Promised Messiah(as) himself. Maulawi Sahib was also given the duty of leading the congregation in the five daily prayers and the Friday prayers, a duty which he preformed throughout his life.

Hadhrat Promised Messiah(as) received revelations concerning

Maulawi Sahib in the words, 'Leader of the Muslims'. Maulawi Sahib once fell seriously ill with carbuncle. The severity of the illness was so great that his recovery and subsequent survival for the period of fifteen days is a miracle and that this was merely a result of the prayers of the Promised Messiah(as) in accordance with divine revelations. However, the recovery from his illness proved to be a temporary one. God had also indicated to Hadhrat Sahib, in repeated revelations that Maulawi Sahib's demise was approaching. On Wednesday the 11th of October 1905 at 2.30pm he breathed his last.

In accordance with the instructions of the Promised Messiah(as) on 12th October 1905, Hadhrat Maulawi Sahib's body was placed in a wooden coffin and he was buried temporarily (imanatan) at the Qadian graveyard. At that time, Hadhrat Masih Mau'od(as) wanted to establish the Bahishti Maqbara in accordance with the command of Allah and it was Hudhur's desire that the first disciple to be buried in this blessed graveyard should be Hadhrat Maulawi Sahib. Thus on 26th December 1905, on the occasion of the Annual Gathering when many Ahmadis from outside had come to Qadian in large numbers and after the noon (Zuhr) and afternoon (Asr) prayer, devotees carrying Hadhrat Maulawi Sahib's coffin on their shoulders entered the Garden, earmarked for the Bahishti Maqbara. The next day at about 10am, Hudhur led his funeral service and Maulawi Sahib was finally laid to rest in the Bahishti Maqbara. In this way, Hadhrat Maulawi Sahib's burial, in affect, constituted the inauguration of the blessed graveyard of Bahishti Maqbara.

Hadhrat Masih Mau'od(as) wrote a very moving ode in Persian for Maulawi Sahib, which was engraved on his tombstone in which he extolled the virtues of this great disciple of his.

Hadhrat Maulawi Abdul Kareem Sahib (May Allah be pleased with him) wrote many valuable books and tracts, including: A lecture entitled 'The Sin'. Lecture entitled, 'The Reformation and Renaissance brought about by the Promised Messiah(as)', *Seerat Hadhrat Masih Mau'od, Isbate-e-Khilafat-e-Sheikhain* (in support of the caliphate of the leaders, i.e. the caliphate of Hadhrat Abu Bakr(ra), Umar(ra) and Osman(ra)), *Khilafate-e-Rashida*, part 1, *Al Qaulul Fasih fil isbat e Haqeeqatul Masih, Da'watun Nidwa, Khutubat-e-Kareemia*, collected by Hadhrat Irfani Sahib, *Al-Furqan (Khilafate Rashida part 2)*.

(4) Maulawi Abdul Mughni of Jhelum (d.1966)

Maulawi Mughni Sahib name has also been recorded in the list of the first 313 Companions of the Promised Messiah(as). He was the son of Maulawi Burhan-ud-Din of Jhelum who was one of the earliest Companions of the Promised Messiah(as).

Maulawi Mughni Sahib was meek and humble of spirit, but austere and strict in the observance of his religious duties. He was Amir of the Ahmadiyya Jama'at in Jhelum till he breathed his last on 10th June 1966.

Maulawi Mughni Sahib did not initially execute a Will because he preferred to be buried by the side of his revered father in the public cemetery of Jhelum. However, when a relative of his, Maulana Abul Ata, conveyed to him that Hadhrat Khalifatul Masih III(ru) desired each and every Ahmadi to make a Will, he set about creating his. When he passed away, he was buried in the Bahishti Maqbara, Qita'a Sahaba (special reserve for the companions of the Promised Messiah(as)) at Rabwah, Pakistan.

(5) Hadhrat Maulana Abdur Rahim Nayyar

Hadhrat Maulana Abdur Rahim Nayyar was a Companion of the Promised Messiah(as) and took covenant of Bai'at in 1901. After Bai'at, he was first sent to London.

Maulana Nayyar Sahib also worked in Sierra Leone, Nigeria and Ghana and was the founder of Ahmadiyya Missions in these countries. In the African countries, he started his journey on 9th February 1921 and arrived in Sierra Leone on 21st February 1921. After a few days stay, he went to Ghana on 28th February. He arranged lectures, public meetings and conversations in these two countries. On 8th April 1921, he went to Lagos, the capital city of Nigeria and stayed there for four months.

Maulana Nayyar Sahib kept moving in these three countries and converted a large number of people to Ahmadiyyat. After consolidating the Ahmadiyya Missions in West Africa, he was posted in London by Hadhrat Khalifatul Masih II(ra) and took charge of the London Mission.

In 1924, when Hadhrat Khalifatul Masih II(ra) visited London for participation in the Wembley Conference, Maulana Nayyar Sahib was also present and attended the foundation-stone laying ceremony of the Fazl Mosque. He accompanied Hudhur on his return journey to Qadian in November, 1924.

Maulana Nayyar Sahib passed away at the age of 65, and was buried in Bahishti Maqbara at Rabwah.

(6) Maulawi Abdur Rahman Fazil (d.1977)

Maulawi Abdur Rahman, son of Shaikh Barkat Ali and nephew of Hafiz Hamid Ali, came from Faizullah Chak, a village some five miles to the south west of Qadian. Hafiz Hamid Ali brought his nephew, Abdur Rahman to Qadian in 1903.

After the sad demise of Maulawi Abdul Karim of Sialkot and Maulawi Burhan-ud Din of Jhelum in 1905, the Promised Messiah(as) proposed to open a theology class to prepare a party of Ulema who were to be well versed in Islamic teachings. Abdur Rahman Sahib was one of the students who formed 'the new class'. Some 20 years later, the school was raised to the status of a Theology College and named the Jamia Ahmadiyya.

After passing his Maulawi Fazil Examination, Maulawi Rahman Sahib was attached to the Madrasa Ahmadiyya in Qadian teaching logic and theology. In addition to his academic responsibilities, he also performed extra mural duties, which occupied much of his time. He was also in charge of the Qaza.

After the partition of the country in 1947, Maulawi Rahman Sahib was allowed to remain behind in Qadian as Amir of the Ahmadiyya Community of Qadian. On the strength of his character and qualities as a man of justice and fair play, he was also elected President of the Municipal Committee of Qadian unanimously by Hindus, Sikhs and Muslims.

Even in his school days, Maulawi Rahman Sahib enjoyed an excellent physique and was an all-round sportsman. He distinguished himself as an excellent footballer. He also played hockey and volleyball. Maulawi Rahman Sahib had a commanding voice and as such he awakened boarders for the morning prayers. Maulawi Rahman Sahib passed away in January 1977.

(7) Babu Faqir Ali, Station Master (Retired) (d.1959)

Faqir Ali Sahib, son of Shadi, belonged to Aujla in the District of Gurdaspur. He passed his Matriculation examination in 1899 in the First Division and later joined the Railway Service in 1900. He became well known for his honesty and truthfulness during his service in the Railways.

From his school age, Faqir Ali Sahib was regular in his daily prayers. Acquaintance between him and Mr. Abdul Ghani of Aujla, who was a staunch Ahmadi, grew into a strong and lasting friendship. Events such as a letter sent to him by post entitled 'Al-Anzaar' to Babu Faqir Ali in Sindh, the terrible earthquake of Kangra in 1905 and the perusal of the Ishtihar, shook the very foundation of Baboo Faqir Ali's life as he seriously started pondering over the claims of the Promised Messiah(as). One day, he decided to study the Holy Qur'an to see what it said about the truth or otherwise of Hadhrat's claim to Messiahship and noted in Ch.12;V.32 that it read: *'He is not a human being; He is but a noble angel'.* Faqir Ali Sahib took this to be a good sign and decided to join the Ahmadiyya Movement. He rendered his written allegiance in March 1905 and visited Qadian personally in November of the same year.

Faqir Ali Sahib sent his two sons, Bashir Ahmad and Nazir Ahmad to join the Talimul-Islam High School, Qadian. In 1927, when the North Western Railway opened the Batala-Qadian section, Babu Faqir Ali was appointed the first Station Master, Qadian.

His second son, Nazir Ahmad Ali, volunteered his service as a Missionary for West Africa where he worked selflessly for the whole of his life. He died there a martyr and was laid to rest in the graveyard of Bo, Sierra Leone on 19th May 1955.

Babu Faqir Ali Sahib died four years after the death of his noble son on 13th December 1959 and was buried in the Bahishti Maqbara, Rabwah. May his soul ever rest in peace.

(8) Hadhrat Bhai Abdur Rahim (Jagat Singh) - (d.1957)

Hadhrat Bhai Abdur Rahim's real name was Jagat Singh before he accepted Ahmadiyyat. It was whilst he was serving in the army when he became interested in Ahmadiyyat as a result of discussions held in his circles.

Abdur Rahim Sahib decided to read some books and pamphlets about Ahmadiyyat and later traveled to Qadian where he met some prominent Companions of the Promised Messiah(as). One day, in 1894, after sincere and earnest prayers, he took Bai'at at the hands of the Promised Messiah(as). He also listened to the recitation of Holy Qur'an from Hadhrat Maulawi Abdul Karim Sahib Sialkoti.

When Hadhrat Rahim Sahib returned to his Army unit, his colleagues criticised him and forced him to come back to their own religion. When his opposition became unbearable, he decided to resign from the services and left to settle permanently in Qadian.

In Qadian, he was fortunate to benefit from teachers like Hadhrat Maulawi Nur-ud-Din(ra) and Hadhrat Maulawi Abdul Karim Sahib. He learned the Holy Qur'an, Hadith and Arabic grammar from Hadhrat Maulawi Nur-ud-Din(ra).

Hadhrat Bhai Abdur Rahim Sahib also served as a teacher in High School Qadian for 29 years. He was separated from his Sikh wife, so the Promised Messiah(as) arranged his marriage with the widowed sister of Mirza Afzal Baig Sahib. He had one son named Dr. Abdur Rehman Sahib who served in the army as a Major.

On the instructions of the Promised Messiah(as), Hadhrat Rahim Sahib served Hadhrat Maulawi Muhammad Din Sahib during his sickness and also performed security duties. He was very fortunate to accompany the Promised Messiah(as) during his journey to Jhelum on 15th January 1903 and also the journey to Delhi in October 1905.

Hadhrat Rahim Sahib wrote many articles in *Alfazl* and served as a teacher at Madrasa Qadian and also as Superintendent of Boarding House. During the 'Tahrik of Shudhee', he traveled to Agra and Mathra.

Hadhrat Rahim Sahib passed away on 9th July 1957 at the age of 84 in Rabwah and Hadhrat Musleh Maud(ra) led his Namaz-e-Janaza. In terms of financial sacrifices, he was amongst the first and devoted a quarter of his income to the community. He was buried at the Bahishti Maqbarah, Rabwah.

(9) Hadhrat Bahi Mahmood Ahmad
(1887-1970)

Hadhrat Bahi Mahmood Ahmad Sahib was born in 1887 and was from Dhinga (Ghujrat). He took bai'at at the hands of the Promised Messiah(as) in 1901 and studied in Talimul Islam High School in Qadian. He first served at the Noor Hospital Qadian and later opened his own dispensary.

After the partition of India-Pakistan, Hadhrat Mahmood Sahib migrated to Sargodha where he established a surgery. He was very successful in his medical profession and had the God-bestowed gift of curing people by his method of treatment.

Hadhrat Mahmood Sahib was a very pious and devoted servant of the Jama'at. He always recited various prayers and was regular in his Tahajjud prayers. He was a very simple, and a noble man who was fond of Tabligh. He loved reading the Holy Qur'an and books of the Promised Messiah(as). During Ramadan, he usually completed the reading of the Holy Qur'an at least seven times.

Hadhrat Mahmood Sahib trained his son, Dr Masood Ahmad as Hafiz-e-Qur'an. During Jalsa Salana, his house was always full of guests and he took much care for their comfort.

Hadhrat Bhai Mahmood Ahmad Sahib died on 29th June 1970 at the age of 83. He was a Moosi.

(10) Hadhrat Chaudhry Bashir Ahmad
(1898-1985)

Chaudhary Bashir Ahmad was born in 1898 at Chahoor Kahlowan, Tahseel Pasroor in the District of Sialkot. His father Chaudhary Ghulam Ahmad joined the Jama'at when Bashir Ahmad was only a student. Bashir Ahmad Sahib was the eldest of four children and along with his maternal uncle was sent to Qadian for early schooling.

When Pandit Lekh Ram met his end, Bashir Ahmad Sahib was one of those who testified that the Promised Messiah's(as) prophecy regarding the Pandit had been fulfilled in its entirety.

Bashir Ahmad Sahib attended schools at Pasroor and Sialkot and passed his Matriculation examination in 1917. He was admitted to the Islamiyya College in Lahore. After graduating in 1921, he joined the Law College in Lahore from where he graduated two years later and started a Law practice in Sialkot under the guidance of his father, Chaudhary Mohammad Ameen, who was by then one of the two top Muslim lawyers in Sialkot.

Chaudhary Bashir Ahmad was blessed on many occasions to be in the company of the Promised Messiah(as). Along with his mother and his grandmother, he had the great honour of staying at the Promised Messiah's(as) house and on one occasion saw the Promised Messiah(as) pick up his younger daughter and embrace her. About two years before Bashir Ahmad Sahib died, he wrote a letter to Hadhrat Sahibzadi Amtul Hafeez Begum telling her of this incident.

Bashir Ahmad Sahib's wife, though inclined towards Ahmadiyyat, joined the Jama'at several years after they were married as a result of a dream in which she had seen the Promised Messiah(as).

In 1927, when he was eligible to practice as an Advocate in the Lahore High Court, he accepted an offer from Hadhrat Chaudhry Zafrulla Khan Sahib to be his Assistant in his Law Practice. He moved to Lahore and the bond with Hadhrat Zafrulla Khan Sahib became ever closer. Thereafter, he continued to rise to several higher offices in Government and industries both in India and later in Pakistan.

Chaudhry Bashir Sahib never retired completely and continued to attend his office until about three weeks before he passed away. He died on 16th November 1985, some ten weeks after the death of his closest friend Hadhrat Chaudhry Sahib.

Chaudhry Bashir Sahib was always closely associated with the activities of the Jama'at and was a Moosi. He was an excellent example not only for his own family but also for all his friends within and outside the Jama'at. His integrity was absolute. He was a well-wisher of all and was always assisted anyone in need. He never asked or expected any reward. He knew his reward would come from the Almighty and it did come to him often and in abundance. Whenever there was an invitation to subscribe for the purpose of construction or repair of a Mosque, he always subscribed liberally. At least half the cost of the Model Town Mosque Lahore was borne by him and his family.

Chaudhry Bashir Sahib was very sensitive in his nature and any bad news affected him immediately. His expression and appearance showed concern. His trust in Allah was of a very high order and he would come to terms with any situation and circumstance very quickly.

Although Chaudhry Bashir Sahib had a very refined taste for food, he led a relatively simple life in accordance with Islamic teachings and would never tolerate waste.

(11) Chaudhry Fateh Muhammad Sayyal – Missionary UK

Hadhrat Chaudhry Fateh Muhammad Sayyal took the covenant of Bai'at in 1899 along with his father Chaudhry Nizamuddin at the blessed hands of the Promised Messiah(as). Due to his great desire for propagation of Ahmadiyyat, he offered to dedicate his life for this purpose and the Promised Messiah(as) graciously accepted his request.

Hadhrat Fateh Muhammad Sayyal arrived in England in July 1913 and initially took up residence at the Woking Mission House. In April 1914, on the instruction of Hadhrat Khalifatul Masih II(ra), he went to London where he stayed till March 1916 before returning to Qadian.

In 1919, Hadhrat Khalifatul Masih II(ra) sent Chaudhry Sahib back to London for two years. During this period, Chaudhry Sahib purchased some land and a house in the Southfields area for the purpose of building a mosque and this is where the present Fazl Mosque now stands.

In 1924, Chaudhary Sahib accompanied Hadhrat Khalifatul Masih II(ra) to London as a delegate in the 'Great Religions Conference' which was held at Wembley, England.

Chaudhry Sahib held important assignments in the organisation of Ahmadiyya Jama'at at Qadian, namely – Nazir Daawat-o-Tabligh, Nazir Taleef-o-Ishaat and Nazir-e-Aala. After the partition of Indo-Pak, he came to Pakistan and served as Nazir Islah-o-Irshad from 1954 to 1960.

He died at the age of 73 and was buried at Bahishti Maqbara Rabwah.

(12) Hadhrat Munshi Fayyaz Ali

Munshi Fayyaz Ali was one of the Companions of the Promised Messiah(as). He originally came from a town called Saraoah in the district of Merath, but later settled in Kapurthala. His name is in the first 313 Companions of the Promised Messiah(as).

Munshi Sahib was indeed a brave person and openly preached Ahmadiyyat. He was always on the lookout for the Arya Samaaj and also confronted the Christian priests in public discussions and never hesitated to talk to them in the matter of religious disputes.

The opponents of Ahmadiyyat in Kapurthala forcefully occupied the Ahmadiyya Mosque and the Ahmadis had no other resort but to go to the court and file a case against the Muslims of Kapurthala. The number of the Ahmadis was very small and none of them held any position of influence. The opposing Muslims held strong hope that the case would be decided in their favour and that the Ahmadis will never get possession of their Mosque. The opposition was very severe. Their opponents blocked even the roads for the Ahmadis. Hafiz Imam Din, the Ahmadi Imam of the Mosque, was badly beaten by the Muslim vagabonds and was dragged along the road. He was bitterly abused and his opponents burned his turban. Calling bad names and abuses of the Ahmadis had become a daily routine.

It was during those bitter days that lasted seven months that Munshi Fayyaz Sahib happened to go to Ludhiana where he mentioned to the Promised Messiah(as) that the Ahmadiyya mosque had been forcibly taken by the non-Ahmadi Muslims and urged him for prayers. The Promised Messiah(as) was greatly disturbed on hearing the news and said: 'If I have truly been raised by God Almighty then you are bound to get the mosque back.'

Munshi Fayyaz Sahib was never afraid of spreading the truth. When he returned from Ludhiana, he told the opponents of Kapurthala what the Promised Messiah(as) had said. For some, it did not seem very wise thing on the part of Munshi Fayyaz Sahib to have uttered those words openly while the case was still in the court. But since Munshi Fayyaz Sahib had heard that news direct from the Promised Messiah(as), he could not even for a moment believe that what the Promised Messiah(as) had said would not come true.

A doctor who was also living in the same street had heard those words from the mouth of Munshi Fayyaz Sahib and said to him that if what he was saying would come true, then he would become an Ahmadi. On the other hand, if what he was saying does not prove to be true, then Munshi Fayyaz Sahib will have to repudiate his faith.

On the day when the decision was to be given, the magistrate on the case made up his mind firmly to give his decision against the Ahmadis and was getting ready to go to the court and announce the judgment. But before he left his home, his heart failed and he passed away instantly. The case was, ultimately, decided in the favour of the Ahmadis by the replacing judge

(13) Sheikh Fazal Ahmad of Batala (1883-1968)

Sheikh Fazal Ahmad was born at Batala in 1883. He joined the Ahmadiyya Movement in 1904 and was an enthusiastic preacher. He used to preach Islam to his British Officers. After retirement, Fazal Sahib served as Mahasib (Finance Secretary) and Sadr Anjuman-e-Ahmadiyya at Qadian and Rabwah.

Hadhrat Sheikh Fazal Ahmad was in the British Army when he first read an article in *The Review of Religions* about the advent of the Promised Messiah(as) and requested the Promised Messiah(as) to send him by registered post all copies of this magazine. After going through some of these, he sent a letter to Qadian requesting the Promised Messiah(as) to kindly accept his Bai'at. Being in the Army, Fazal Sahib was constantly on the move but succeeded ultimately to be in the presence of the Promised Messiah(as) in 1907.

Fazal Sahib was a zealous preacher of Ahmadiyyat. He was once asked how many people had joined Ahmadiyyat through his efforts and very humbly remarked: 'Over a hundred', and this was while he was heavily engaged in the British Army.

Fazal Sahib had a very close relationship with the Khilafat-e-Ahmadiyyat. During the First Khilafat, he sacrificed his service in the army. He was holding a highly paid job in his core as Finance Officer but when his immediate officer, a major in the army, objected to observance of his prayers, Sheikh Fazal Ahmad Sahib resigned immediately and went to Qadian. It was a huge sacrifice for the sake of Allah. After a year or so, Hadhrat Khalifatul-Masih I(ra) advised him to rejoin army. His senior, a major in the British Army was so much impressed of his righteousness, that he regularly asked Fazal Sahib to say some of his daily prayers at his office in his very presence.

Fazal Sahib once went to Kashmir and brought a prayer mat as a gift for Hadhrat Sheikh Sahib. Hadhrat Khalifatul-Masih II(ra) has described this incident in his book *Sair-e-Ruhani*.

Fazal Sahib was a great scholar of Persian and Urdu languages and enjoyed poetry. Though he hardly ever composed any poetry himself, he knew by memory many Persian and Urdu poems which praised God and the Holy Prophet (peace and blessings of Allah be on him). Fazal Sahib was very fond of reading and almost knew by heart, *Mathnawi Maulana Rome*.

In the early 1960s, Fazal Sahib became very ill. Hadhrat Maulana Rajeki Sahib came to visit him and raised his hands to pray. After a few minutes, Hadhrat Maulana said aloud: 'Allah-O-Akbar Allah-O-Akbar' (God is the Greatest), and said 'I have seen right now in a vision, the angels were descending on you the baskets of Noor (light).' He explained that this vision could be interpreted in two ways: 'Firstly, the time of your life span has come to an end and you will be rewarded in the heavens abundantly. If this happens at all, I request you to convey my Salam to Hadhrat Masih-e-Mau'od, the Promised Messiah(as), or the buckets of Noor (light) may also mean that you would recover miraculously.' After this Fazal Sahib started recovering and by the grace of Allah, within six months he was as energetic as ever.

In 1942, Fazal Sahib called one of his sons from Delhi and took him to Hadhrat Khalifat-ul-Masih II(ra) and said: 'I want him to devote his life for the sake of Allah'. Hudhur replied: 'He is yet only seventeen.' The following year, again Sheikh Sahib called his son and offered him to Hudhur. Fazal Sahib felt extremely honoured and lucky when Hudhur accepted his request. This son was Maulana Laiq Ahmad Tahir who is presently working as a missionary in the UK.

(14) Maulawi Hafiz Fazal-ud-Din of Kharian
(b.1854)

Hadhrat Hafiz Maulawi Fazal-ud-Din was born in 1854. His father's name was Hafiz Abdullah and he came from the Gujjar family. Fazal-ud-Din Sahib, his father and two brothers were all Hafiz of the Holy Qur'an. Fazal-ud-Din Sahib was known as a saintly person who possessed an eminent personality.

Fazal-ud-Din Sahib was always very keen and eager to seek religious knowledge so he left for Saharampur to pursue this aim. He gained admission for two years at an Islamic school of Malawi Mazhar-ud-Din. However, during this period, his brother Hafiz Ilam-ud-Din became unwell and Fazal-ud-Din Sahib was subsequently summoned back to Kharian.

In Kharian, different religious leaders and scholars confronted Fazal-ud-Din Sahib on various issues but on each occasion, Fazal-ud-Din Sahib was blessed with success and gained victory on them.

Fazal-ud-Din Sahib was known for his intellectual capability and intelligence by the scholars of his time. Hindus and Sikhs also treated him with respect and admiration and admired his esteemed knowledge, wisdom and ability.

Before the advent of the Promised Messiah(as), the area of Kharian was dominated by the A'arian's agnostic activities against Islam. People would say insults on the Holy Prophet Muhammad(saw) and used foul and disgraceful language towards Muslims and the Holy Qur'an.

Fazal Din Sahib prayed fervently to Almighty Allah for redemption from the A'arians hostilities against Islam. He saw in a dream, that dust had risen from a very far distance in the East and sought its meaning. Somebody replied that the Promised Messiah's(as) armies had defeated the armies of non-believers who had escaped leaving dust behind. Then he saw that as clouds of dust were cleared, a saintly person was sitting in a tent at a piece of land. He entered the tent and submitted to him. The saintly person taught him – *'La Ilaha Illallaho Muhammad-ur-Rasoolullah'* (There is none worthy of worship but Allah and Muhammad is His Messenger). The reading of this verse was said with full passion. As he woke up, Fazal-ud-Din Sahib was in tears reciting the Kalima and mentioned said that he had been enjoying the spiritual taste of this dream for a week. On Friday, he narrated his dream and its interpretation was that a man of God was to appear in support of Islam.

After some time, Fazal-ud-Din Sahib received a book titled *Surma Chashm-e-A'ria* which strongly refuted A'riaism. He also thought that according to his dream, the author of the book, Hadhrat Mirza Ghulam Ahmad(as) would stand in support of Islam but Fazal-ud-Din Sahib remained silent since the Promised Messiah(as) had not yet announced his appointment yet.

Fazal-ud-Din Sahib's father, Hafiz Abdullah also read the book and became fond of its author. However, his father died before Hadhrat Mirza Ghulan Ahmad made the claim of being the Promised Messiah(as).

Hadhrat Malawi Burhan-ud-Din Jehlami Sahib was a devoted companion of the Promised Messiah(as). He was a pillar of Ahmadiyyat in Kharian and his nobility and piety was admired by both his supporters and opponents. Non-Muslims often appointed him as their arbitrator in various matters.

When Hadhrat Maulawi Burhan-ud-Din Jehlami visited Kharian, he took an immediate liking to Fazal-ud-Din Sahib and told him about the Promised Messiah's(as) claim. Fazal-ud-Din Sahib signed a covenant of Bai'at with the Promised Messiah(as) at Qadian in September 1891.

Upon his joining the Jama'at at Kharian, Fazal-ud-Din Sahib faced a lot of hostilities from the opponents of Ahmadiyyat. He had held many debates with the opponents in the neighbouring villages of Kharian and was particularly successful at Doga Malka. One written debate concerning the death of Jesus Christ(as) continued for seven days with Mehmood Gunjwi. Another successful debate was held with Maulawi Abraham Sialkoti on the death of Jesus Christ(as). These religious debates had contributed tremendously towards the establishment of many Jama'ats in the neighbouring villages of Kharian. In private meetings with Fazal-ud-Din Sahib, many people accepted the truth and joined the Jama'at. Hadhrat Ghulam Shah of Nawrang, a known scholar, accepted Ahmadiyyat as a result of a meeting with Fazal-ud-Din Sahib. He later established an active Jama'at Nawrang.

Hadhrat Promised Messiah(as) had great affection for Fazal-ud-Din Sahib. During his stay at Qadian, whenever Fazal-ud-Din Sahib requested permission to go back to Kharian, the Promised Messiah(as) would say: 'stay more, you are not permitted to go yet.'

When he joined Ahmadiyyat, Hadhrat Promised Messiah(as) told Fazal-ud-Din Sahib three things.

1. To improve concentration and humility, to recite 'Iyyaka na'abudo wa Iyyaka nasta'een,' repeatedly in prayers.
2. To recite 'Istaghfar and Durood' repeatedly.

3. To observe Tahajjud prayers whenever possible.

Fazal-ud-Din Sahib whole-heartedly observed and practised all these three things till his death.

The Promised Messiah(as) wrote the name of Maulawi Hafiz Fazal-ud-Din Sahib at number two in the list of his beloved (313) companions.

(15) **Mian Fazal Muhammad of Harisan** (1866-1956)

Mian Fazal Muhammad of Harisan joined the Ahmadiyya Movement in 1896. After his initiation into the Movement, he had a dream in which he was told that he would live up to the age of 45. He narrated the dream to the Promised Messiah(as) who remarked that God Almighty had the power to double the number.

Accordingly, Fazal Muhammad Sahib lived up to the age of 90. He frequently visited Qadian and enjoyed the company of the Promised Messiah(as) and could recall numerous anecdotes of his holy life. Fazal Muhammad Sahib migrated to Qadian in 1914 and had a house built in Dar-ul-Fazl near the Talimul Islam High School. His eldest son, Maulawi Abdul Ghafoor Fazil was one of the gifted students in religious studies at Qadian College. All his sons are devoted to the cause of Ahmadiyyat.

Fazal Muhammad Sahib died in 1956 and was buried among the Companions of the Promised Messiah(as) at Rabwah.

(16) **Sayyad Fazal Shah** (d.1924)

Sayyad Fazal Shah Sahib visited Qadian around 1884 where he remained for eight months. He requested the Promised Messiah(as) to pray for him as he had some problems that were agitating him. The Promised Messiah(as) asked Fazal Shah Sahib to stay with him for six months in Qadian and during this period, a close friendship between the two developed.

On the last day of the six-month period, Sayyad Sahib reminded the Promised Messiah(as) of his promise to pray for him to which he replied: 'Do not be afraid of the trouble, there is yet one more night.' On the following day, the Promised Messiah(as) said to Sayyad Fazal Shah: 'You have done your part, now I would do mine.' Overnight, Sayyad Fazal Shah had found to his great joy that the trouble which had kept him in turmoil for a long time had melted in thin air and he was free from all cares. He said to the Promised Messiah(as): 'Sir, there is nothing to pray for me now, for the ailment which troubled me is over and I am quite happily relieved.'

Sayyad Fazal Shah was a sincere and faithful follower of the Promised Messiah(as). One day he was massaging the feet of the Promised Messiah(as) when the latter fell into a state of trance and the revelation of God descended on him. Some of the sentences were audible enough for him to hear very clearly. When the trance was over, the Promised Messiah(as) wrote down what had passed between him and his God. Sayyad Sahib said that he had also heard some of the sentences of the Wahi (revelation). In this way, he was fortunate enough to hear the revelation of God, the nature of which he was anxious to know. Sayyad Fazal Shah afterwards lived in the blessed company of his spiritual Master.

Sayyad Fazal Shah passed away on 1st February 1924 and was buried in the Bahishti Maqbara.

(17) **Chaudhri Haji Ghulam Ahmad of Kariam** (1875-1943)

Ch. Ghulam Ahmad, son of Gamman Khan, belonged to a Rajput family of Kariam. He was born in 1875. He was a very generous man and his house was a haven of rest and repose for the poor and needy. Ghulam Ahmad Sahib was from the early age very particular about his daily prayers, and fasting during the month of Ramadan and received lessons in the Holy Qur'an from Hafiz Karim Bakhsh.

The study of two books, *Izala-i-Auham* and *Aeena-i-Kamalat-i-Islam* by the Promised Messiah(as) was instrumental in drawing Ghulam Ahmad Sahib's attention to the study of the Ahmadiyya Movement. He fervently prayed to God to be guided on the right path. In a dream, he saw the words 'Promised Messiah' written in bold golden letters. In another dream, he saw a number of people dressed in white attire as if they were angels. An outsider came up to the assembly and said: 'It is the time of the Promised Messiah'. 'What is the proof?', said the other. The outsider replied: 'A reformer always appears at the head of every century. None has claimed to be the reformer for the present century except Hadhrat Mirza Ghulam Ahmad of Qadian. This is the proof.' The questioner confirmed the statement. Ghulam Ahmad Sahib was now firmly convinced of the truth of the claimant.

Haji Ghulam Ahmad Sahib made up his mind to join the Ahmadiyya Movement and proceeded to Qadian in January 1903 where he stayed for a month. This gave him opportunities to study Ahmadiyyat closely. What impressed him the most was the mode of life Ahmadi Muslims led at Qadian including listening to the discourse of Promised Messiah(as) in his morning walks and evening sittings, the Qur'anic commentary by Hadhrat Maulawi Nur-ud-Din(ra) in the Aqsa Mosque, the recitation of the Holy Qur'an by Maulawi Abdul Karim of Sialkot, Sayyad Ahmad Noor Kabul's call for prayers in the stillness of night etc. In February 1903, he pledged allegiance to the Promised Messiah(as) and later returned to his native town altogether a changed man.

Chaudhri Ghulam Ahmad Khan's life was a practical demonstration of the teachings of the Ahmadiyya Movement. He became a zealous preacher of Islam and Ahmadiyyat and worked with a missionary spirit for the rest of his life. He preached Ahmadiyyat in collaboration with Ch. Feroz Khan of Rahon and Ch. Abdus Salam of Kathgarh. Together they were successful in establishing Ahmadiyyat Jama'ats in these two districts.

Chaudhri Ghulam Ahmad Khan proceeded on a pilgrimage to Makkah in 1911. He set up an Ahmadiyya School at Kariam and personally bore all the expenses. He took a keen interest in the affairs of the school and succeeded in obtaining government recognition, grant-in-aid and also some financial help from Sadr Anjuman Ahmadiyya, Qadian.

Ch. Ghulam Ahmad Sahib volunteered his services for the Malkana campaign 1923 in Mathra district where he successfully worked to reclaim the Malkana Rajputs back to Islam. He acquired a piece of land for the construction of a mosque for the Kariam Jama'at and undertook a major part of the expenses from his own pocket.

Ch. Ghulam Ahmad Sahib passed away on 3rd July 1943 at Kariam. His body was brought to Qadian where he was buried in the Bahishti Maqbara along with the old Companions of the Promised Messiah(as).

(18) **Malik Ghulam Fareed** (d.1977)

Hadhrat Malik Ghulam Fareed was the elder son of Hadhrat Malik Noor-ud-Din (also a Companion of the Promised Messiah(as)) and was the first among those who responded to the call of Hadhrat Khalifatul Masih II(ra) to join the scheme of life devotees (Waqfeen Zindagi).

Malik Ghulam Fareed Sahib served the Jama'at as a Missionary in Germany and then in England. He edited the magazines *Sun Rise* and *The Review of Religions*. He was the Secretary of the College Committee and for a lengthy period, served Hadhrat Khalifatul Masih II(ra) as his Private Secretary. He was also an Acting Nazir Talim. His great achievement and service to Islam was his *English Translation and Commentary of the Holy Qur'an* which he prepared in association with Hadhrat Mirza Bashir Ahmad(ra) and Hadhrat Maulana Sher Ali.

Hadhrat Malik Ghulam Fareed died at the age of 79 on Friday 7th January 1977 in Lahore. Being a Moosi and a Companion of the Promised Messiah(as), he was laid to rest in the special plot of Bahishti Maqbara, Rabwah the same day after Asr Prayer. The Namaz-e-Janaza was led by Hadhrat Khalifatul Masih III(ru).

(19) **Dr. Sayyed Ghulam Ghaus** (1868-1957)

Sayyyed Ghulam Ghaus, son of Sayyed Habib Bakhsh, was born at Bijah, District Ludhiana, in 1868. After passing his Middle School Examination, he joined the veterinary school in Lahore and qualified as a veterinary assistant.

During the course of his voyage to Mombassa, he conversed extensively with Dr. Rahmat Ali, elder brother of Hafiz Roshan Ali about the claims of Hadhrat Mirza Ghulam Ahmad of Qadian as the Messiah and Mahdi and after which he decided to join the Movement. and wrote a letter of allegiance to the Promised Messiah(as) at Qadian in 1900. He also sent some money requested for the Minara-tul-Masih and *The Review of Religions*.

In 1913, Ghulam Ghaus Sahib came to India on four months leave and visited Qadian with his wife and children. He stayed there for a year and witnessed many signs at the hands of the Promised Messiah(as).

Sayyed Ghulam Ghaus Sahib was a meek, selfless man of great piety. He often had dreams and visions which came true. He was sincerely devoted to the cause of Ahmadiyyat, the Promised Messiah(as) and Khilafat.

Sayyed Ghulam Ghaus bequeathed one-third of all his property for the spread of Islam.

He migrated to Qadian in 1928 and after the partition of the country he settled in Rabwah.

Ghulam Ghaus Sahib died on 19th February 1957 and was buried in the Bahishti Maqbara, Rabwah.

(20) **Mahr Ghulam Hassan of Sialkot** (d.1956)

Mahr Ghulam Hassan and Ghulam Ali of Arazi Yaqub, Sialkot, together with their father joined the fold of Ahmadiyyat in the year 1896. Before joining, they were zealous members of the Ahl-e-Hadith. Mahr Ghulam Sahib one day had a vision in which he saw a man flying a kite. He saw that an aeroplane appeared and hit the kite but strangely enough, the aeroplane and not the kite, was torn to pieces and fell to the ground. In another vision, he saw that the same gentleman who was flying the kite, was now reciting the Holy Qur'an in a Hindu Mohallah of Sialkot City. The person he saw in the dream was Hadhrat Mirza Ghulam Ahmad of Qadian(as). After mutual consultation, the whole family offered their allegiance to the Promised Messiah(as) in 1896.

Mahr Ghulam Sahib had another vision in which he saw that his friend, Maulawi Hafiz Faiz-ud-Din of the Kabutran Wali Masjid, Sialkot had also joined the fold of Ahmadiyyat. He went to see his friend and narrated what he had seen in the vision. Maulawi Sahib laughed and scorned at the idea. But eight years later, Maulawi Sahib joined the fold of Ahmadiyyat and for 20 years was a devoted follower of the Promised Messiah(as) until he passed away in 1924 and was buried in the Bahishti Maqbara at Qadian.

Mahr Ghulam Hassan sent his son Nazir Ahmad Mubashar to join the Madrassa-e-Ahmadiyya, Qadian. He later served Islam and Ahmadiyyat in Ghana, West Africa for 26 years from 1936 to1961.

Mahr Ghulam Hassan died on 17th September 1956 and was buried in the Bahishti Maqbara in Rabwah.

(21) **Chaudhary Ghulam Muhammad B.A (1877-1961)**

Chaudhary Ghulam Muhammad was born in October 1877. He passed his Primary School in the year 1894 and later his Matriculation examination in 1901 from Sialkot.

Chaudhary Sahib's mother passed away when he was an infant and he married in 1893 at the young age of 16 whilst he was still a student.

In 1905, Chaudhary Sahib went to Qadian for the Annual Gathering and took his Oath of Initiation at the blessed hands of the Promised Messiah(as).

For many years, Chaudhary Sahib worked as a schoolteacher at Khushaab, Shahpur and Daska. Having obtained his BA Degree from Aligarh in 1909, he came to Qadian as a member of Talimul Islam High School staff and settled there. He began serving the Sadar Anjuman-e-Ahmadiyya from where he obtained his pension in the year 1938. Chaudhary Sahib used to teach science and mathematics to students in Matriculation classes. He also was in-charge of the hostel of the school at Qadian and later the Manager of Nusrat Girls School, Qadian.

Chaudhary Sahib had the honour of translating into English the book *Aaeena-e-Kamalat-e-Islam* which was published in the *The Review of Religions*. He also translated the book of the Promised Messiah(as), *Chashmah-e-Maseehi* into English, which was also published in the year 1918.

He was very fond of learning Arabic language and he published the book *Tasheel-ul-Arabiyya* which became very popular.

Chaudhary Sahib was a good preacher and many of his family members accepted Ahmadiyyat through him.

Chaudhary Sahib passed away on 7 August, 1961 at Lahore. He was a Moosi and is buried Bahishti Maqbara at Rabwah

(22) Hadhrat Sufi Ghulam Muhammad (1898-1985)

Hadhrat Sufi Ghulam Muhammad was a dedicated and sincere member of the Ahmadiyya Jama'at. His father, Hadhrat Mian Muhammad Din Patwari was also a Companions of the Promised Messiah(as).

Hadhrat Sufi Ghulam Muhammad was born on 19th October 1898. He entered Talim-ul-Islam School, Qadian in 1905. From 1905 to 1908, he remained in regular contact with the Promised Messiah(as) and it was this close relationship which made him a kind, generous, pious and God-fearing person. Because of his character and qualities, he was called 'Sufi' and this became a part of his name.

In 1917, when Hadhrat Khalifatul Masih II(ra) launched a scheme and demanded that young members should dedicate their lives, Sufi Ghulam Sahib was among the early members who responded to the call. After dedicating his life, he was instructed by Hadhrat Khalifatul Masih II(ra) to complete his college education.

From 1926 to 1931, Hadhrat Ghulam Sahib resided at the Ahmadiyya Hostel, Lahore where he was a popular and respected student. In 1932, he was appointed a teacher at Talim-ul-Islam High School in Qadian, where he taught mathematics, geography and science.

In 1935, Hadhrat Ghulam Sahib had the honour to be appointed Private Secretary to Hadhrat Khalifatul Masih II(ra) for a period of a few months. In 1936, he entered Aligarh University for his BT degree.

In 1947, he moved to Chiniot, Pakistan, where he continued to teach at the Talim-ul-Islam High School, Rabwah. After his retirement, Hadhrat Ghulam Sahib was appointed Naib Nazar Baitul Mal and subsequently Nazar- Aala Thani by Hadhrat Khalifatul Masih IV(ru). He continued to serve in both capacities till his demise on 23rd April 1985. He also served in other auxiliary organisations of the Jama'at.

Hadhrat Ghulam Sahib also served, on a number of occasions as the administrator of Langar Khana during the Annual Jalsa in Qadian and Rabwah. In a letter dated 12th August 1984, Hadhrat Khalifatul Masih IV(ru) expressed his great pleasure at the services rendered by Hadhrat Sufi Ghulam Muhammad.

Hadhrat Ghulam Sahib had promised to dedicate his son, Mubarik Muslehuddin before his birth.

Hadhrat Sufi Ghulam Muhammad died on 23rd April 1985 and was buried in Bahishti Maqbra Rabwah on 24th April 1985. In the Friday Sermon of 26th April 1985, Hadhrat Khalifatul Masih IV(ru) paid tribute this tribute to Sufi Ghulam Muhammad:

'A tragic news which I am

conveying to the Jama'at is that an extremely dedicated and sincere person, Sufi Ghulam Muhammad had passed away. *(Inna Lillahi Wa Inna Illahe Rajioon)*. Sufi Sahib was a selfless and humble worker of the Jama'at. When I entered school, Sufi Sahib was my teacher and was respected and loved by his colleagues. He had great sympathy and love for children. On the other hand, he was strict as far as discipline is concerned. He had served the Jama'at in several capacities. Humbleness, selflessness, and loyalty were deeply rooted in him. I have been very close to him. I had worked under him and along with him. He had also worked under me. He was a lovable person who has departed. He was 87 years old and served the Jama'at till his last breath. He never took leave from work, perhaps that was what he had prayed for and desired for. Being a companion of the Promised Messiah(as) and Nazar-i-Aala Thani, the Jama'at has an obligation. After the Juma Prayers, there will be a Namaz Janaza Ghaib. Remember him in your prayers and in future pray for his soul and his children that they may remain steadfast.'

(23) **Maulawi Ghulam Nabi Misri** (1874-1956)

Maulawi Ghulam Nabi Misti was born in 1874. He was the son of Mohkam Din and came from the Chaurian village in Patiala State. His father employed a Maulawi to teach him the Holy Qur'an.

In later years, Ghulam Nabi Misri Sahib studied medicine in Delhi. After the death of his father, he came to Ludhiana where he studied theology. He then went to Amritsar for a while and then to Qadian where he worked as a dispenser in Hadhrat Maulawi Nur-ud-Din's(ra) clinic.

The great physician, Maulawi Nur-ud-Din, was a great lover of books and possessed a large library at Qadian. He sent Maulawi Ghulam Sahib to Bhopal to copy some rare books from the state library of the Begum of Bhopal. Maulawi Sahib did his job very diligently but some of the books could only be found in the library at Cairo, Egypt. He proceeded to Cairo via Basra on foot and arrived in Cairo safe and sound. It was only then that he informed his master at Qadian of his adventure. As a rule, nobody was allowed to enter the library with a pen. Maulawi Ghulam Sahib therefore took a pencil with him and copied some of the books, which he needed for his master.

Maulawi Ghulam Sahib also attended Arabic classes at the Al-Azhar University and openly preached Ahmadiyyat in Cairo. He learnt the Egyptian style of writing and adapted well into their cultural. Around the year 1906, he returned to India via Makkah. Hadhrat Maulawi Nur-ud-Din(ra) was very pleased at his adventure.

Maulawi Ghulam Sahib was appointed a teacher of Arabic and theology in the Talimul Islam High School, Qadian. He also taught in the Madrassa Ahmadiyyat in Qadian for a number of years. The greatest of his literary achievements is his translation from Urdu into Arabic of some of the books written by the Promised Messiah(as) - *Barahin-e-Ahmadiyya,* (first four parts), *Fathe Islam*, *Tauzih-I-Maram* and *Izala-e-Auham*.

Munshi Habib Ahmad of Saharanpur, UP visited Qadian around the year 1907. During the course of his talk with Hadhrat Maulawi Nur-ud-Din(ra), he said that he had two daughters whom he wanted to marry to two brothers so that the two girls could live in the same locality. Hadhrat Maulawi Sahib had two sons, Ghulam Nabi and Ghulam Mohammad and offered them both as marriage proposals. The gentleman consented and married his elder daughter, Sakina to Ghulam Nabi and the younger one, Maimuna to Ghulam Muhammad.

Maulawi Ghulam Nabi passed away on 27 April 1956. He was buried in the Companion's enclosure of Bahishti Maqbara at Rabwah.

(24) **Hafiz Ghulam Rasul of Wazirabad** (1854-1944)

Hafiz Ghulam Rasul, son of Hafiz Muhammad Hussain, was born in 1854 at Dhirke, District Gujrat. In1886, whilst he was a student of theology at Lakhoke in the Ferozepur District, he heard about Hadhrat Mirza Ghulam Ahmad(as) of Qadian when Abdur Rehman, son of Hafiz Muhammad of Lakhoke was intently reading a book. Hafiz Sahib asked him: 'What book is it you are reading so intently?' Abdur Rahman said: 'It is the *Barahin-e-Ahmadiyya* by Mirza Ghulam Ahmad of Qadian, the Mujaddid (Reformer) of the age.' Ghulam Sahib then asked: 'What is a reformer?' Abdur Rehman responded by showing him: the 'Mishkat' and read the tradition: 'God will appoint, at the head of every Century one who would revive the religion of Islam for Muslims.' Ghulam Rasul asked another question, 'Where is the reformer?' Abdur Rehman replied: 'He is at Qadian, Gurdaspur District'. Soon after, Hafiz Ghulam Rasul made his way towards Qadian and met Hadhrat Mirza Ghulam Ahmad(as) at his house. The Promised Messiah(as) and Ghulam Rasul Sahib both had a meal together and a heart-to-heart talk about his claim as the Mujaddid (Reformer). From this, Hafiz Ghulam Rasul became convinced of the Promised Messiah's(as) claim as Mujaddid.

Hafiz Ghulam Sahib was an eye-witness to the historical eclipse of the sun and the moon in the month of Ramadan in 1894. He also witnessed that the Promised Messiah's(as) essay on the physical, moral and spiritual conditions of man was unanimously declared to be superior to all other essays read at the 'Religions Conference,' at Lahore in 1896.

Hafiz Ghulam Sahib joined the Ahmadiyya Movement in 1897 together with his younger brother Hafiz Ghulam Muhammad and Maulawi Najam-ud-Din of Shadiwal, District Gujrat.

Hafiz Ghulam Sahib related that one day the Promised Messiah(as) was talking to some of his friends at his house on the necessity of sending their sons to join the Ahmadiyya School. Hafiz Ghulam Sahib offered his son, Hafiz Ubaidullah, who was later sent as an Ahmadiyya Muslim Missionary to Maurtius where he worked for seven years. His son died in Mauritius and was laid to rest there in a foreign land leaving his wife and a son of four years. Hafiz Ghulam Sahib bore the loss of his only son with patience and undertook a long journey in his old age to Mauritius and brought back his grandson and daughter-in-law to Qadian, India.

Hafiz Ghulam Rasul Sahib had a charming personality. His talk was sweet, beautiful and penetrating. He recited the Holy Qur'an melodiously. He was a poet of good repute and master of the Punjabi language. He was a very pious man and Allah the Almighty often answered his prayers.

Hafiz sahib passed away in 1944. He was buried in the Bahishti Maqbara at Qadian.

(25) **Hadhrat Maulana Ghulam Rasul**

Hadhrat Maulana Ghulam Rasul Rajeki writing about his family stated that:

> 'It was purely by the grace of God Almighty that the family that He selected for my birth was so renowned for its piety, virtue and selflessness that to this day it is known as the family of 'Seven Generation' (*Saat peerhion Waliyon Ka Khandan*). They had such an ardent love of the Holy Qur'an, that at times there were up to ten Hafiz in a single generation. Another example of the piety of the family was that it was the practice of many of our women that they would not breast-feed their children unless they had performed the wuddoo i.e. ablutions.'

Ghulam Rasul Sahib's exact date of birth is not known. He was born between 1877 and 1879 in Rajeki. His father's name was Mian Karam Deen and his mother's name Amina Bibi. Both his parents believed in the truth of the Promised Messiah(as) but unfortunately neither of them took the Bai'at (the oath of allegiance). Before his birth, his mother saw a dream that a lamp was lit in their home which illuminated the whole house.

In his early childhood, Maulana Rajeki Sahib read the Holy Qur'an at the local village school. He gained some secondary education but his father arranged for him to study Persian at home. During this period, he also read the book *Masnawi Maulan Roum* with Hadhrat Maulawi Imamuddin of Goleki.

During his youth, Maulana Rajeki Sahib used to undertake long periods of meditation and worship in the wilderness according to the traditions of the Qadriya school of Sufism. In those days, he also undertook long periods of fasting.

Even after having accepted Ahmadiyyat, for some time Maulana Rajeki Sahib continued his meditation and recitation of prayers in the tradition of the old Sufi school. After a while, he felt he should ask for the approval of the Promised Messiah(as) with regard to these practices. In reply to his query, the Promised Messiah(as) made some observations that are summarised below:

a) Meditating on persons who are themselves creatures, can only result in shirk (making partners with Allah).

b) Recitation of the name of Allah should suffice for His remembrance and there is no need for complicated prayers in order to glorify the Lord.

c) With regards to reciting the

Durood, the best is the one taught by the Holy Prophet(saw) and which has been incorporated in our daily prayers.

As soon as Maulana Rajeki Sahib received this letter, he abandoned all his previous ways and conducted his devotions in the manner prescribed by the Promised Messiah(as). As a result of this, the Glory and Omnipotence of the Almighty became so indelibly inscribed on the mind and soul of Maulana Rajeki Sahib that he seemed in a state of perpetual remembrance of the Almighty from then onwards.

Once, while Maulana Rajeki Sahib was reading the Masnawi of Maulana, Jalaluddin Rumi with Maulawi Imam Deen, a policeman came into the mosque. This man had a book with him and Maulana Rajeki Sahib expressed a desire to read it. The man declined saying that the book had been written by his spiritual leader which he might not be able to tolerate. Maulana Rajeki Sahib, however, assured him that this was not the case and having obtained the book, *Aine-e Kamalat-e-Islam*, read it and almost immediately wrote a letter to the Promised Messiah(as) declaring his allegiance. The letter was written in September or October 1897. After a few days, he received the reply about the acceptance of his Bai'at. His teacher, Maulana Imamud Deen Sahib suggested that Maulana Rajeki Sahib had acted with haste in taking the Bai'at .

However, Maulana Imamud Deen soon himself investigated the claims and teachings of the Promised Messiah(as) and once he was satisfied, both teacher and pupil set off for Qadian to take the Bai'at at the hands of the Promised Messiah(as). When they reached Qadian, the Promised Messiah(as) was in Masjid Mubarak. Hadhrat Maulawi Imamud Deen Sahib leapt up the stairs in his keenness to see him, while Maulana Rajeki Sahib lagged behind to extract some money from his pocket so that he could present it as a gift to the Promised Messiah(as). Although the Promised Messiah(as) had no knowledge of their coming, as soon as he met Imamud Deen Sahib, he asked him: 'Where is the boy who has accompanied you here, call him forward'.

Hadhrat Maulana Rajeki Sahib describes his first meeting with the Promised Messiah(as). He says: 'When I shook his blessed hand for the first time, I was overcome with emotion and I fell weeping at his feet and my whole body was racked with emotion. Whilst I lay there, Hudhur kept gently stroking my head and back in an attempt to console me. When I finally recovered slightly, I got up from his feet and Hadhrat Maulawi Imamud Deen and I took the Bai'at at Hadhrat Sahib's hand along with some other people.'

At the time of the Bai'at, Maulana

Rajeki Sahib was about 18 or 19 years old. On reaching home, he began preaching the good news. Despite the fact that everyone was aware of the piety and spirituality of Hadhrat Maulana Ghulam Rasul Rajeki, they began considering him as the black sheep of the family and began complaining to his elders since in their view, the good name and reputation of the family was at stake. The elders of the family decided to invite some religious scholars to talk to Maulana Rajeki Sahib in order to bring this 'young rebel back in to the path of the faith'. In this gathering of the elite and scholars, Maulana Rajeki Sahib presented eloquent arguments on the truth of the Promised Messiah(as). The invited scholars declared him to be a 'heretic' and urged the people to impose a 'social boycott' on him. A cousin of Maulana Rajeki Sahib stood up on this occasion and began reviling the unfair and totally un-Islamic attitude of these so-called scholars and the gathering was thus dispersed. Maulana Rajeki Sahib states: 'It was a direct result of this proclamation of his heresy, by the scholars that the true meaning of the unity of God and the practical implications of saying 'La Ilaha Illallah' became manifest to me. What I failed to learn from years of ritual prayer and practices, was taught to me in a single moment there.'

At this time Maulana Rajeki Sahib received the following revelation, which proved to be the turning point in his life: 'Maulawi Ghulam Rasul; pious youth full of miracles.' *(Mauvi Ghulam Rasul, Jawan-e-Sualeh, Karamati)*. After having received this revelation, Maulana Rajeki Sahib was blessed with amazing success in religious discussions and debates with Hindu pundits, Christian priests and Missionaries and Muslim scholars. As a result of the direct blessings of the Promised Messiah(as), Maulana Rajeki Sahib became a living miracle of the manifestation of God.

God graced Maulana Rajeki Sahib with a deep knowledge and understanding of the Holy Qur'an and its exegesis, (i.e. Tafseer). Maulana Rajeki Sahib states: 'Once I saw a dream in which I was shown a tall tree on which the words of the Holy Qur'an are written from bottom to top. I start reading these verses and at the same time, start climbing up the tree. When I reach the top of the tree and have completed the whole Qur'an, I start inviting people to it. Alhamdolillah.'

Despite the lack of formal education, God had granted him with such eloquence in the Arabic language that both his Arabic prose and poetry are without parallel. He has written poems, which do not contain any of the letters of the Arabic alphabets with dots and the others in which every word used had a dotted letter.

Maulana Rajeki Sahib himself states: 'Once in a dream, during the time of the Promised Messiah(as), I was visited by an angel in the form of one of my ancestors, Hadhrat Mian Noor Ahmad Chenabi, and he said to me that it would have been a good thing if I could study some Arabic. I replied saying that I had a dislike for the traditional learning of Arabic skills as was the practice at the time. On hearing this reply, the angel presented me with a journal and asked me to read from it. When I had read only three lines, he took it away, saying: "For you these three lines are sufficient."

Maulana Rajeki Sahib was also very well versed in the science of interpretation of dreams. He himself states: 'It is a special grace and a favour of the Almighty God, that as a result of the blessings of the Promised Messiah(as), I have been graced with the knowledge of the interpretation of dreams.'

Hadhrat Maulana Ghulam Rasul Rajeki states: 'Despite numerous weaknesses and errors, by the Grace of Allah the Almighty, I have seen Allah on many occasions and have seen His Angels and have listened to them talking and seen many of His esteemed Prophets and have listened to them speaking. Most of all, on many occasions, I have been blessed with the vision of the Holy Prophet(saw) and have also heard his blessed speech.

I have also toured the heavens and in visions I have met the Promised Messiah(as), Hadhrat Khalifatul Masih I and the Promised Reformer (May Allah be pleased with them) and have often sought their guidance in several matters.'

The life of Maulana Rajeki Sahib is full of such miraculous events. These are detailed in his autobiography entitled *Hayat-e-Qudsi*, which is compulsory reading for anyone wishing to step into the realm of true spirituality

From the day he took the Oath of Allegiance (Bai'at), to the day of his demise, every moment of his life was devoted to the service of the Ahmadiyya Movement. He followed the commandments of the Promised Messiah(as) and his successors with loyalty, zeal and devotion.

Hadhrat Maulana Ghulam Rasul Rajeki passed away on 15th December 1963 and was buried the following day in the 'Qita e Sahaba'.

(26) Hadhrat Maulana Ghulam Rasool

Mirza Ghulam Rasool Sahib was born in the village Pindi Laala in the district of Gujrat in the province of the Punjab. He passed his BA examination from the Islamic College, Lahore. He used to visit Qadian occasionally when he was a student. He joined the fold of Ahmadiyyat in the year 1907.

Mirza Ghulam Rasool often said that he was deeply impressed by the pious life of the Promised Messiah(as) and the sense of honour that he had about the faith of Islam.

On the occasion of election of the second Khalifa, Ghulam Rasool Sahib did not immediately take the Oath of Initiation until he understood the true notion of Khilafat and its status whereafter he pledged his allegiance.

When Hadhrat Khalifatul-Masih II(ra) asked for volunteers for the Shuddhi Movement of Arya Samaaj, Ghulam Rasool Sahib was one of those who joined and even gave up his service for this important task. During his stay at Malkana, the Arya Samaj arranged a public meeting in which they openly accused him of misleading the people of the Arya Samaaj. As the result of their speeches, more than thirty people attacked and beat him with sticks and caused his hut to be dropped on him. Then they dragged him out and tried to kill him but some of the Malkana people whom he had been treating intervened and saved his life.

The Arya people then asked him to leave the village but Ghulam Rasool Sahib replied that Hadhrat Khalifatul-Masih II(ra) had sent him to the village and he would not leave without his command.

On many occasions, Allah helped Ghulam Rasool Sahib against the Aryas and they were humiliated due to his success in matters of faith. When he went back to the village, he resumed his duties and stayed in the same grass hut near to the small mosque. He again started his preaching work. About a month later, a great number of Malkaana people of the district of Uspaar rejoined the faith of Islam and the prayers of Ghulam Rasool Sahib were accepted by God Almighty.

Ghulam Rasool Sahib used to say his Tahajjud prayer regularly and recite the Holy Qur'an in a very pleasing manner. He was always inclined towards helping the poor and the needy. He believed spending money in the path of God Almighty was indeed a source of national progress and used to also subscribe to each and every appeal that was made in the name of the true faith.

Qazi Muhammad Yusuf, the Amir of the Frontier Province, stated that Ghulam Rasool Sahib used to pay all his dues regularly and never denied subscribing to the local needs of the community. Once money was needed for the publication of the book

Haqeeqat-ul-Masih. Ghulam Rasool Sahib learnt about this and went to his wife and said that a certain important book has to be published for which money was needed. His wife was also a very sincere Ahmadi. She took off her golden ornaments and gave them to her husband and said: 'Sell these so that the book might be published.'

Ghulam Rasool Sahib passed away on 5th October 1949.

(27) Dr. Syed Habib Ullah Shah

In 1903, Hadhrat Dr Syed Abdul Sattar Shah Sahib, sent both of his sons (Syed Zain ul Abedin Wali Ullah Shah Sahib and Dr Syed Habib Ullah Shah Sahib) to Qadian for education during the lifetime of the Promised Messiah(as). Both his sons had the good fortune to become his Companions.

Dr Syed Habib Ullah Shah Sahib had a profound love of the Holy Qur'an. Whenever he heard anyone reciting it, he was always moved to tears. He had unfathomable love and respect for the Jama'at.

Dr. Habib Sahib worked at the Jail Department and retired as Deputy Inspector General of Jails. He held the rank of Major at the time of his pension and was decorated with the title of MBA while serving as the Superintendent of Central Jail of Multan.

Mr Veerander, the editor of *Daily Partap* of Jullundur, who was a staunch member of Arya Samaj, was imprisoned due to his political activities, together with Mr Shorash Kashmiri (who was an opponent of Ahmadiyya Community). Both unanimously praised Dr. Habib Sahib saying that he used to treat all prisoners equally, regardless of caste or creed and looked after their basic human rights.

In the history of cruelties of jailers, one person by the name of Lala Chaman Lal, Jailer of Punjab Jail, surpassed all others. His own son was appointed as Deputy Superintendent of old Central Jail of Multan where Dr. Habib Sahib was the Superintendent. Once a political prisoner belonging to Congress party complained that his quilt was short and did not have enough cotton to keep him warm. Mr Chaman Lal rejected the complaint saying that he was a liar and a troublemaker, but Dr. Habib Sahib ordered a replacement quilt.

In the jail, there were Sikh prisoners of the opposition parties. One day they had a fight among themselves and Chaman Lal arrested the two leaders and ordered the guards to beat them severely with sticks and put them in separate cells without blankets. As a result of the severe cold, one of the leaders was found dead in the morning. Chaman Lal tried to hide the truth by making false statement, but Dr. Habib Sahib ordered a post-mortem because he believed in justice and fairness. It was proven that the Sikh had died of pneumonia. Dr. Habib Sahib called the then Inspector General of Jails and after investigating the case, Chaman Lal was jailed for five years.

While Chaman Lal was serving his sentence, he one day asked Dr. Habib Sahib to provide him with a bigger and better quilt as he was too tall for the short quilt. Dr. Shah Sahib rejected his request and reminded him of the similar request made by the Congressman, who had been told by

Chaman Lal that he was a liar and a troublemaker.

Once, an Anglo-Indian lady who was concerned about her somewhat darker skin, asked Dr. Hashmatullah Sahib for a treatment. Dr Habib Ullah Shah Sahib was present at that occasion and said to her that Dr Hashmatullah Sahib could not prescribe any remedy at all, as in this world the dark colour would remain as it was, but he could prescribe for her what was written in the Holy Qur'an. He read out the translation of the verses *'Whosoever leads a pious life in this world, his/her face will be white on the Day of Judgement.'* So if you live your present life in accordance with Qur'anic guidance, on the Day of Judgement your face would be white. Hadhrat Khalifatul Masih II(ra) mentioned this incident in his book *Seer-e-Roohani*, Vol. I.

Dr Syed Habib ullah Shah Sahib died in Sialkot on 8th April 1953 at the age of 60 and was buried in Bahishti Maqbarah, Rabwah.

(28) **Munshi Habib-ur-Rehman Raees Hajipura**
(1867-1930)

Hadhrat Munshi Habib-ur-Rehman was born in Sarawa, District Meerath in India, in 1867. He belonged to a very traditional and eminent Muslim family that had made great contributions towards the propagation of Islam, like opening religious schools and building mosques in their area. During the time of Muslim rule in India, the Mughal Empire delegated his family the responsibility of 'Kanoon Goi' (law pronouncement). In recognition and appreciation of good services of the family, the Maharaja of Kapoorthala, granted them a large land where a village named 'Haji Pura' was developed. After his uncle's death, Hadhrat Habib Sahib inherited all properties and consequently became 'Raees' (the Chief) of Haji Pura.

Hadhrat Habib Sahib gained his elementary education at home and memorised part of the Holy Qur'an. He also completed his basic education in Persian and Arabic and gained admission at an English School in Kapoorthala. Within three years, he was well versed in the English language.

Hadhrat Habib Sahib's uncle, Haji Mohammad Wali-Ullah Sahib, was promoted from Commissioner of Finance to Session Judge and also performed the duties of an interpreter. On completion of his education, he was offered the position of Tehsildar in the state, which he refused to accept due to certain bad practices attached to the position.

Hadhrat Habib Sahib had a sentimental attachment with Kapoorthala Mosque. He became the custodian of the Mosque after his uncle's death. The Mosque was forcibly taken away by the opponents of Jama'at but was returned to Ahmadis fulfilling the prophecy of the Promised Messiah(as) in which he said: 'If I am righteous and my mission is true, then you shall get your mosque back.'

Hadhrat Habib Sahib was one of the blessed 313 Companions and his name appears on serial 169 on the list. His name is also mentioned in two books of the Promised Messiah(as) – *Ainae Kamalate Islam* and *Anjame Aatham*, in which he referred to them as like the 'Ashab-e-Badar'.

Hadhrat Habib Sahib was greatly honoured to have attended the first Jalsa Salana held in Qadian on 27th December 1891. He participated in security duty during the debate between the Promised Messiah(as) and Maulawi Seyyad Nazir of Jamia Mosque, Delhi. He was also present during his debate with Abdullah Aatham at Amritsar, at the case of Karam Din and at the time of delivery of Khutba Ilhamia by the Promised Messiah(as).

Hadhrat Habib Sahib was a devoted

follower of the Promised Messiah(as) and whenever he wished to see him, he used to travel from Haji Pura to Qadian. Hadhrat Habib Sahib often used to arrange meals for the entire entourage of the Promised Messiah(as).

Hadhrat Habib Sahib was always anxious to contribute to the fund raising schemes of the Jama'at and often made special pledges and regular payments for Tahrik Jadid. He also contributed towards the construction of Minaret-ul-Masih and his name is inscribed on the minaret.

Hadhrat Munshi Sahib was blessed with six sons, four of them were also Companions of the Promised Messiah(as). These were Munshi Kazeem-ur-Rehman (Sadr Anjuman Ahmadiyya, Qadian and Rabwah); Sheikh Abdul-ur-Rehman (Nusrat Jahan Reserve Fund); Sheikh Abdul Sahab, (Deputy Election Commissioner and Ameer Jama'at Islamabad) and the youngest son, Sheikh Khalil-ur-Rehman (Secretary Ziafat for Jama'at Ahmadiyya, Karachi).

Hadhrat Habib Sahib was a true follower, and dedicated faithful servant of the Promised Messiah(as) and served the Jama'at very sincerely during his whole lifetime. He died on 1st December 1930 at the age of 63 years. His funeral prayer was led by Hadhrat Munshi Zafar Ahmad and was buried in his orchard at Haji Pura in accordance to his Will. The Indian Government later cemented his grave and inscribed the name plate on it bearing, 'Grave of a Muslim Saint'.

(29) **Hadhrat Chaudhary Hakim Ali Panhiar** (1872-1942)

Hadhrat Chaudhry Hakim Ali, a chief of Chak Panhiar, District Gujrat, Pakistan belonged to the Warraich family. He was born in 1872 in Chak Panhiar. His father's name was Allah Wadhaya. Chak Panhiar consisted of 500 acres of land, which belonged to Chaudhary Hakim Ali's father and uncle.

In 1897, when Hakim Ali Sahib visited Qadian, he came across an advertisement in which the Promised Messiah(as) gave an invitation that whoever wishes to seek God in a true sense should contact him. Hakim Ali Sahib was deeply religious so he proceeded to Qadian and met the Promised Messiah(as) and subsequently joined the fold of Ahmadiyyat.

Before returning to his village, the Promised Messiah(as) advised Hakim Ali Sahib to observe three things. Firstly, he should recite the Holy Qur'an and read its translation and commentary every day even if it is a single verse. Secondly, he should offer the Tahajjud prayer regularly even if he had to say two raka'ats and thirdly, he should maintain correspondence with him. Chaudhary Hakim Ali showed an excellent example by observing the advice of the Promised Messiah(as). He bought a copy of the Holy Qur'an with translation before he reached his village. He built a mosque in the compound of his house, always prayed vehemently, wrote regularly to the Promised Messiah(as). He also visited Qadian frequently and eventually settled there.

Chaudhary Hakim Ali had extraordinary blessings from Allah – most of his prayers were accepted and he used to have visions of several forthcoming events. In 1901, when the canal irrigation system was established in Punjab, he purchased about 600 acres of land at Chak 9 North, District Sarqodha. Since most of the early settlers of this village were his family members, the village became known as Chak 9 Panhiar. Chaudhary Hakim Ali Sahib retained a small part of land for himself and divided the rest among his family members. He was once offered the post of soldier but he rejected it and preferred to stay in Qadian and remained near the Promised Messiah(as) for 11 years.

Chaudhary Hakim Ali Sahib was among the 101 companions of the Promised Messiah(as) who had donated 100 rupees or more towards the construction of Minaratul Masih.

After the demise of the Promised Messiah(as), Chaudhary Hakim Ali Sahib remained very dedicated to Khalifatul Masih I(ra) and Khalifatul Masih II(ra).

Chaudhary Hakim Ali Sahib was appointed officer of Langar Khana, and a member of Drul-Qaza. He was so deeply passionate about preaching that on one occasion, he missed several trains at a railway junction having became so engrossed in Tabligh.

Chaudhary Hakim Ali's first marriage took place when he was around twenty years of age. After he joined Ahmadiyyat, his first wife Hakim Bibi followed him soon after. He had three sons and two daughters from his first marriage. His second wife was Ayesha Begum, daughter of Hadhrat Ahmad Jan of Peshawar. He had three sons and four daughters from this second marriage. One of his sons, Chaudhary Samiullah is the son-in-law of Hadhrat Mirza Abdul Haq, Amir Punjab Province. One of his grandsons, Naseem Ahmad Bajwa is a missionary who has served the Jama'at for several years in Pakistan and Scotland. He is presently serving in England.

Chaudhary Hakim Ali Sahib died on 6th January 1942 in Qadian and was buried in Bahishti Maqbara.

Qazi Zahooruddin Akmal, the then editor of *Al Fazl* wrote an excellent poem dedicated to his memory.

(30) **Hakim Muhammad Hussain – 'Marham -e-Isa'** (d.1954)

Hadhrat Hakim Muhammad Hussain was from the well-known Mian family of Lahore. He was more popularly known as 'Marham-e- Isa'. This family were the remnants of the Mughal household who migrated from Punjab and beyond during the disintegration of the Mughal empire in the beginning of the 18th century.

Muhammad Hussain Sahib studied medicine during the early years of his life and acquired considerable knowledge and experience by the time he was thirty. Hadhrat Hakimul-Ummat Maulana Nur-ud-Din(ra) who later became the First Successor of the Promised Messiah(as) met the promising young Hakim sometime in 1892. He recognised his talent and accepted Muhammad Hussein's request for apprenticeship with him. Soon, Muhammad Hussain became a renowned Hakim and occupied a prominent position among the physicians of Lahore.

Hadhrat Hakim Muhammad Hussain heard about the claims of the Promised Messiah(as) and without much arguments and hesitation took the covenant of Bai'at in January 1892. He was the second person to become an Ahmadi from his extended family. The first to convert was Mian Mairajuddin Umar who later became the owner and the editor of *Al-Badr* publication.

Hakim Muhammad Hussain Sahib was a great preacher and a living example in his own way of the beauties and truth of Ahmadiyyat. When the Promised Messiah(as) passed away at Lahore on 26th May 1908, Hakim Sahib was greatly shocked with grief and was seriously hurt when he fell down on hearing the sad news.

Hakim Muhammad Hussain Sahib's famous ointment 'Marham-e-Isa' caused a stir both in India and abroad. This ointment was originally used by the early Christians for healing the wounds of Jesus Christ(as) after his unsuccessful crucifixion by the Jews. Hadhrat Hakim Sahib took great pains to trace this ointment in the ancient books of medicine. Eventually he prepared this ointment and distributed it across India and other parts of the world. Soon after this, the Christians of Lahore lodged a lawsuit against Hakim Sahib. In the Lahore Chief Court, it was stated that a poster containing an advertisement about Marham-e-Isa had hurt the religious feeling of the Christian Community. As a result of this, Hadhrat Hakim Sahib made some changes to the advertisement but the name – 'Marham-e-Isa' was retained with reference to the crucifixion of Jesus Christ(as). This was a victory for Hakim Sahib. God had already informed the Promised Messiah(as) about this victory and Hadhrat Hakim Sahib subsequently became known as 'Hakim

Marham-e-Isa.'

Hadhrat Hakim Muhammad Hussain was a great writer and published many books. He was the editor also of a monthly journal *Hakim-e-Haaziq* published from Lahore. |This journal was mainly devoted to the promotion of medicines but a portion of the magazine was always reserved for Tabligh. Hadhrat Hakim Sahib was an ardent lover of the Holy Qur'an and could be heard reciting the Holy Qur'an morning and evening regularly. He was also a great Arabic scholar.

Hadhrat Hakim Sahib travelled throughout India many times in connection with great religious public debates in Bombay, Calcutta, Madras, Delhi, and other Indian cities. When mentioning the services rendered by the Mian family of Lahore to Ahmadiyyat in the early years, Hadhrat Khalifatul-Masih II(ra) particularly mentioned the name of Hadhrat Hakim Muhammad Hussain.

Hakim Muhammad Hussain had the privilege to witness some of the signs of Allah while he was in the company of the Promised Messiah(as). Once on a dark night in1904, the Promised Messiah(as) had to travel to Qadian from Gurdaspur. As the caravan of the 6 to 8 bullock carts passed out of the city, a patch of bright light appeared from nowhere and led the caravan from Gurdaspur city to the Yakka stand at Qadian – a distance of about 23 miles. Hakim Sahib was also in the caravan along with his younger brother Mian Abdul Aziz Mughal.

Hadhrat Hakim Muhammad Hussain died at Lahore in 1954 at the age of 94 years. Hadhrat Musleh Mau'od(ra) led his Janaza prayer. He was buried at the Bahishti Maqbara, Rabwah, Pakistan.

Hakim Sahib was the eldest son of Charaghuddin 'Rais-e-Aazam', Lahore. He left behind 11 sons and 4 daughters. His eldest son, Dr. Abdul Hameed Chughtai was a great scholar and a physician. One of the sons, Mian Idris Chughtai was the first to arrive in the UK (Birmingham) and his youngest son Abdul Wasi, known as Adam Chughtai, is a well know poet and a devout Ahmadi in the UK and part of his house was used as the first Ahmadiyya Centre in Birmingham from 1962 to 1975.

Today, by the grace of Allah, the number of Ahmadis from the Mian family exceeds one thousand. They had the distinction of having the largest number of Companions of the Promised Messiah(as) within one family.

(31) Hadhrat Hakim Mohammad Ismail Sekhwani

Hadhrat Hakim Mohammad Ismail Sekhwani was not only one of the 313 Companions of the Promised Messiah(as) but his father, Mian Jamal-ud-Din, his grandfather Mian Siddique and two of his uncles were also among the first 313 Companions. Hadhrat Jamalud-Din was among the members of the deputation proposed by the Promised Messiah(as) to go to Nasibin for the investigation of the travels of the Messiah of Nazareth to Kashmir (the deputation could not leave for some reasons).

Hadhrat Ismail Sahib was brought up in pious surroundings. His interest in worldly affairs was merely to provide the minimum essentials for himself and his family. He passed his days with most time spent in the remembrance of Allah. He followed the commandments of the Holy Qur'an and those of the Holy Prophet(saw) in every aspect and made the best use of the literature written by the Promised Messiah(as).

Hadhrat Ismail Sahib always arrived punctually at the mosque for congregational prayers. Many of the elders used to relate that they tried their best to reach the mosque before him but never succeeded. Hadhrat Ismail Sahib used to talk about his time with the Promised Messiah(as) with such a remarkable clarity that the listeners would feel that they were actually present in those sittings.

Hadhrat Ismail Sahib's father and his uncle used to pay frequent visits to Qadian. Quite often, after finishing the day's work at Sethwan, they would walk to Qadian for night-duty and then return to Sethwan the next morning to continue their normal work.

Once the Promised Messiah(as) went to court relating to a case along with some of his companions. Hadhrat Ismail Sahib took a hand-held fan and used it to provide some cool air for the Promised Messiah(as). Hudhur at that point remarked: 'Look he has also partaken of the reward'. Hadhrat Ismail Sahib used to relate this incident with such enjoyment that it would almost leave us with a feeling of loss of not being present at the time.

Hadhrat Ismail Sahib led a simple life and took a keen interest in preaching. As a Hakim, he had knowledge of many rare and effective medicines known to the Promised Messiah(as) and Hadhrat Khalifatul-Masih I(ra) but he never attempted to make commercial gain from this. His motto remained as 'service for mankind' and he used to go on foot or horse to see his patients accepting only the actual cost of the medicine and any extra remuneration freely given by the patient's guardian. He firmly believed that medicine was only a tool and the actual cure lay in the hands of God alone.

Obedience to the institution of Khilafat and the office bearers of the Jama'at was extremely important to him. His contributions to Chanda, particularly of Wassiyat, were very generous and in far excess of the minimum one tenth of his income.

Hadhrat Ismail Sahib was extremely patient and forbearing. He suffered many losses during his life including the death of a young son and a daughter, but he bore all this with great courage and fortitude. During his protracted illness, he never uttered a word of complaint and remained grateful to God in all situations.

(32) **Hadhrat Mir Hamid Shah of Sialkot** (1859-1918)

Hadhrat Mir Hamid Shah of Sialkot belonged to an educated family. His father, Hadhrat Mir Hassam Uddin was an old Companion of the Promised Messiah(as). Both father and son were devoted and staunch Ahmadis. Hadhrat Mir Hamid Shah was a gifted person and was well reputed for his pious life and public service.

After completing his basic education, Hamid Shah Sahib took up service in the District Court of Jammu and then at Sialkot where he remained until retirement. He served first as an Superintendent and then as a Registrar of the Courts where he enjoyed a reputation of honesty and dignity by all fellowmen.

Hamid Shah Sahib devoted all his spare time to Jama'at's activities. He wrote several poems and books. His poems were compiled as *Rubaiat-e-Hamid* and were frequently recited at the Jalsa Salana.

The Promised Messiah(as) said the following about Hamid Shah Sahib:

> 'Syed Ahmad Shah Sahib Sialkoti is the son of my devoted friend and is a true lover of faith. God has given him special power in poetry and this is evident to the readers of *Qaul-e-Fassih* which is evidently a picture of truth, faithfulness and love. I hope he will be able to serve Islam to a great extent with his poetry and writings. I cannot fully gauge the extent of his warmth and true love. I am only too happy to say that he is the son of my old and famous friend from Sialkot Mir Hassam Uddin Sahib.' (*Aazala-e-Auham*, page 319).

Hamid Shah Sahib kept himself in good health. His was very kind-of-heart and his words and actions were always of a righteous nature.

(33) Hadhrat Master Muhammad Hassan Dehlavi (1889-1955)

The ancestors of Hadhrat Master Muhammad Hassan Sahib belonged to the Chistia Movement of Sufis. His grandfather once gave a copy of the book *Barahin-e-Ahmadiyya* written by the Promised Messiah(as) to his father, Maulawi Mahmoodul Hassan. There was an advertisement in the book in bold writing that attracted his attention in which the Promised Messiah(as) challenged other anyone who doubted the truth of the Holy Qur'an and Islam. Maulawi Mahmoodul Hassan thought that a person who dares to challenge others with such courage is surely sent by Allah.

Muhammad Hassan Sahib was initiated into the Jama'at at the hands of the Promised Messiah(as) in April 1900. The Promised Messiah(as) has mentioned the name of Maulawi Mahmoodul Hassan in *Azalai Oham Part II* and the supplement to *Anjam-i-Atham*. He was a very active member of Patiala Jama'at and was regular in paying his contributions.

Hadhrat Master Muhammad Hassan was born in Patiala in January 1889. He had the good fortune of being in the company of the Promised Messiah(as) many times during his childhood through various sessions and listened attentively to the blessed sayings of the Promised Messiah(as) and read his books regularly. Muhammad Hassan Sahib had an extraordinary zeal for preaching the message of Ahmadiyyat.

Despite being a literary person and a famous writer, Master Muhammad Hassan Sahib never let this hinder his religious pursuits and the training of his children. He used his literary capabilities mostly to spread the truth. He always used decent language in his stories and fiction articles. His stories were broadcast regularly from the All India Radio station.

Once Muhammad Hassan Sahib went to the house of a famous nobleman named Nawab Khawaja Abdul Hamid to introduce Ahmadiyyat. Nawab Khawaja Abdul Hamid was annoyed and spoke very rudely and told Hadhrat Hassan Sahib and his colleagues to get out of his house. Hadhrat Hassan Sahib replied politely in a Persian verse the following: 'To turn away your face from the truth because of arrogance and wealth is not nobility. A real wealthy person is the one who is enriched with the truth.' However, at a later date, Khwaja Hamid's son asked Hadhrat Hassan Sahib how he had become an Ahmadi. Muhammad Hassan Sahib was delighted to have the opportunity to preach Ahmadiyyat to Nawab's son and his friends. He was happy that he had redeemed the humiliation he had earlier received at Khawaja Sahib's house.

Hadhrat Khalifatul Masih II(ra)

mentioned Master Hassan Sahib in his Friday Sermon on 23rd September 1955 saying that when Hudhur launched the scheme of Waqf-e-Zindgi (dedication of life) there were hundreds of well-to-do members of the Jama'at who were unable to dedicate their children for the service of Ahmadiyyat. However, Muhammad Hassan Sahib dedicated four of his sons out of his seven children. Though he was not well-off financially, Muhammad Hassan Sahib made great sacrifices for his children's education and they all graduated well. He also taught them well for the service of Ahmadiyyat and four of his children, dedicated their lives for the service of Ahmadiyyat in different parts of the world. Hudhur said: 'If they had not dedicated their lives for the service of Ahmadiyyat, Master Hassan Sahib would have been remembered for a decade or two, but now when my sermon will be published, thousands of Ahmadis will praise and admire Master Hassan Sahib'.

Muhammad Hassan Sahib migrated to Pakistan in 1947. He stayed mostly in Lahore. He died on 25th August 1955, aged 65, at the residence of his son Mahmood Ahmad Khan Sahib. Hadhrat Maulana Jalaluddin Shams Sahib led the funeral prayer on 26th August 1955. He was buried in the special plot reserved for the Companions of the Promised Messiah(as) in Bahishti Maqbara, Rabwah, Pakistan. Hadhrat Mirza Nasir Ahmad Sahib(ru), Khalifatul Masih III, led the prayers at his grave after burial.

(34) **Baba Hassan Muhammad of Aujla** (d.1949)

Baba Hassan Muhammad was a cousin of Munshi Abdul Aziz of Aujla. His initial attitude towards the Ahmadiyya Movement was hostile but as a result of sincere prayers he was shown in a vision a view of Qadian, the Aqsa Mosque and the Promised Messiah(as) which convinced him of the truth. Upon this, he hastened to Qadian to join the movement.

Baba Hassan Sahib migrated to Qadian in 1902. After the sad demise of Maulawi Abdul Karim of Sialkot in 1905, the Promised Messiah(as) drew the attention of the community to dedicate their sons so that they might fill in the gap which had been caused by the deaths of Maulawi Abdul Karim of Sialkot and Maulawi Burhan-ud-Din of Jhelum. Baba Hassan Muhammad offered his only son, Rahmat Ali for this purpose. His son proved to be one of the most successful Ahmadiyya missionaries of Islam in Sumatra and Java where he founded Ahmadiyya Jama'ats. His sincerity and his simple habits won the hearts of those who came in contact with him. He had gained complete mastery over the Indonesian language and was a personal friend of the late Dr. Soekarno (who was Dr. Soekarno).

Baba Hassan Muhammad also had the honour of being the first Ahmadi to undertake Wasiyyat and offered one-tenth of his property in 1905. His Wasiyyat is numbered one. Baba Hassan Sahib was a very pious and learned person and taught the Holy Qur'an to women-folk and regularly preached from house-to-house at night.

After the holocaust of I947, he migrated to Pakistan and settled in Chiniot near Rabwah. passed away on July 20, 1949 and was buried in the Bahishti Maqbara, Rabwah.

(35) **Hadhrat Doctor Hashmat Ullah Khan** (1887-1967)

Hadhrat Dr. Hashmat Ullah Khan was born in Dhaka in the year 1887. When he was about five years old, he was sent with his brother Malik to learn the reading of the Holy Qur'an at a mosque. He later started learning Urdu and Persian.

Dr. Hashmat Sahib started school in the year 1896 when he was nine years old and passed his Matriculation examination in 1907. In April 1920, he joined the Medical School.

Dr. Hashmat Sahib married at a young age but his wife passed away soon after the marriage. He married again in 1910 to his cousin named Fatima Ama-tul-Hafeez and she bore him four daughters and three sons.

In 1899, when Dr. Hashmat Sahib was twelve years old, he accompanied his grandfather and father when they took the Bai'at at the hands of Maulawi Abdul Qadir. When he reached the age of fifteen, Dr. Hashmat Sahib himself developed a great urge to do Bai'at but wanted to at the hands of the Promised Messiah(as). He was indeed a very devote follower and together with Sheikh Afzal of Batala and Khuda Buksh, who were also students, Dr. Hashmat Sahib wrote to the Promised Messiah(as) to request their Bai'ats. This was granted and later announced in the *Al-Hakam* newspaper.

When Dr. Hashmat Sahib was eighteen years old, he had a great urge to visit the Promised Messiah(as). He prayed fervently and humbly to Allah for this to happen and a few days later, following a dream about this, he made his way to Qadian in the month of August 1905. It was the first time he had seen the Promised Messiah(as) and Dr. Hashmat Sahib took his Bai'at at the hands of Hadhrat Mirza Ghulam Ahmad(as).

The Holy Prophet(saw) had foretold that the Promised Messiah(as) will descend together with two angels on a white minaret in the East of Damascus. The Promised Messiah(as) had also written that he or his successor would be travelling to Damascus.These two angels were the said Dr. Hashmat Khan Sahib and Maulawi Zulfiqar Ali Khan.

After having obtained his medical Degree, Dr. Hashmat Sahib joined the staff of a major hospital at Patiala. When the Promised Messiah(as) was suffering from influenza, Dr. Hashmat Sahib attended to him continuously for three months until he was fully recovered.

Dr. Hashmat Sahib was also the personal physician of Hadhrat Khalifatul Masih II(ra) and accompanied him during his journey to Europe in 1924. In 1955, he again assisted Hadhrat Khalifatul Masih II(ra) as his personal physician during Hudhur's tour of Europe.

Dr. Hashmat Sahib continued his

medical services until 1954 representing over 42 years of service. By the grace of God, he was also a Moosi and his name was included in the first 5,000 contributors to Tahrik Jadid. He also contributed a large sum towards the Minaratul Masih construction.

Dr. Hashmat Sahib also served as the Secretary of the Ahmadiyya Community in the year 1907 and again from 1912 to 1918. When he settled permanently at Qadian, he was made the Officer-in-Charge of the Noor Hospital of Qadian where he made a number of improvements. Every year, he was always elected as a member of the Advisory Council (Shura).

Dr. Hashmat Sahib had also written quite a few articles that were published in the *Al-Fazl* and *Al-Hakam* newspapers.

Dr Hashmat Khan Sahib was indeed quite a pious man and showed full of sympathy for his fellow beings. He rendered all possible help to whosoever came to him for treatment. He passed away on 13th April, 1967 and was buried in Bahishti Maqbara, Rabwah, Pakistan.

(36) **Maulawi Muhammad Ibrahim Baqapuri**
(1873-1964)

Maulawi Muhammad Ibrahim belonged to a Zamindar family who were all devoted to the acquisition of knowledge. Maulawi Ibrahim Sahib was born in October 1873 at Chack Chattah in the District of Gujranwala. In 1884, he went to Lahore and studied Theology with the Ulema of the Madrassa Rahmania. In 1889, he went to Ludhiana in and stayed with Maulawi Abdul Qadir for two years. He then proceeded to Saharanpur in 1893 to complete his studies in Theology. While still a student, he had the honour of saying his Asr Prayers with the Promised Messiah(as). He was also a witness of the Sign of the Eclipse of the Sun and the Moon in 1893.

Muhammad Ibrahim Sahib paid frequent visits to Qadian but hesitated to join the Ahmadiyya Community for a number of years until 1905 when he finally decided to submit his allegiance to the Promised Messiah(as). Although Muhammad Ibrahim Sahib was slow to join the fold of Ahmadiyyat, he strove hard to make up the deficiency. He stood firm and made rapid strides in spirituality. His dreams and visions always came true and as he advanced in years, he was gifted with revelations.

Muhammad Ibrahim Sahib was a sincere and selfless missionary of Islam. He preached Islam and Ahmadiyyat in Punjab from 1909 to 1922 and in Sindh from 1923 to 1928. Hadhrat Khalifatul Masih II(ra) granted him permission to initiate people into the Ahmadiyyat Movement on his own behalf. He served as the local preacher and teacher in the Headquarters. He retired in 1938.

Muhammad Ibrahim Sahib wrote his own autobiography called *Hayat-e-Baqapuri* in five volumes. It contains a number of his spiritual experiences.

I shall be failing in my duty if I omit to narrate my own experience of the efficacy of his prayers. I had some shares amounting to Rs.3000 in the Mechanical Industries Ltd, in Qadian 1947. After the partition of country, the then director of the company did nothing to safeguard the interests of shareholders. But the manager, Mr Mahmud-ul- Hassan, himself a shareholder, filed a claim in the court at Sargodha and as a result of his sustained efforts, he succeeded in winning the case in favour of the shareholders. I, for one, got a bona-fide compensation book duly signed by the Deputy Settlement Commissioner Chiniot. The Rehabilitation authorities announced that holders of compensation books amounting to less than Rs. 5,000 would receive cash payment provided they deposited their compensation books in their respective Tahsils. Mine was a genuine case. I deposited my compensation for my claim. I frequented Settlement offices at Chiniot, Lyallpur and Jhang but there was no trace of my compensation book. I visited Lahore more than once in connection with my missing book but nothing came out of it. I was dismayed and in my anxiety, I related the whole story to Maulana Baqapuri and asked him to pray for me. He did pray for me but still there was no response from any quarter. Again I asked the Maulana to pray for the same. He again prayed for me and then said: 'There is something in the air.' The remarks were very encouraging. I again went to Jhang and met the clerk in-charge. My joy knew no bounds when he told me that the compensation book had been traced out. I thanked God and thanked the clerk. In due time, I received a cheque for Rs.3,149/ from the National Bank, Chiniot. I got the money by the grace of God. My faith in the efficacy of prayer was immensely increased. I also thanked Maulana for his efficacious prayers.

Maulana Baqapuri Sahib passed away in 1964. He was buried in the Bahishti Maqbara at Rabwah.

(37) **Hadhrat Munshi Imamuddin** (1863-1939)

Hadhrat Munshi Imamuddin Sahib Patwari was born in 1863. He joined the fold of Ahmadiyyat as a result of preaching by his brother-in-law, Munshi Abdul Aziz Sahib in 1894. He was from a place called Qila Darshan Singh. He became known as Sekhwani because he had left Qila Darshan Singh and settled down in Sekhwan. After his primary education he came to Gurdaspur for further education. He worked as a Patwari, (Land Registrar) for 35 years.

Hadhrat Munshi Abdul Aziz Sahib relates that Imamuddin Sahib was of a rather stern disposition and was always feared. At one time Imamuddin Sahib denied Ahmadiyyat, and there seemed no hope in trying to convince him. However, by Divine design, such a situation was created that Imamuddin Sahib decided to take the bai'at on his own. He describes this occasion of his bai'at in the following way:

'After the evening prayers, Munshi Abdul Aziz Sahib pointing towards me requested Hadhrat Masih Mau'od(as) to administer the bai'at. I was taken to the Baitul Fikr, (this is the name given to the room in which the Promised Messiah(as) used to do most of his writing work). Hadhrat Masih Mau'od(as) made me sit at the head of the Charpoi (traditional bed which has a hammock-like structure woven between a wooden frame) and despite my protests, he himself sat towards the foot end of the bed. This made a lasting impression on me, because usually the spiritual leader or master sits at the head and makes his disciple sit at his feet, whereas this was a complete reversal.'

After accepting Ahmadiyyat, Hadhrat Imamuddin Sahib became so active in preaching the message of Ahmadiyyat, that his own family and four whole villages nearby entered the fold of Ahmadiyyat. These were Qila Gilanwali, Talaundi, Jhunglan and Loh Chak. Even after having migrated to Qadian, he used to go back to his village to continue preaching.

Once Hadhrat Imamuddin Sahib went to Phero Cheechee. The non-Ahmadi opponents threw him out of the village using violence. Hadhrat Imamuddin Sahib said: 'Now I have really enjoyed preaching, when I was still employed (as a government servant) people did not treat me badly.'

Hadhrat Imamuddin Sahib was extremely fond of preaching the message of Ahmadiyyat. When Hadhrat Khalifatul Masih II(ra) expressed the desire that every Ahmadi should convert at least one person to Ahmadiyyat per year, Imamuddin Sahib was unwell. So whenever some non-Ahmadi came to enquire about his health, Imamuddin Sahib used this opportunity to start preaching to them and from this, many people were converted.

Hadhrat Imamuddin Sahib states that once when he was in the company of the Promised Messiah(as), he had the desire to ask a question. The question had barely entered his mind when the Promised Messiah(as) changed the topic of what he was saying and started answering Imamuddin Sahib's question (the question he had wanted to ask was, whether the Messiah and Mahdi were the same person or not?)

Hadhrat Imamuddin Sahib relates that during the trial of Maulawi Muhammad Hussain Batalvi, the head of the police station, Mohammad Bukhsh Thanedar once said: 'In the past Mirza (meaning the Promised Messiah(as) has always managed to get away, but this time he will feel my hand.' Hadhrat Masih Mau'od(as) said: 'Mia Imamuddin you will see that his hand will be severed.' Hadhrat Imamuddin Sahib related that soon after this incident, Muhammad Bukhsh Thanedar developed a severe pain in the palm of his hand and died soon afterwards.

On the occasion of the 1908 Jalsa (after the death of the Promised Messiah(as) which took place on the 26th May 1908), Maulawi Muhammad Ali Sahib (who later led the split of the movement at the death of Hadhrat Khalifatul Masih I(ra) and was among the founders of the Lahori Jama'at) gave the responsibility of providing fire-wood at the eleventh hour when only a few days were left for the Jalsa to begin, to Hadhrat Mirza Bashir-ud-Din Mahmood Ahmad (who later become Khalifatul Masih II(ra)) so that in the event of his failure to do so, he would be embarrassed. Hadhrat Imamuddin Sahib had a great deal of foresight, and he understood the intentions behind this scheme and took over the responsibility from Hadhrat Mirza Bashir-ud-Din Mahmood Ahmad and personally took the labourers to cut and gather the fire-wood and completed the work within a very short period of time. During his stay in Qadian, he was the Officer-in-Charge of the kitchen at the time of the Annual Gatherings.

On the death of Hadhrat Khalifatul Masih I(ra), the Paighamis (name given to the Lahori Jama'at because of their publication named *Paigham-e-Sulah*) tried very hard to convince Hadhrat Imamuddin Sahib to join them, but Hadhrat Imamuddin Sahib's steadfastness did not falter the breadth of a hair.

Hadhrat Imamuddin Sahib was so fond of offering his prayers in congregation that if due to some difficulty he was absent from the mosque, the other members of the congregation used to become worried about his absence. He had immense love for the members of Hadhrat Masih Mau'od's(as) family. He used to say to his children, that as long as you remain associated with this family, you will always profit and progress in the world.

In 1928, when the railway line was being laid down through Qadian, it was in the interest of the Jama'at that the tracks should enter Qadian from the South. The opponents of the Jama'at, however tried to get it laid from the Westerly direction. Hadhrat Mirza Bashir Ahmad Sahib(ra) appointed Hadhrat Imamuddin Sahib as his deputy in presenting the Jama'at's case to the authorities. Hadhrat Imamuddin Sahib worked very hard in this matter and finally the Jama'at's opinion prevailed by the grace of God.

When the building of a slaughterhouse was proposed in Qadian, the non-Muslims, planned to create civil unrest. Hadhrat Imamuddin Sahib was assigned to diffuse the situation in which he was instrumental in avoiding any disturbances by entering into negotiations with the neighbouring Sikh Community.

Hadhrat Imamuddin Sahib was in the habit of smoking the Huqqah. Once when Hadhrat Khalifatul Masih II(ra) spoke against this habit, he immediately gave it up but this caused him to fall ill. His friends tried to persuade him to stop smoking gradually and not to give up suddenly, but Hadhrat Imamuddin Sahib refused saying: 'Once I have given it up, come what may, I will not touch it again.'

Hadhrat Imamuddin Sahib could tolerate a great deal of pain and suffering – once he was supposed to be operated upon for a carbuncle, but he refused anaesthesia and was operated upon without any anaesthetic. He was a very hospitable person and looked after his guests very well.

Because of his very close association with the family of the Promised Messiah(as), Hadhrat Ummul Momineen (the wife of the Promised Messiah(as)) invited Hadhrat Imamuddin Sahib's family to attend the wedding ceremony of Hadhrat Nawab Mubarika Begum Sahib (the eldest daughter of the Promised Messiah(as)).

Hadhrat Imamuddin Sahib died on 26th July 1939 and was buried in the special plot for the Companions of the Promised Messiah(as) in Bahishti Maqbarah, Qadian. India.

(38) **Maulawi Imam-ud-Din of Goleki** (1851-1940)

Maulawi Imam-ud-Din of Goleki was born in 1851 at Goleki, which was the centre of learning in those days in the Gujrat District. Students from far and wide flocked towards this place for seeking knowledge. By the time he was twenty, Maulawi Sahib had picked up knowledge of Arabic, Persian, Urdu and Theology.

After the death of his father in 1871, Maulawi Imam-ud-Din Sahib felt an urge for a spiritual guide. He paid a quick visit to Qadian and had a brief interview with the Promised Messiah(as) who told him to seek guidance from God through prayers and supplications. Maulawi Imam-ud-Din Sahib did just that and became convinced of the truth of the Promised Messiah and Mahdi(as) and pledged himself at his hands in 1895.

Maulawi Imam-ud-Din Sahib devoted himself wholly and solely to propagating the message of the movement in his neighbourhood. In 1903, when the Promised Messiah(as) visited Jhelum to appear as witness before a court, the railway platform was thronged with visitors who came from long distances to have a glimpse of him. Maulawi Imam-ud-Din Sahib, accompanied by a large number of Ahmadis and non-Ahmadis also proceeded to Jhelum.

People gathered at the house where the Promised Messiah(as) was staying and wanted to see him and were impatient to have a look at his holy face. The Promised Messiah(as) seated himself in an easy chair on the roof of the house. On that day, over one thousand people joined the fold of Ahmadiyyat As a result of this visit, many Ahmadiyya communities sprang up in the villages of Jhelum, Gujrat and Gujranwala districts.

Maulawi Imam-ud-Din Sahib was a scholar in many branches of theology and his pupils included a large number of Muslims and Hindus.

In 1925, a year after the death of his wife, Maulawi Imam-ud-Din Sahib migrated to Qadian. He had deep and warm affection for the family of the Promised Messiah(as). He willed a large proportion of his property to be assigned to the Sadr Anjuman Ahmadiyya, Qadian, for the spread and propagation of Islam.

Maulawi Imam-ud-Din Sahib composed poems in Arabic, Persian, Urdu and Punjabi. His only son, Akmal of Goleki, was a renowned poet in Arabic, Persian, Urdu and Punjabi.

Maulawi Imam-ud-Din Sahib passed away at the age of 91 on 12th April 1940. He was buried at Bahishti Maqbara, Qadian.

(39) Hadhrat Mian Imam-ud-Din Sekhwani

Hadhrat Mian Imamu-ud-Din was the second eldest of three brothers. He was the father of Maulana Jalal-ud-Din Shams and paternal grandfather of Maulana Munir-ud-Din Shams. He was also Additional Vakil Isha'at and the maternal grandfather of Amatul Majid Chaudhary Sahiba, the ex-Managing Editor of *The Review of Religions*.

Imam-ud-Din Sahib had settled in Sekhwan after migration from Kashmir. He took the initiation soon after the announcement of the first Bai'at by the Promised Messiah(as). He used to relate that when the names of 313 companions were proposed by the Promised Messiah(as) and were written down, unaware to the Sekhwani brothers was that some people made requests for them to included in the list. One day, when the three brothers went to Qadian from Sekhwan, the Promised Messiah(as) told them: 'We have recorded your names among the 313 companions.' Mian Imam-ud-Din Sahib's number in this blessed list is at 32.

Imam-ud-Din Sahib was a pious and selfless devotee of Ahmadiyyat. He was very punctual in prayers, regular in Tahajjud and chanda payments and very enthusiastic in Tabligh. He played an important role in the establishment of the most of the Ahmadiyya Jama'ats in Gurdaspur District. During his stay at Sekhwan, Imam-ud-Din Sahib was secretary of the Jama'at. He was compelled to shift to Qadian after his son Maulana Jalaluddin Shams Sahib left for England.

Imam-ud-Din Sahib was a member of the deputation that Hadhrat Khalifatul Masih II(ra) sent to the Jama'at of Sekhwan and Gurdaspur District to resolve a problem.

When the Promised Messiah(as) expressed a need for Rs.150 for religious purpose, Imam-ud-Din Sahib along with his brothers and Munshi Abdul Aziz Sahib of Patwar collected the amount and offered it to the Promised Messiah(as). The Promised Messiah(as) was very pleased and published a poster in which their names were mentioned as having acted like Hadhrat Abu Bakr(ra).

Due to his devotion and love for the Promised Messiah(as), Imam-ud-Din Sahib often visited Qadian. When Imam-ud-Din Sahib's son Bashir Ahmad fell ill of a soar in the thigh, some people thought it was plague. Imam-ud-Din Sahib went to see the Promised Messiah(as) who was already aware of his son's ailment. As soon as the Promised Messiah(as) saw Mian Imam-ud-Din approaching, he said to Imam-ud-Din Sahib: 'It is only minor and not the plague'. The Promised Messiah(as) then added very enthusiastically: 'Look, whom we know, can never suffer from the plague and who knows us as well can never be inflicted with plague.' On hearing this, he returned to Sekhwan and Bashir Ahmad fully recovered after a few days.

Once under the instruction of Hadhrat Musleh Mau'od(ra) some preachers were sent to Tehsil Shakar Bash. As a result of Tabligh, many Hindu Mahashas showed an interest and willingness to accept Islam. Hadhrat Khalifatul-Masih II(ra) was informed about the situation and Hudhur selected Hadhrat Mian Imam-ud-Din to take the initiation at Shakar Bash. Sheikh Abdur-Rahman Misri said that Hudhur insisted on Imam-ud-Din Sahib being sent on that mission saying: 'You do not see the value of the Companions of the Promised Messiah(as). They used to preach and deliver the message of truth when there were no regular preachers.' Mian Imam-ud-Din Sahib stayed there for many days.

Hadhrat Mian Imam-ud-Din was a preacher in District Gurdaspur. He established the Jama'at of Hussein, a village only two miles away from Sekhwan. Once during the lifetime of the Promised Messiah(as), two or three non-Ahmadi Maulawis came to Hussein and started to use bad language against the Promised Messiah(as) in the mosque. The people of the village called upon Mian Imam-ud-Din to go and talk with them. Hadhrat Mian Sahib directly went to Qadian to get permission for Manazrah from the Promised Messiah(as). The Promised Messiah(as) said: 'No permission for Manazrah.' On hearing this, all of them were surprised and refused to embark upon any debate. Ultimately the Maulawis started to provoke by saying: 'The Ahmadis do not have the courage to face us in discussion.' Hadhrat Mian Sahib went again to Qadian, explained the situation and asked the Promised Messiah(as) permission for Manazrah. The Promised Messiah(as) again said: 'No permission for Manazrah.' They returned again to the village and spent the whole day outside the village but refused any discussions with their opponents who continued their abuse. The effect of the Promised Messiah's(as) decision was that eventually, a non-Ahmadi of the village drove the Maulawis out of their village due to their foul language. Soon after, about 16 non-Ahmadi men of Hesian went to Qadian to attend the next Friday prayer to observe with their own eyes whether the person whom the Maulawis abused was really such a man. After the prayer, all of them met the Promised Messiah(as) and expressed their desire for initiation and entered the fold of Ahmadiyyat.

Hadhrat Mian Imam-ud-Din used to say that it is there belief that if the Manazrah had taken place, maybe no one would have accepted Ahmadiyyat. Because there was holiness and blessing in the words of the Promised Messiah(as) and their restrain from discussion resulted in an impact on the villagers, many people were guided to the right path and accepted Ahmadiyyat.

(40) **Hadhrat Seth Ismael Adam** (1874-1957)

Hadhrat Seth Ismael Adam Sahib belonged to a well-known, affluent and respectable Indian Memons community among the Muslims. Seth Adam Sahib was born in 1874 in Bombay. He grew up and was engaged in the family business. His shop was adjacent to the Jami'a mosque and he was known as 'the trader with the blue umbrella.' His father was a disciple of renowned saint, Pir Rasheed-ud-din Sahib, popularly called 'Pir Jhande Wale' of Saeedabad, District Hyderabad, Sindh.

Ismael Adam Sahib's father took him to Pir Sahib in his childhood and requested Pir Sahib to accept his pledge. Before taking the pledge, Ismael Adam Sahib enquired from Pir Sahib that how will he actually benefit from it. Pir Sahib had a good look at him, asked for water, recited something over it and gave to him to drink. Then addressing his father he said: Your son will have the blessing of pledging his allegiance (Bai'at) to a great Divine person.

The background to Ismael Adam Sahib's taking the pledge of allegiance to the Promised Messiah(as) is very inspiring. He learned about the claims of Hadhrat Masih Mau'od(as) through newspapers from Punjab which were generally hostile to the Promised Messiah(as). Ismael Adam Sahib enquired from people about the Promised Messiah(as)'s claims and studied some of his writings and soon the truth dawned on him clearly. Before taking the decisive step, he wrote a letter in Persian to Pir Sahib saying:

> 'I am a worldly person and am spiritually blind. You are a leader and guide hundreds of thousands of people and endowed with knowledge. Therefore, I want you to tell me, on oath, whether Mirza Ghulam Ahmad of Qadian is true or false in his claim to be the Mahdi and the Messiah. If you tell me not and he happens to be true and thereby we are deprived of guidance, you will be responsible to God. On the other hand if he is false and we accept him through our ignorance and are thus misguided, our sin will be on your head'.

The Pir Sahib wrote back most respectfully with three testimonies, which are recorded below:

First Testimony:

'It is our routine that, between Maghrib and Isha prayers, we sit with our disciples in a circle for remembrance of Allah. During one of these sessions, I saw the Holy Prophet(saw) in a vision and asked him: "O, Hadhrat, Who is this man, Mirza Ghulam Ahmad?" The Holy Prophet(saw) replied: "He is from us."'

Second Testimony:

'This is our family tradition that after Isha prayers, we do not converse with anyone and go to sleep, that being the Sunnah of the Messenger of Allah. Once I saw the Holy Prophet(saw) in a dream and said to him: "O Hudhur, the maulawis have issued fatwas of 'kufr' about this man and call him a liar." He replied: "He is possessed by our love."'

Third Testimony:

'Our dispensation and our family have been regular in Tahujjud prayers. Every night we get up after 3am and after Tahujjud prayer we lie on our side and offer Fajr prayer with the same wudu (ablution), that too being the Sunnah of the Messenger of Allah. One day in the same position, I was overtaken by light sleep when the Holy Prophet(saw) appeared. I said: "O, Messenger of Allah, not only the whole of India but the Ulema of Arabia have also issued Fatwas of 'kufr' about him." The Holy Prophet(saw) with great dignity, repeated three times: 'He is true, he is true, he is true."'

'This is the true testimony, I have. Now I am free of the burden of your oath. To believe or not to believe – that is up to you.'

Signed: Rasheed-ud-din Sahib-ul-'alam.

(*Quoted by Maulana Abdul-Malik Khan Sahib, Al-Fazl, 29th Jan 1958)*

Hadhrat Masih Mau'od(as) has mentioned about his correspondence with Hadhrat Pir Rasheed-ud-din Sahib-ul-'alam in his books, including *Anjaam-i-Atham (Zamima)*:

'And second is the Pir Sahib-ul-'alam, who is one of the renowned divines of Sind with a following of more than a hundred thousand. He is well versed in Arabic knowledge and is one of the established scholars. He has given the following testimony about me: "I saw the Messenger of Allah(saw) in a vision and enquired him of you, saying: Explain to me, O Messenger of Allah, is he a liar – an impostor or true? The Messenger of Allah(saw) replied: He is true and from Allah. Thus I realised that you are on manifest truth and since then have had no doubts about you, and entertain no uncertainty about your station and we will do as you order. If you command us to go to America, we shall certainly go there, and we put ourselves completely at your disposal and you will find us of the obedient ones.'

This is what his Khalifa – the late Abdul-Latif, and Sheikh Abdullah Arab have told me verbally and testified to it when my close friend, Seth Saleh Muhammad Haji Allah Rakhkha Sahib, went to see him in Madras. He stood up in a general gathering, with a rod in his hand, declared to those present, in a loud voice, that he believed me to be true in my claim. I have also seen that in a vision. His son has declared that he cannot deny what has been verified by his father.

(Ruhani Khazain, Vol 11 p.344)

Hadhrat Masih Mau'od(as) has also mentioned this in *Tohfa Golarwiya (Ruhani Khazain*, Vol.17 p.463) and *Haqiqatul Wahy* – sign no 16 (*Ruhani Khazain*, Vol.22 p.210).

With the letter of Pir Sahib, the truth fully dawned upon Ismael Adam Sahib, he pledged his allegiance to Hadhrat Masih Mau'od(as) in writing around July or August 1896. His joining the fold brought him strong opposition from many quarters but he faced all difficulties admirably. Once, some Ulema wrote to him that they would see him privately to explain things to him, he agreed to this suggestion, but they ended up being preached by him at length.

Once Ismael Adam Sahib wrote to Hadhrat Masih Mau'od(as) that when he attends the mosque for Zuhr, Asr and Maghrib prayers, he is badly abused every time. Hadhrat Masih Mau'od(as) replied: 'You should offer Juma prayers with Zain-ul-'Abideen Sahib, the engineer – he is a sincere Ahmadi. You can offer other prayers at your shop.'

Ismael Adam Sahib arrived in Qadian in 1898 for the first time and again in 1900 when he had the honour of listening to the Arabic Sermon, known as the *'Khutaba ilhamiyya'.* On this occasion a group photograph, including Hadhrat Masih Mau'od(as) and his Khuddam was taken. Seth sahib joined in. Ismael Adam Sahib had this photograph in his house with the inscription: *1st April 1900, after Asr prayers on the occasion of 'Khutaba ilhamiyya'.*

Ismael Adam Sahib studied Urdu and Gujrati at a basic level but he was very fond of religious knowledge, general studies, reading papers, magazines and books. He attained a very high status in the field of knowledge and understanding.

In 1902, when Hadhrat Musleh Mau'od(ra) was married for the first time to the daughter of Dr. Rasheed-ud-din Sahib, he had a very fine, red, velvety Turkish cap prepared and had it embroidered with the words of the following ilham: *'Mazharul-Haqqi wal-'ula ka-ann-Allaha nazala min-as-samaa'* and requested Hadhrat Masih Mau'od(as) that the cap be worn by the groom at the time of Nikah ceremony. Moreover, he had a silken headwear, bordered with golden tape, prepared for the bride. Hadhrat Masih Mau'od(as) wrote back with his own hands, as follows:

In the name of Allah the Gracious, the Merciful

My dear brother Seth Ismael Adam sahib

Assalamo-alaikum wa rahmatullahi wabarakaatuhu,

Your letter and the gift that you have sent for Mahmud (and Bashir) on his wedding i.e., the cap and the headwear have been received. I thank you for your friendly gift, and pray for you, that Allah may reward you in both religious and worldly matters. Amen.

It is all well here.

Wassalaam,
Mirza Ghulam Ahmad.
(20 Oct 1902)

Seth Sahib had with him many letters from Hadhrat Masih Mau'od(as) but he was so attached to this one that he never wanted to part with it.

Ismael Adam Sahib played a facilitative role in the 'Bai'at' of Ghulam Yasin 'Maulana Abu-al-Nasr Aah' the elder brother of Maulana Abu-al-Kalam Azad. Ismael Adam Sahib states that in 1902 Maulana Abu-al-Nasr Sahib saw a dream, which he narrated in the following words: 'Me and my younger brother, Abu-al-Kalam Azad are in Qadian. ... We met Mirza Sahib and discussed some religious matters with him. During the discussion my brother spoke harshly to Mirza Sahib. A respected divine seated nearby got greatly offended and reprimanded Abu-al-Kalam, saying: 'Be quiet! Do you know who you are talking to so disrespectfully? One who was praised by the Messenger of Allah(saw)!'

That respected divine spoke in a loud and powerful voice that struck terror and woke me up.

When Maulana Abu-al-Nasr narrated that dream to me, I told him: I have a group photograph which includes Mirza Sahib and myself. If I showed you that photograph, will you be able to recognise that divine? He said yes, he remembered his face very well. A few days later, Seth Sahib took that photograph to him; he looked at it very carefully and, pointing at it with his finger, said: This is Mirza Sahib and this is the divine, with the glasses, who reprimanded my brother. Seth Sahib told him that he was Maulawi Abdul-Karim Sialkoti and that had a loud voice, and that it was he who read out Mirza Sahib's lecture in the world religions conference held in Lahore in 1896. Three years later, on 2nd May 1905, accompanied by his brother, he went to Qadian, arriving there before Zuhr prayer. Most respectfully he went to see Hudhur, in the garden where he was staying at that time. After general enquiries, Hudhur blessed him most beneficial exhortations, which impressed him very much and he took the pledge of allegiance (bai'at).

(Tareekh-e-Ahmadiyyat, Vol.3 pp. 408-409)

Hadhrat Seth Sahib had the distinction of being host to Ahmadis when they sojourned with him on their overseas voyages. He had the honour of being host to Hadhrat Khalifa-tul-Masih II(ra) on his way to Makkah and Egypt. During this journey, Hadhrat Mir Nasir Nawab Sahib was also his guest. On another occasion, Hadhrat Mirza Sultan Ahmad Sahib stayed with him as his guest.

On 8th September 1934, when Hadhrat Mirza Nasir Ahmad Sahib arrived at Bombay, on his way to England, he had breakfast with Seth Sahib. Hadhrat Sheikh Ya'qub Ali Sahib Irfaani was also with him. *(Tareekh-e-Ahmadiyyat, Vol.7, p.198)*

On 16th October 1938, when Hadhrat Khalifatul-Masih II(ra) arrived in Bombay from Karachi by ship, the Bombay Ahmadiyya Jama'at, Hadhrat Seth Ismael, Adam Sahib and local missionary Hadhrat Maulana Abu-al-Ata Sahib gave him a very warm welcome. Hadhrat Seth Sahib had the honour of being host to Hadhrat Khalifatul-Masih II(ra) on this occasion.

Hadhrat Khalifatul-Masih II(ra) greatly respected Ismael Adam Sahib. In 1933, Hadhrat Sheikh Ya'qub Ali Sahib Irfaani was the Ameer of Bombay Jama'at. But in 1935, Hudhur replaced him with Ismael Adam Sahib who then held this office till 1948 except for the short period when he left for Puna, because of his business commitments.

In spite of his old age, he used to participate regularly in Jum'a prayers and other Jama'at gatherings. When Chaudhry Abdullah Khan Sahib was elected as Ameer of Karachi Jama'at for the first time, the meeting was presided by Hadhrat Seth Sahib.

Ismael Adam Sahib was a very good-mannered, sociable and hospitable person. He respected and looked after those coming from Markaz. He was full of sympathy for mankind and was always pleased to help deserving people. Khawaja Muhammad Ismael Sahib, in his treatise 'Hadhrat Seth Ismael Adam of Bombay' writes:

> 'I can say it with certainty, based on personal experience, that whenever I had the opportunity of visiting and enjoying the company of the Sahaba, who had the blessing of keeping company with Hadhrat Masih Mau'od(as) or visiting him frequently, I found that they were illumined with the special light of faith, and Hadhrat Seth Sahib had his major share of that.'

Ismael Adam Sahib was devoted to worship and every Friday, for Juma prayers, he would close his business to go the mosque and lead the prayers. He regularly paid his various chandas and attended Jama'at meetings. He was very hospitable to those coming to Bombay on Jama'at duty. Allah had blessed him with a very generous heart and he happily performed whatever duties were assigned to him.

In Bombay, his shop was in a very good location and both his retail and wholesale business were very successful. In 1938, he started his business in Colombo as well and sent his sons – Adam Ismael Sahib and Hashim Ismael Sahib. In 1942, during the Japanese shelling, the two brothers had to leave in fear of their safety. In the same year, Ismael Adam Sahib had to close down his business in Bombay because of losses. This grieved him a lot, but he bore this with steadfastness.

After the partition with India in 1948, Ismael Adam Sahib migrated to Karachi. His health started deteriorating in 1953 and he passed away on 7th December 1957 and was buried in the graveyard of the Memon community. He was a Moosi, therefore an epitaph was installed in the Bahishti Maqbara of Qadian.

He married five times and was survived by four sons.

(41) **Hadhrat Jahan Khan** (the Last Companion of the Promised Messiah)

At a Question/Answer session in Germany, Hadhrat Khalifatul Masih IV(ru) was asked about the identity of the last Companion of Hadhrat Promised Messiah(as).

Hudhur suggested the name of Jahan Khan Sahib. A person sitting in the gathering suggested a possible other name. Hudhur then asked Maulana Dost Muhammad Sahib Shahid who was among the audience, to carry out an investigation in this matter and he then sent the following authentic article.

This authentic witness was to verify that Hadhrat Choudhary Jahan Khan Sahib was the last Companion of the Promised Messiah(as) comes from Hadhrat Maulana Ghulam Rasool Rajeeki who visited the Promised Messiah(as) one or two days before the demise of the Promised Messiah(as) and got Jahan Khan Sahib initiated at his hands.

It is written on page 85 of the *Hayyat-e-Qudsi* (Part III) printed in January 1954 by the Taj Press of Haidevabad Dakkan that:

> 'Choudhary Jahan Khan joined the fold of Ahmadiyyat at the time when the Promised Messiah(as) last visited Lahore. I presented Choudhary Jahan Khan to Hudhur just one or two days before Hudhur's demise and got him initiated. To my knowledge, no other person had the opportunity after that to have initiated at the hands of the Promised Messiah(as) because the Promised Messiah(as) suddenly fell ill and passed away a day or two later. Therefore in my opinion Choudhary Jahan Khan is the last companion of the Promised Messiah(as)'.

(42) **Hadhrat Munshi Jalaludin (b.1830)**

The Promised Messiah(as) wrote the names of his first 313 companions in his book *Anjam-e-Athem (The Fate of Athem)*, published in January 1897. The fist name to appear was that of Munshi Jalaludin of village Balami Kharan, District Gujrat. The following is a short biography by Hadhrat M Sheikh Noor Ahmad Sahib with the assistance of Mirza Mohammad Ismail, a staff member of Tahrik Jadid.

Hadhrat Munshi Jalaluddin was born in 1830 in Balami District Gujrat. His father died when he was only seven years old and he was then looked after by his maternal uncle Mirza Zainul Abedee who hired the best teachers for his education. As a result of this, Munshi Jalaludin Sahib became very well versed in Arabic and Persian.

Munshi Jalaludin Sahib was very fond of reading the newspaper and once read an article and concluded that the writer must be the Promised Messiah(as) whose coming was foretold by the Holy Prophet(saw). Soon after reading this article, Munshi Jalaludin Sahib set off for Qadian. Along the way, he stopped in the town of Batala where a man named Mian Sahib stopped him from going to Qadian. Munshi Jalaludin Sahib prayed to Allah for help. Once Munshi Jalaludin Sahib saw the Promised Messiah(as) in a dream and became very restless and prayed again. But once again, in a second dream he saw the Promised Messiah(as).

When Munshi Jalaludin Sahib met the Promised Messiah(as) for the first time, he immediately recognised him from his earlier dreams. The Promised Messiah(as) met him with great love and Munshi Jalaludin Sahib requested him to take his Bai'at. Upon this, the Promised Messiah(as) said: 'I have not been ordered to take Bai'at.' Munshi Jalaludin Sahib then returned back his home. From then onwards, whenever Munshi Jalaludin Sahib took leave from his work, it was normal for him to first go to Qadian and then to his family. He developed a deep spiritual attachment with the Promised Messiah(as) which was reciprocated by the Promised Messiah(as) himself. When Bai'at was announced, Munshi Jalaludin Sahib immediately came and took Bai'at and his name was among the first 313 Companions mentioned in *Anjame Athem*.

Once, as Munshi Jalaludin Sahib was passing through an unpopulated area at about midday, he felt very thirsty and hungry. He prayed to Allah and soon after he saw a tent. When he approached it, he saw a table full of food and also a comfortable chair in a corner. He ate some food and had a rest. When he woke up, the tent and its contents were nowhere to he found. This was a miracle from God for his servant.

In 1891 or 1892, Munshi Jalaludin

Sahib saw a vision that the Promised Messiah(as) has read his 'Nikah' with a virgin. He related this dream to the Promised Messiah(as) who advised him to perform a service to the religion and assigned to him a task to write a book about the Holy Qur'an.

Munshi Jalaludin Sahib married at a young age. He had four daughters and four sons.

(Rendered by Sheikh Noor Ahmad ex Missionary, Middle Eastern Countries)

(43) **Hafiz Jamal Ahmad – Missionary Mauritius**

Hafiz Jamal Ahmad was among the youngest Companions who accepted the Promised Messiah(as). The first time he met the Promised Messiah(as) was in May 1908 at Lahore.

Hafiz Sahib writes: 'My father had accepted the Promised Messiah(as) through a letter. I was about fifteen or sixteen years old when I first saw the Promised Messiah(as) and that was when he last came to Lahore. Only a fortnight later, the Promised Messiah(as) passed away.'

Hafiz Jamal Ahmad had the distinction of having served as an Ahmadiyya Missionary in Mauritius continuously for twenty-one years. It was on 27th July 1928 when he reached Mauritius from Qadian. He passed away on the 27th December 1949 in Mauritius and was buried in the graveyard known by the name of St. Perry.

When the news of the demise reached Hadhrat Khalifatul-Masih II(ra) at Rabwah, he mentioned his services in his Friday Sermon on 30th December 1949 in the following affectionate words:

> 'The passing away of Hafiz Jamal Ahmad was indeed a very special event. When he was sent to Mauritius the financial state of the Ahmadiyya Jama'at was indeed very weak. The Community at Mauritius could not pay the travelling expenses of their Missionary. In this situation the name of this very competent person Hafiz Jamal Ahmad was suggested
>
> Another reason for selecting him was that the former Ahmadiyya Missionary of Mauritius was Sofi Ghulam Muhammad who knew the Holy Qur'an by heart. So to replace him another Hafiz, Hafiz Jamal Ahmad was posted at Mauritius.
>
> Hafiz Jamal Ahmad was married to the daughter of Maulawi Fateh Deen who was closely related to the Promised Messiah(as) before his proclaiming of Messiah.
>
> Although the financial position of the Ahmadiyya Jama'at was not at all very sound and Hafiz Jamal could not leave his family behind, I did give him permission to take his wife and children along with him on the condition that he would have to stay at Mauritius throughout his whole life. He, therefore agreed to stay at Mauritius permanently.
>
> After quite a long time, when his sons as well as his daughter had grown up, he wrote to me stating that as his children have grown up and he has to arrange for their marriages, he should be permitted to come back to Pakistan.
>
> But I did remind him of the promise that he had made to stay

at Mauritius permanently. He wrote to me that it was also necessary that his children should get married. I therefore reconsidered his case and decided that he should be allowed to come back in order to benefit from the new centre (Rabwah).

But God Almighty did not allow that Hafiz Jamal Ahmad should break his promise. He, therefore, caused him to die in Mauritius.

All these facts and occurrences I believe are indeed Signs from God Almighty. A certain person makes a promise and does keep that promise faithfully for many years. Owing to certain circumstances beyond his control, he wishes to come back for a short time and seeks permission to come back and keeps quiet after his request is not approved.

He had also said that the education of his children was suffering quite a lot. I wrote back to him stating that he should send his children back to Pakistan. Consequently one of his sons is studying at Lahore and is being supported by the Ahmadiyya organisation. A little later, I did grant him permission to come back. But God Almighty did not like that he should break his promise and did cause him to die.'

That was how he joined the distinguished party of the blessed people. There are many more who are waiting to fulfil their promises. Hadhrat Khalifatul Masih II(ra) further said that there are indeed quite a few among our community who do make up similar promises. There are some among them who have fulfilled their promises, while there are others who are waiting to do the same.

Mauritius is the country where the Khalifa of the Ahmadiyya Muslim Community sends our Missionaries. That country also deserves to have the tomb of some Companion of the Promised Messiah(as) and of the one who had seen a Companion.

(14) **Hadhrat Chaudhri Karam Ilahi 'Kanoongo'** (1883-1968)

Chaudhri Karam Ilahi was born in Talwandi, Khajoorwala, District Gujranwala, Punjab in 1883. He took the covenant of Bai'at at the blessed hands of the Promised Messiah(as) in 1900. He was the first Ahmadi in Talwandi Khajoorwala and through his efforts many people joined the fold of Ahmadiyyat.

After taking Bai'at, Karam Sahib frequently visited Qadian and enjoyed the company of the Promised. Messiah(as). When the Promised Messiah(as) went to Sialkot in 1904 and stayed there for eight days, Karam Sahib was also present and when the Promised Messiah's(as) written lecture, *The Philosophy of the Teachings of Islam* was read out by Maulawi Abdul Karim of Sialkot. Karam Sahib also had the honour to accompany the Promised Messiah(as) during a visit to Lahore.

Chaudhri Karam Ilahi always kept himself busy. He frequented the small town of Talwandi Khajoorwala on a daily basis to preach the message of Ahmadiyyat with utmost vigour and earnestness. His efforts in this regard quickly bore fruit and many local families accepted Ahmadiyyat.

Karam Sahib served as Amir Jama'at of Talwandi for a short time and up to the time of his death. He had special love and regard for all the members of the family of the Promised Messiah(as).

Karam Sahib gained some elementary education in District GuJranwala and later became a 'Patwari' in the same district. He remained a Patwari for almost 15 years. The job of the Patwari was normally considered a corrupt job but Karam Sahib never succumbed to temptation. He had a large family but always lived within his means. God blessed his household and always provided for him.

Karam Sahib regularly attended the Annual Gathering at Qadian and was exceptionally regular in his daily prayers. He usually gathered all his children after Isha prayers and held a session consisting of important information about Ahmadiyyat and Islam. One of his sons, Maulana Fazal Ilahi Bashir is a missionary and life-devotee is presently living at Rabwah.

At the time of Hadhrat Chaudhri Karam's death, his progeny were counted as seventy-one. He passed away in 1968 and was buried at Bahishti Maqbarah Rabwah, Pakistan.

(45) **Mian Khair-ud-Deen of Qadirabad** (1889-1949)

Mian Khair-ud-Deen was born in 1889. His father, Mian Muhammad Bukhsh also joined the Ahmadiyya Jama'at in the very early stages.

The village where he lived was quite close to Qadian and was often frequented by the Promised Messiah(as) and his family members.

Mian Sahib was a carpenter by trade and during his training, the Promised Messiah(as) prayed for his success after receiving a request from Deen Sahib's family.

Mian Sahib was a witness to the Signs of the truth of Promised Messiah(as). He says: 'When the plague spread in India, a great many people fell ill. Among them was my father. My mother and I, both went to the Promised Messiah(as) and told him about the condition of my father. The Promised Messiah(as) prayed for him and then he opened the drawer of his table and gave her some medicine and told her to apply it over the inflammation. He also gave her a small amount of money and asked her to keep on repeating the following prayer: "My God Almighty, whatever is on the Earth does obey Thee: O my God, do keep me safe, and help me and show Thy Mercy to me."'

My mother said to the Promised Messiah(as): 'I will soon forget this prayer, so do please be kind enough to write it on a piece of paper.' He, therefore, wrote that prayer on a piece of paper. After we returned to my father, we took his bed outside our house and placed it under the shade of a tree close by. We also told our neighbours to do the same. All those who did listen to us were saved. But those who did not listen to what we said, all of them died because of the plague. We also advised all our neighbours and friends to remain in their houses and keep on reciting the above prayer. That is how our father was saved as we did exactly what the Promised Messiah(as) had advised us.

Mian Sahib had the good fortune of taking part in the construction of buildings in Qadian. But after the partition of India, he had to forsake his home and went to stay at Ahmadnagar near Rabwah where he worked as the Secretary Ziafat (Hospitality) for three years. He was also the President of the Ahmadiyya Community of Quadirabad

Mian Sahib was a man of very humble nature and did his best in serving the Ahmadiyya Community. He was very regular in performing his daily prayers and spent a lot of time reading the Holy Qur'an. He was particularly fond of reminiscing to others the time when he was living not very far from Qadian and often seeing the Promised Messiah(as).

The revered Mia Khair Deen Sahib passed away at Ahmad Nager, Distt. Jhang on 4th July 1949

(46) Hadhrat Mian Khair Deen of Sekhwan (1869-1949)

Hadhrat Mian Khair Deen was born in 1869. He was one of the earliest Companions of the Promised Messiah(as). He had great respect and regard for the Promised Messiah(as) and took his Oath of Initiation at his hands on 23 November 1889.

The Promised Messiah(as) included Khair Deen Sahib in the list of the 'three hundred and thirteen' from among his faithful followers and his list number is 198.

In 1899, the Promised Messiah(as) sent a deputation to Naseebain and its surroundings to find out the travels of Hadhrat Isa(as) in that country. That journey was done to make further enquiries regarding the journey of Prophet Jesus(as) to Kashmir. Concerning the financial contribution made by Mian Khair Deen Sahib and with regards to this, the Promised Messiah(as) wrote:'The financial contribution of these four men from amongst all our brethren is indeed exceptional. They all are certainly not well-off people but they could be likened to Hadhrat Abu Bakr(ra), God be pleased with them, they have brought with them what they did possess. They have accomplished to do what they had promised in their oaths of initiation'.

In 1900, the Promised Messiah(as) asked all his companions to contribute Rs.100 each for the construction of the Minaratul-Masih. Mian Khair Deen Sekhwani and his brother along with their mother requested that their names be considered as one of the contributors but four of them could only contribute Rs.100 in total. The Promised Messiah(as) accepted their request. When the Minaratul-Masih was completed during the time of Hadhrat Khalifatul Masih II(ra), the names of those three brothers and their mother were also inscribed on it.

The Promised Messiah(as) very rarely led the daily prayers in the mosque. However, Mian Khair Deen Sahib had the honour of being one of those who offered some prayers that were led by the Promised Messiah(as) himself. Deen Sahib was very regular in his prayers.

Mian Khair Deen Sahib had also participated in the 'Al-Wasiyyat' system as well as the Tahrik Jadid.

In 1947, Deen Sahib left Qadian to reside in Jehlum. Whilst in Jehlum, he was involved in a railway carriage accident and as a result passed away on 17th March 1949 at the age of eighty years. He was buried at the Bahishti Maqbara, Rabwah, Pakistan.

(Note: Mrs. Safya Hayat, the respected wife of our beloved Late Bashir a Hayat Sahib (the author of this book) is grand-daughter of Hadhrat Mian Khair Deen Sahib).

(47) **Dr. Khalifa Rashid-ud-Din of Lahore** (d.1926)

Khalifa Rashid-ud-Din Sahib belonged to a very respectable family of Lahore. He joined the Ahmadiyya Movement in 1892 when he was a student of the Medical College in Lahore. He was one of those devotees whose pleasure it was to offer all their monthly income to their spiritual Master, retaining only a paltry sum for their domestic needs.

In 1902, the Promised Messiah(as) wrote to Dr. Sahib asking for the hand of his eldest daughter, Mahmuda Begum in marriage with his son Sahibzada Mirza Mahmud Ahmad(ra). In spite of the opposition of some (non-Ahmadi) members of the family, Dr. Sahib willingly gave his consent to this alliance. In those days, Dr. Sahib was posted at Roorki in U.P. It was mutually agreed that the marriage should be solemnised at Roorki. Accordingly Hadhrat Sahibzada Mirza Mahmud Ahmad(ra) proceeded to Roorki accompanied by Hadhrat Maulana Nur-ud-Din(ra), Maulawi Muhammad Ahsen, Mir Nasir Nawab, Mufti Muhammad Sadiq and Dr. Noor Ahmad. On October 5th, the party returned to Qadian and congratulated the Promised Messiah(as) on the solemnisation of the marriage alliance. Hadhrat Mahmuda Begum Sahiba (the bride) had the honour of being the first daughter-in-law of the Promised Messiah(as).

Rashid-ud-Din Sahib was an exemplary person and noted for his pleasant disposition and philanthropy. He sacrificed his personal ease and comfort when his professional duties required immediate attention and care in emergency cases. His patients, whether rich or poor, received selfless services from him in treatment, care and attention.

Rashid-ud-Din Sahib exhibited in himself an inspiring example for his fellow-beings during his meeting in the Darbar of Nawab of Rampur (UP) where the Nawab was responsible for ruining the life of a poor Ahmadi family in his State. Dr. Rashid-ud-Din Sahib, being the Medical Advisor to the British Resident, accompanied the above-mentioned Ahmadi to the Darbar where he met the Nawab and with courage explained to him the atrocities caused to the Ahmadi family.

After his retirement, Rashid-ud-Din Sahib settled in Qadian and served the Jama'at in various capacities. He sacrificed a great deal to provide good education to his sons and daughters. His eldest son, Khalifa Alim-ud-Din was a pensioner of the British Indian Government. His second son, Col. Taqi-ud-Din is a pensioner of the Pakistan Government and his third son, Wing Commander Khalifa Muneer-ud-Din passed away as a martyr during the Indo-Pak War of 1965.

Dr. Khalifa Rashid-ud-Din passed away on July 1st,1926 and was buried in the Bahishti Maqbara, Qadian.

(48) Hadhrat Hakim Khalil Ahmad Mongheri (1874-1970)

Hadhrat Hakim Khalil Ahmad accepted Ahmadiyyat by post in 1905/1906 and remained in regular contact with Hadhrat Promised Messiah(as) through correspondence. Hadhrat Hakim Sahib always cherished the memory of receiving a gift from Hadhrat Promised Messiah(as) which was his new publication *Haqeeqatul Wahi (Reality of Revelation)*. The parcel arrived wrapped in cloth on which Hadhrat Promised Messiah(as) himself had written the name and address.

Hadhrat Hakim Khalil Ahmad was born in 1874 at Mongher, Bihar State, India. His father Mohammad Faiz, a religion scholar, physician and a Sufi poet died when Hadhrat Hakim Sahib was only three years old. After studying Urdu, Persian, Arabic literature and Islamic Jurisprudence, Hadhrat Hakim Sahib obtained a Physician's Degree from Medical College, Lucknow.

In 1903, Hadhrat Hakim Sahib set up a clinic in Mongher that became extremely popular. He was specially appointed as the physician for the Maharaja of Bihar and was held in great esteem. In recognition of his public service, he was awarded the title of 'Fakhru Attiba' (the Pride of Physicians) by the Bihar State Council of Aurvedic and Unani medicines. He treated patients without discrimination of wealth or status. He received a special award from the Bihar Government for his exceptional and selfless service during the First and the Second World Wars and played an important role to keep peace between Muslims and the Hindus during the partition of the India subcontinent and had set up a peace committee in the area.

Hadhrat Hakim Sahib was an active member of the Anjuman Himayate Islam of Mongher. He was also a member of the Muslim League committee and a member of the Municipal Council.

Hadhrat Hakim Sahib was introduced to Ahmadiyyat when he attended the annual gathering of Anjuman Himayate Islam. An opponent, Maulawi Abdul Wahhab spoke against the Promised Messiah(as) and was ridiculing his commentary on these verses of the Holy Qur'an from Chapter Al-Takveer: 'When the she-camels shall be discarded, when the seas are made to flow into one another, when the people are brought together.' But the interpretation of Hadhrat Promised Messiah(as) made sense to Hadhrat Hakim Sahib's logical mind and he decided to study the Promised Messiah's(as) books for himself. Soon a boy came to Hakim Sahib's and discussed the death of Hadhrat Jesus Christ(as). Hakim Sahib wrote:

'I considered the boy an angel of

guidance for me. I requested him to bring me some books of Mirza Sahib (i.e. Hadhrat Promised Messiah(as)). His father, Mahboob Ali was the only Ahmadi in Mongher, who sent me some books in Arabic, Persian and Urdu. First I read *Taryaqul Qulub (An Antidote for the Hearts).* The more I read, the deeper that influenced my heart'.

Hakim Sahib heard from his mother and elder sister, the Will of his late father which stated that 'the time of appearance of the Mahdi is near, you must accept him.' There was also much talk about sign of the solar and the lunar eclipse. Soon Hadhrat Hakim Sahib was convinced of the truth of Hadhrat Promised Messiah(as) and sent his letter of Bai'at to him. Hakim Sahib wrote:

'After Bai'at, Allah blessed me with true dreams and granted me spiritual blessings. Once I saw in a dream that the Holy Prophet Muhammad(saw) was sitting in his chamber and he offered me a glass of delicious drink. I drank it with deep pleasure and enjoyment from the blessed hand of the Holy Prophet(saw). Suddenly I saw that his face was the same as that of Hadhrat Mirza Ghulam Ahmad Qadiani(as)'.

In the next Annual Gathering of Anjuman Himayate Islam, Hadhrat Hakim Sahib spoke in support of the beliefs of Hadhrat Promised Messiah(as) which created an immense uproar. Hadhrat Hakim Sahib faced extreme opposition and there was a boycott of his clinic. The severer the oppression, the more firmly rooted was his faith. He was deeply devoted to the truth and he began to devote all his time to spread the message of Ahmadiyyat. Hakim Sahib wrote: 'I developed a sort of madness for preaching unconcerned of my physician's profession and I invested all hours in this field'.

It was as a result of his devotion and enthusiasm that prominent Ahmadi scholars from Qadian were sent to such remote areas as Bihar. In May 1911, a famous debate took place in Mongher between Ahmadi and non-Ahmadi Muslims. Around 150 non-Ahmadi scholars had come from all parts of India who insisted that the debate should be conducted in Arabic. However, when Hadhrat Maulawi Ghulam Rasul Rajeki spoke in eloquent and fluent Arabic, they were stunned and began to create disturbance to disrupt the gathering. However, by the Grace of Allah, some educated young men accepted Ahmadiyyat.

Once, the Hindu organisation known as Arya Samaj challenged the Muslims of Mongher for a debate. Despite the fact that Hakim Sahib was an Ahmadi, the Muslims approached him to represent them.

Hadhrat Hakim Sahib was able to express himself well both in Urdu and Persian. He once organised an All India Mushaira (poetry recital) in Mongher. Among the top poets of the day who attended the function were Josh Malih Abadi and Jigar Muradabadi Jigar enquired as to who was the central figure among the organisers of the event and was told that it was Hakim Sahib who was also the founder of the literary group – Bazm Nau Adab. Someone also mentioned to him that Hakim Sahib belonged to the Qadiani sect. At this Jigar Muradabadi exclaimed: 'A Qadiani and a poet?'.

When Hadhrat Hakim Sahib learnt of this remark, it moved him deeply and for the honour for Ahmadiyyat, he wrote a lengthy poem with the title 'Longing for a Glimpse.' As he recited the poem, it overwhelmed the gathering and was regarded the top poem of the meeting.

In this Urdu poem comprising 114 lines, Hakim Sahib has experienced all mystical concept of the existence of God and the unsuitable desire of a wayfarer to experience Him with all his senses.

Hadhrat Hakim Khalil Ahmad Sahib also endured many trials and tribulations. His clinic was boycotted and an attempt was made on his life while he preached the message of Ahmadiyyat in Madras. His first wife died without bearing a child and his house was demolished by an earthquake in 1934. But nothing could deter Hakim Sahib to continue his journey with deepest devotion.

In 1914, Hadhrat Khalifatul Masih II(ra) appointed Hakim Sahib(a full-time Missionary) and asked him to conduct a tour of Bengal. At a later date, Hakim Sahib also preached in U.P. Delhi, Bombay and the Punjab and played a leading role in stabilising the Jama'at in Madras. After his success in public debating, opponents of the Jama'at planned to murder him. Hakim Sahib was badly beaten but with the Grace of Allah, he survived the attack and went to Mongher for treatment and stayed there and continued to serve the Jama'at in Mongher as Amir.

Hakim Sahib also established a printing press and laid the foundation of an Ahmadiyya Mosque. He wrote quite a few books – *Burkey Asmani*, and *Israrey Nihani* are among them.

After the death of his first wife, Maimoona (a German lady who converted to Islam by Hakim Sahib), he married Sahibzadi Zubaida Begum, the daughter of Hadhrat Maulawi Zulfiqar Ali Khan. His first wife bore him no child but he had several children from his second wife. Some died in infancy but six sons and three daughters survived. His children are deeply devoted to Islam and Ahmadiyyat. His eldest son, Professor Shakil Ahmad Munir is serving the Jama'at in an honourary capacity as

Amir and Missionary In-charge Australia since 1985. One of his sons, Syed Rashid Ahmad died in 1991. His other sons are: Syed Jamil Ahmad, Syed Mohammad Jalil (alias Mubasher Ahmad), Monawwar Ahmad Noori who is serving in various capacities in the UK Jama'at. His daughters are: Nuzhat Hafeez, Saadat Hameedi, and Qudsia Begum.

In 1952, Hadhrat Khalifatul Masih II(ra) appointed Hakim Sahib as Nazir Talimo Tarbiyyat and Additional Nazir Dawat-e-Tabligh in Qadian. To take up these posts, Hadhrat Hakim Sahib left Mongher with his family and settled in Qadian. He was regular speaker at the Annual conventions and on occasions was also appointed Acting Amir in Qadian.

In view of the wish of his children who had since settled in Pakistan, Hadhrat Khalifatul Masih II(ra) gave permission to the ageing Hakim Sahib to move with them. He left Qadian on 19th January 1962 and settled with his children in Karachi, Pakistan where he continued to serve the Jama'at. Whilst in Karachi, Hakim Sahib had the honour of a personal visit to his home by Hadhrat Khalifatul Masih III(ru).

Hadhrat Hakim Khalil Ahmad passed away aged 96 years on 13th December 1970 (may Allah be pleased with him). He was buried in the special enclosure of Bahishti Maqbra Rabwah.

His own line of poem in engraved on his gravestone:

'The death for the Lovers is nothing but a change of abode. Grieve not the parting for I leave to live in the Hereafter.'

(49) **Hadhrat Mian Khuda Bakhsh of Bhera** (d.1877)

Hadhrat Mian Khuda Bakhsh of Bhera has reported: 'In the year 1889, I was twelve years old and I recall that my father Hadhrat Mian Allah Ditta Sahib, although not an Ahmadi, used to read the books of the Promised Messiah(as) with great interest. He often used to spend all day and sometimes all night long reading Hadhrat Sahib's(as) books. He spent six years reading Hudhur's books and finally took the oath of allegiance at the blessed hand of the Promised Messiah(as).'

As I was his eldest son, he took me with him as he left Bhera for Qadian. We reached Batala a little before the time for the late night (Isha) prayer. As was the custom in those days, we went to a local mosque to spend the night. After having said evening prayers, the members of the congregation inquired where we had come from and where we were heading. My father told them that we had come from Bhera and were on our way to Qadian. On hearing the word "Qadian" they immediately became agitated, abusive, very angry and violent. They started abusing us and physically threw us out of the mosque. We were very shocked and came into the local bazaar and in this state remained sitting there for almost two hours. After a while we went back to the mosque and this time finding it deserted, as everyone had left for the night, we lay down in the courtyard of the mosque, where we spent the night, and quickly left the mosque in the morning before anyone returned. When we were approximately one mile out of Batala, my father said to me that we should ask someone the way to Qadian.'

As we were new to this place, we were also very conscious of the event in the mosque the night before. Eventually we met a Sikh gentleman, and my father asked him the way to Qadian. This Sikh gentleman told us the way to Qadian with great politeness and affection. In those days the road to Qadian was a difficult one to travel on. We did not have any real means of transport and walking on foot was also not that easy.

We finally reached Qadian where the majority of the people were Sikhs. We made our way to the Masjid-e-Aqsa. At about midday we left the mosque to go to Hadhrat Promised Messiah's(as) house. There was a small mosque adjacent to Hudhur's house and below the mosque, there used to be a small room called the 'Round Room' where Hudhur's guests used to come to meet him. We also went and sat down there. After a while, the Azan was said and we went to the mosque in order to say our prayers. In the mosque, we found Hadhrat Maulawi Nur-ud-Din Sahib(ra). Since he was also from Bhera, we told him of our intention.

Hudhur's(as) house and the mosque were adjacent and shared a wall in which there was a small window, through which Hudhur(as) used to enter the mosque. As soon as we saw Hudhur's(as) glowing face, our hearts were filled with happiness. With the permission of Hudhur(as), the prayers were led by Hadhrat Maulawi Abdul Karim Sahib. Hudhur(as) had already been informed of our arrival before the prayers and so after the prayers were over, Hudhur(as) remained seated in the mosque. Hadhrat Maulawi Nur-ud-Din(ra) told Hudhur(as) that these two gentlemen are from his hometown of Bhera and that they wish to take the Bai'at at Hudhur's(as) hand. After that, Hudhur(as) kept talking to us for quite a while. Regarding the Bai'at, Hudhur(as) said that we should stay in Qadian for a few days. That stay in Qadian proved to be the most precious blessing for us. During this time, we got the opportunity to meet Hudhur(as) almost every day. We said our prayers in his company and used to have long conversations with him. At that time the Langar Khana, the communal kitchen of the Jama'at did not exist, and the food for the visitors used to come from the household of Hadhrat Masih Mau'od(as). It would be appropriate here to mention an incident, which took place during our stay there. Hadhrat Masih Mau'od(as) used to have a very loyal and simple-minded servant called Peera. It used to be his duty to bring the meals for the guests from Hadhrat Sahib's(as) household and Hudhur(as) used to eat his meals along with the guests. One day we were having our meal with Hudhur(as), when Peera brought some milk for Hadhrat Hakeem Fazal din Sahib of Bhera. Hadhrat Hakeem Sahib took one sip and whispered to Peera saying "Mian Peera, there should be some sugar in the milk." Hudhur heard this and immediately got up, went home and brought some Batashas (which are sweet drops made from sugar and could probably be described as the alternative to sugar cubes) wrapped in a napkin and said to Hakeem Sahib "here you are Hakeem Sahib add some sugar to your milk." we were all surprised as to how Hadhrat Sahib was able to hear this whisper.

Another day, when Hudhur's(as) mail was brought to him, it included a letter, which had several abusive remarks written on the front of the envelope. When Hudhur(as) showed this to one of those present, the person suggested that Hudhur(as) should sue the man for libel, specially as there was proof in the form of this letter. Hadhrat Masih Mau'od(as) replied: "We have not been commissioned by God to drag people through the courts, our job is to call people to spread the cause of Islam. However please see to it that this letter is sent back to the person who wrote it." Thus we stayed in Qadian for a week or ten days and then asked Hudhur's[(as)] permission to leave, upon which he took the Bai'at from us and we returned back home.

Some time later I again accompanied my father on a visit to Qadian and this time we stayed with Hadhrat Hakeem Qutubuddin Sahib. At that time I was approximately twenty-three years of age in about the year 1900. Hudhur[(as)] in those days was busy writing one of his books and the Zuhr and Asr prayer services were being performed together. This time too we had the opportunity of saying our prayers in the company of Hadhrat Sahib[(as)]. Every day Hudhur[(as)] used to go for a walk which used to be a mile or two long and we used to accompany him on these walks."

Here I would like to recall an incident, which took place during our stay. We were staying with Hakeem Qutubuddin Sahib. One day Hakeem Sahib came home and announced that Hudhur[(as)] was unwell and that his doctors had suggested the use of goat milk as a remedy. Some people suggested that a goat should be kept and one of us should be given the responsibility of taking the goat out for grazing and generally looking after it. This suggestion was implemented. A goat was bought and given to a person who used to take it to graze, milk it and deliver the milk to Hadhrat Sahib[(as)]. On request from this person, he was paid some compensation for this assignment. "

(This article has been submitted by Mrs. Hafiz Mohammad Akram Sahib Hafeez)

(50) **Hadhrat Maulana Mahboob Alam**

(Pioneer Missionary in the Kashmir Valley)

Hadhrat Maulana Mahboob Alam came from the Chak Pirana village in Gujrat District of Punjab from where he migrated to Kashmir. He was blessed with true dreams and visions and Allah frequently accepted his prayers. Knowledge and virtue, devotion and piety, attention to worship and religious exercises and his relationship with Allah were the salient features of his personality. People called him a saint and stood up for him out of reverence.

Maulana Mahboob Alam was a descendant of one of India's well-known religious guides and Sufis, Hadhrat Hafiz Sadruddin, who had propagated Islam in the sub-continent. Hafiz Sahib originally belonged to Delhi from where he travelled to Punjab to preach the Word of God and settled in Miana Chak Dhaw village in Gujrat District. The residents of about forty villages became his followers and he set up a Gaddi – (a religious center for his dispensation) and acquired a big estate. The people sought his guidance and arbitration in their disputes. The members of this family were known with the titles of Maulana, Mian, Qadhi, Ustad, and Chaudhry etc. in the whole region.

Maulana Alam Sahib was born to Mian Sharfuddin Sahib – a descendant of Hafiz Sadruddin in about 1850. Being himself a knowledgeable person, Mian Sharfuddin paid special attention to the education of his son. Following the advice of his father, Maulana Alam Sahib undertook several long and laborious journeys and faced many hardships including periods of starvation. His accomplishment and academic superiority was recognised by his contemporaries. Judges would seek his help in deciding several disputes. His decisions were based on truth and justice and the parties accepted them whole-heartedly. Once Justice Thakur Das had Maulana chair the court proceedings on his behalf in a serious dispute involving Muslims.

After completing his education in about 1875, Maulana Alam Sahib toured Kashmir. He was much grieved by the condition of the region and chose it for propagation of Islam. He spent most of the time teaching and preaching in Kashmir, visiting Gujrat for a month or so in a year to keep an eye on his property there.

Qadhi Fazal Din, who had migrated from Rajoori to Salwah in Poonchh district, met Maulana Alam Sahib and was much impressed by his righteousness and gave his daughter Sarah Bibi in his marriage. Sarah asked her father to arrange Qur'an tutorials for the rest of her life as the Haq Mehr during Nikah. The couple dedicated their lives to teaching of Qur'an and spreading its light in the area. Sarah was a pious, righteous and austere lady from her early life and her prayers were accepted by Allah. Everybody addressed her as 'Ammanji'. She loved the Promised Messiah(as) and his family and expressed her emotions in some verses, which were unfortunately lost during partition. She died in 1947.

In view of the prevailing conditions, Maulana Alam Sahib said that the times demanded a Divine Reformer. Through repeated dreams and visions, Allah made it clear to him that the Imam Mahdi had appeared and accordingly he turned his attention to the Promised Messiah(as). In search of truth, he undertook an arduous journey on foot through Kashmir to Jehlum where he met Maulawi Burhan-ud-Din and said that the latter had acted precipitously in taking the oath of allegiance. He suggested that both of them should have acted together after proper scrutiny in the light of signs mentioned in Hadith. Hadhrat Burhan-ud-Din replied that he had taken the Bai'at and 'you can scrutinise as you like'. Thereafter Maulana Mahboob Alam went to Lahore, where the Promised Messiah(as) was then stationed, intending to hold a debate with the latter. The Maulawis had created uproar and prevented people from seeing the Promised Messiah(as) saying that he was a sorcerer and would cast a spell. It occurred to him that one of the signs mentioned by the Holy Prophet(saw) was that the Imam Mahdi would be opposed and denied by the Maulawis. The clamour by the Maulawis clearly indicated their attitude and suggested the possible truth of the claimant. Some tried to stop him while others would let him go hoping that he would cast his spell to bring Mirza Sahib to the right path. He seated himself close to the Promised Messiah(as) and had the Hadith in his mind, which mentioned stammering and stroking of thigh when talking as two signs of the Mahdi. He witnessed these signs, believed in the truth of the Promised Messiah(as) and gave up the idea of a debate. He impatiently waited for the end of the Promised Messiah's(as) talk then he threw himself at his feet sobbing and with tears flowing down his eyes. When he regained his composure, he cried out:

> 'O, Allah's true Imam Mahdi, this humble servant of Muhammad(saw) has come down the mountainous terrain of Kashmir, at times crawling on the knees because of fatigue, and presents the salutations of 'Assalamo-Alaikum warahmatullahi wabarakatohu' from Muhammad(saw).'

After he accepted Ahmadiyyat, the Promised Messiah(as) advised him: 'You have many disciples and pupils in Kashmir. Go and deliver the message to them.' This started a new phase in the propagation of Ahmadiyyat in Kashmir. He dedicated himself to preaching, day and night. After making the pledge of giving preference to matters of faith over temporal matters, he gave up his annual visits to his hometown and would only visit Qadian for Jalsa Salana. On his return after the Bai'at, he took up preaching starting with his wife. She refused to listen to any arguments and only wanted to know if he had performed the Bai'at. When told 'yes', she replied, 'I do not need arguments. I am with you. Write a letter of my Bai'at. Allah has already informed me of the appearance and truth of Imam Mahdi through some dreams.' Later his nephew – Maulawi Abdul Haye Sahib, his brother – Mian Naik Alam Alias Maulawi Abdul Halim Sahib, his brothers-in-law – Qazi Abdullah and Qazi Ibrahim and many other relatives accepted Ahmadiyyat. Then he turned to others and by the Grace of Allah, many people from various groups and schools of thoughts joined Ahmadiyyat. The list included Maulawi Allah Ditta, Choudhry Gaddi, Choudhry Mangu, Maulawi Hassan Muhammad, Mian Gamma, Maulawi Imam Din, Qazi Firozuddin, Qazi Bahadur Ali, Qazi Nuruddin, Mian Firozuddin alias Mian Khoju, Mian Raju, Mian Karam Din Khokhar, Haji Amir Alam, Munshi Ilam Din, Master Alif Din, Maulawi Faqir Muhammad, Ms Rani and Ms Jatti. They accompanied Maulawi Mahboob Alam Sahib and had the honour of performing Bai'at at the hands of the Promised Messiah. Qazi Feroz-ud-Din suffered from asthma. He requested the Promised Messiah(as) for prayers at this occasion and was cured soon after.

He used to prepare a terrace in a village, under the trees near a spring, and started his work from there and worshipped there. Once a Jama'at was established there he would move on to the next village. Thus, he spread the message of Ahmadiyyat from village to village. He also trained and supervised the new converts.

A Golden Advice

Several chieftains of Kashmir offered him estates and properties but he did not accept any of such offers. Rejecting one offer he said: 'Do you want me to gain estates and thus make my descendants subservient to the ruling class. I gave up my properties in Gujrat. Thanks for your offer but I will never accept it. My descendants are devoted to preaching the word of Allah. They will serve the faith and will be provided from heavens.' Keeping that advice in view, both his sons, Maulana Ahmad Din and Maulana Abdul-Rehman devoted their lives to service of Islam.

Obedience to the Khalifa

In compliance with the instruction from the Promised Messiah(as), he was so absorbed in his preaching that he completely forgot his home. However, after the demise of the Promised Messiah(as) he thought of returning to his hometown to preach to his near and dear ones. For that he sought permission from Hadhrat Khalifatul-Masih I(ra) but the latter declined saying: 'You have organised the Tabligh and Ta'lim-o-Tarbiyyat in Kashmir. No one else can handle that so well. Therefore, you better stay there.' He submitted to the orders from the Khalifa and bade farewell to his home permanently. On his way to and from Qadian for Jalsa Salana, he would spend a few days in Gujrat and preach.

He was a high ranking and competent physician. Many hopeless patients were miraculously cured with his treatment, to the amazement of many doctors.

Hadhrat Maulawi Sahib was an eloquent Persian poet. He wrote several Urdu and Arabic poems but his Persian verses were particularly popular. Unfortunately, during the 1947 upheavals this work was lost along with his great book collection.

Maulana passes away

Allah had informed Hadhrat Maulana Mahboob Alam about his impending departure from this mortal world through various revelations, dreams and visions. Before departure for Jalsa Salana in 1923, he received the revelation: He will surely bring you back to the ordained place of return. He narrated this revelation to several friends and added that it was time to meet the Lord. On leaving for Jalsa, he left a note for his household saying: Farewell! We are unlikely to meet again. After attending the Jalsa, Maulawi Sahib went to his ancestral home in Chak Pirana, Gujrat and following a brief illness died there on 4th January 1924.

(The above article has been extracted from a long article written by Mr. Abdul Wahab Ahmad, Published in monthly 'Ansarullah', Rabwah, September/October 1998).

(51) Hadhrat Hafiz Syed Mahmood Ullah Shah (1900-1952)

Mahmood Ullah Shah Sahib was born in December 1900. He qualified as a Hafiz-e-Qur'an when he was eight years old. Once he stated that he had the honour of meeting Hadhrat Masih Mau'od(as) in 1907 and many a time he recited the Holy Qur'an before him. Hudhur(as) used to give him sweets and Beatle leaves (Paans).

Mahmood Ullah Sahib passed his Matriculation examination from Qadian in 1917 and later graduated from Islamia College, Lahore. On his return from England, he passed his B.T. Course, from Ali Garh University, and commenced teaching in high school of Qadian.

Hadhrat Musleh Mau'od(ra) sent him to England on 25th November 1922 for the study of Railway Engineering. On the eve of his departure, Hadhrat Musleh Mau'od(ra) gave him many valuable advices that guided him throughout his stay in England and he practiced the precious advices to the last letter.

After the death of his first wife, he re-married to the daughter of Hadhrat Maulawi Syed Muhammad Sarwar Shah Sahib. She died on 31st October 1923. He married once again to Farkhanda Akhtar Sahiba, daughter of Sheikh Niaz Muhammad (a companion of Promised Messiah(as)) She served as the Principal of Nusrat College, Rabwah.

Services in East Africa

In 1929, with the permission of Hadhrat Musleh Mau'od(ra), he left Qadian for Nairobi, Kenya, where he taught as a teacher in an Indian High School for 15 years. He was very much loved and respected by both Ahmadis and non-Ahmadis.

Mahmood Ulah Sahib organised the local Jama'at's affairs with the assistance of other members so well that the local Jama'at requested the centre (Qadian) to send a qualified Missionary on their expense. Until that time there was no Missionary there. This request was granted and Maulana Sheikh Mubarak Ahmad Sahib was sent as a Missionary in November 1934 and the first Ahmadiyya Mission was established in that country.

Hadhrat Shah Sahib(as) served the Jama'at by holding various responsible offices and by delivering Dars-e-Qur'an and speeches. He was a living example of an obedient servant of the Promised Messiah(as).

Construction for Tabora – Fazal Mosque

Hadhrat Musleh Mau'od(ra) expressed his wish to have as many Mosques as possible in East Africa. At the time it was not an easy task for the Jama'at. In 1942, the Jama'at found a piece of land in very convenient and pleasant surroundings and by the grace of Allah, the construction of the Mosque was completed in 1944 at a cost of 35,000 shillings. Syed Mahmood Ullah Shah, Syed Abdul Razzaq Shah, Mr Fazal Karim Lone, Mr Abdul Karim Butt, Mr Akram Khan Ghouri, and other Asian and African Ahmadies' helped the construction of the Mosque.

Once, the members of the Jama'at went to meet Mahmood Ullah Sahib and express condolence at the sad demise of his sister Hadhrat Umme-Tahir (the beloved mother of Hadhrat Khalifatul Masih IV(ru)). He informed them: 'Today in the morning I had been told in the vision that the tragic events have commenced for the destruction of this world. Then I started praying.'

After this vision Mahmood Ullah Sahib decided to travel to Qadian, as his health was deteriorating. He sent letters to Hadhrat Masih Mau'od(as) and Hadhrat Mirza Bashir-ud-Din Ahmad Sahib(ra) for prayers. Due to the event of the Second World War, the letters were intercepted by the Government and Shah Sahib was prosecuted under the Defence Acts. The lawyers advised him not to admit that the letters were sent by him as the onus was on the police to prove it but he refused to do so and told them that he will tell only the truth and nothing but the truth.

There appeared before the court, as Shah Sahib's witness, an Englishman named Mr. Edward Lincoln. This gentleman had served for 30 years in the Punjab Government as Deputy Commissioner, Acting Commissioner and other high posts. He had also served in the District Gurdaspur (Punjab) as a Deputy Commissioner. He was well associated with Dr. Mir Muhammad Ismail Sahib the brother of Shah Sahib, Major Dr. Habibullah Shah Sahib and Hadhrat Choudhury Muhammad Zafrulla Khan Sahib. He told the Court that these intercepted letters were not addressed to the ordinary relatives but to the Head of the Ahmadiyya Community. The members of Ahmadiyya Community have great faith in the prayers of their Khalifa; therefore, Mr. Shah wrote to the Khalifa to pray for him and the safety of the whole Community.

In the opinion of the British Government, the whole Community was extremely faithful and sincere to the Government. The Courts kept in view the services being rendered by Shah Sahib to the Government during this War. Hadhrat Shah Sahib was a man of superb character and was very popular among the Asian and European community. They backed his innocence but the court refused to withdraw the allegations.

Consequently, the Jama'at lodged an appeal to the His Excellency, the Governor of Kenya, whose attitude was very sympathetic and looked into the whole case very attentively. Shah Sahib continued praying for the victory of the British, even though he suffered a great deal of hardships by the stubborn attitude of the authorities. Only a pious and God-fearing person can possess such super quality. During this period, Shah Sahib became very ill and left for Qadian in 1944.

In Qadian, Hadhrat Musleh Mau'od(ra) appointed him the Headmaster. By the Grace of God, within a few months the educational and moral standard of students leapt to a very high level as Shah Sahib introduced a lot of reforms. After the partition of India, T.I High School was re-established in Chiniot District Jhang and Shah Sahib re-built the Old Standard and the school flourished once again to the top of fame so much so that non- Ahmadi parents transferred their children from other schools to the T.I High School.

In 1952, when the school was re-established in Rabwah, the Matriculation results of the Punjab University were achieved by the students so brilliantly that 1st, 3rd, 6th, 7th positions were declared in favour of T.I. High School, Rabwah. The Divisional Inspector of schools visited the school and observed the high standards of education and morals of students. He was so impressed that he remarked: 'This is an exemplary school and a unique school, where the students receive a proper Islamic education and he also praised the noble teachers'.

Mahmood Ullah Sahib Sahib created a special relationship between the teacher and students, a bond of trust and respect. Never in the whole history of T.I. High School, were so many successes achieved as during the time of Hadhrat Shah Sahib. He was a great organiser and administrator and a man of vision and charismatic charm.

Hadhrat Shah Sahib passed away on 16th December 1952 due to heart failure. He was buried in Bahishti Maqbarah, Rabwah, Pakistan.

(52) **Master Faqir Ullah**
(1876-1965)

Master Faqir Ullah Sahib was born on 7th June 1876. At school he was known as a good footballer. He was equally good in academic subjects and a master in mathematics. In 1896, he borrowed one of the books of the Promised Messiah(as) entitled *Izala-i-Auham* from Maulawi Ghulam Hassan Khan of Peshawar, which he read with great interest.

The following year (1897) he proceeded to Qadian where he remained for the rest of his life. He was posted as a teacher of mathematics in Talim-ul-Islam High School. He was also Superintendent of the Boarding House attached to the School. He was appointed as the Manager of the English magazine, *The Review of Religions* and served as Assistant Accountant of Sadr Anjuman Ahmadiyya. Faqir Sahib had the great fortune to be the tutor of Hadhrat Khalifatul Masih II(ra) in his school days.

In 1914, when there occurred a split in the Ahmadiyya Community, Faqir Ullah went over to the secessionists at Lahore. But in 1944 when Hadhrat Khalifatul Masih II(ra) declared on oath that he was actually the Promised Reformer as mentioned in the Sabz Ishtiher of the Promised Messiah(as), Faqir Sahib retraced his steps and pledged himself at the hand of the Promised Reformer. After the partition of the country, he came to Rabwah and served the Community.

Faqir Ullah Sahib passed away on 9th August 1965 and was buried in the Bahishti Maqbara, Rabwah.

(53) **Hadhrat Maulawi Burhanuddin** (1830-1905)

Hadhrat Maulawi Burhanuddin Sahib was born in 1830. At the age 25 years, he went to Delhi for religious studies.

In 1865, he returned to his hometown and became an ardent proponent of the Ahle Hadith school of thought. From the year 1867 to 1886, he remained in search of a true scholar and reformer of the time. He first became a disciple of a pious man in Bowli Shareef and then spent several years under the influence of Hadhrat Maulawi Abdullah Sahib Ghaznavi. After this, he became a disciple of Hadhrat Peer Kotha Shareef, but he finally found the truth in the person of the Promised Messiah(as). In 1886, he presented himself to Hadhrat Masih Mau'od(as) in Hushiarpur and asked Hadhrat Sahib(as) to accept his Bai'at. Hudhur(as) at the time replied that he had not yet been permitted to accept the Bai'at. However, in 1892, he took the Bai'at at the hands of the Promised Messiah(as).

After his Bai'at, Maulawi Sahib used to come to Qadian every year. Hadhrat Sahib(as) used to say: 'Maulawi Sahib's arrival is a source of great relief to me'.

In 1904, when Maulawi Sahib was in Sialkot with the Promised Messiah(as), a lady had thrown ashes onto Hadhrat Sahib(as) while he was passing below her house. Hadhrat Sahib(as) passed safely, but the ashes fell on Hadhrat Maulawi Burhanuddin Sahib's head as he was following behind Hadhrat Sahib(as). He was so entranced in the love of the Promised Messiah(as) that he shouted out to the Punjabi woman in Punjabi 'Pa Maeya, hore Pa' i.e. (please throw some more, old woman some more!)

Whenever Maulawi Sahib(as) visited Qadian, Hadhrat Sahib(as) used to ask him to move permanently to Qadian, but he used to reply that he was not worthy of any service and was afraid that he may become a liability on Hudhur(as). On his way back from Qadian, Maulawi Sahib invariably returned to Jehlum via Amritsar and Lahore and used to preach to his friends and meet members of these Jama'at's.

Maulawi Sahib was well versed in various religious branches of knowledge including Hadith, Jurisprudence and Tafseer of the Holy Qur'an. He knew traditional medicine and was fluent in Urdu, Persian, Arabic and Pushto. He could write very well in these languages and was also a good debater and used to preach to his students. Three of his students who accepted Ahmadiyyat were Maulawi Mubarak Ali Sahib of Sialkot, Maulawi Abdul Rehman Sahib of Khewal and Maulawi Muhammad Qari Sahib of Jehlum.

Maulawi Sahib led a very simple life and always trusted in God to fulfill his needs. He passed away on 3 December 1905 after a short illness.

(54) **Hadhrat Maulawi Fazal Deen**

Hadhrat Maulawi Fazal Deen came from Gujranwala. His early education was at Hafizabad and he had great interest in learning geography. His parents, however, had the desire that he should learn the Holy Qur'an and as a result, he joined the company of Hadhrat Maulawi Ghulam Rasool Sahib Rajeki and proved to be a great lover of the Holy Qur'an. He often used to pray to God saying 'O God I am not an educated person but help me to understand your Kalam' (i.e. Qur'an). Maulawi Fazal Sahib was not educated from school or passed any Arab examination. He gained great know-ledge by being in the company of Hadhrat Maulawi Ghulam Rasool Rajeki. Maulawi Fazal Sahib eventually became a Missionary and remained very close to the Head of the Community.

On the day when the organisation of Ansarullah was established, Hudhur invited all the Ansar. Khan Ferzand Ali introduced himself first and then others followed. In his heart Maulawi Fazal Deen said: 'I shall not introduce myself because neither I am a scholar nor a rich person and I do not have any position of responsibility.' When Maulawi Sahib's turn came Hudhur himself stood up and said: 'This man who is sitting is not an ordinary man. He loves the Qur'an and for this purpose he is staying with Rajeki Sahib. He is the only one among the large Jama'at of Manget Oonchay who can read and had such an enthusiasm of preaching that every week I receive a large list of new converts from him.'

In 1912, Ferzand Ali Khan Sahib wrote to Maulawi Sahib: 'O brother, I hope you will give true answer to my question without omitting any details. The question is this: 'You come to Qadian every Sunday and meet Hudhur. I truthfully ask you what things have you done that you have taken such a place in Hudhur's heart.' Maulawi Sahib replied: 'I swear to God that I even do not know that Hudhur likes me so much and remembers me so much. The only thing I can say is that I am very much fond of preaching and I keep doing it. Secondly, I love the Qur'an and I keep reading it. There is nothing else in me that I can put as a reply to your question.'

Maulawi Ghulam Rasool Rajeki Sahib was a great lover of the Qur'an and so was his student Maulawi Fazal Deen. There is an interesting story about them. Maulawi Rajeki Sahib often used to say to Maulawi Fazal Deen: 'You can come to me for reading at any time without hesitation. Even if I am very ill and weak and you ask me a question about the Qur'an at that time. I hope that I will explain to you the meaning of the verse provided my tongue could speak.' It so happened that once Maulawi Rajeki Sahib who used to deliver Dars (commentary) of the Holy Qur'an was suffering from fever. At that time Maulawi Fazal Deen was staying with him and remembered what he used to say, so he started reciting the Holy Qur'an and his teacher (i.e. Rajeki Sahib) uncovered his face. Maulawi Fazal Deen asked the meaning of the verse. Rajeki Sahib started explaining the verse and gradually his enthusiasm grew stronger and stronger. Then he got up and said Qur'an is really a healer for the people. My fever has gone during the time I was explaining to you the meaning of the verse.

Hadhrat Khalifatul Masih II(ra) appointed him as a teacher at a school in Manget Oonchay. During his stay there, Maulawi Fazal Sahib established six schools. He also served in the Finance Department for some time but could not stay there very long. In 1928, he started teaching again in Sheikhopura. During this time another interesting incidence happened. One day a senior judge by the name of Saeedud Deen sent his servant with a message asking Maulawi Sahib to see him as he wanted to talk to him. Although this judge was a Shia, he asked Maulawi Sahib to teach his children and prepare them for 'Maulawi Fazil' examination. Maulawi Sahib said: 'Delivering a Dars is quite different from getting the pupils ready for the examination. I am not suitable person for that purpose. Moreover, there are so many other people with 'Maulawi Fazil' degrees who are prepared to teach your children". But the judge insisted that he should teach his children. So Maulawi Sahib started teaching. There were two children of the judge and two from his sister-in-law. Maulawi Sahib used to work hard as well as pray for them. When the time came for sending admission forms for the examination the judge asked whether it was all right to send the admission forms for all the children. Maulawi Sahib said I could see only one who can pass. On hearing this, the judge became very happy and said: 'I will do whatever you will say.' So only one of the children's admission form was sent and he passed his examination.

(55) **Hadhrat Maulawi Fazal Deen (2)**
(1883-1968)

Hadhrat Maulawi Fazal Deen Sahib took the Oath of Initiation at the hands of the Promised Messiah(as) in the year 1901. He came to reside at Qadian some time in the year 1916-1917.

God Almighty graciously granted him the honour of serving the Jama'at for quite a long time. In the beginning, Maulawi Fazal Deen Sahib, had been teaching Arabic to boys of the Ahmadiyya School in Qadian. Hadhrat Mian Bashir Ahmad Sahib appointed a number of persons as the Examiners of the Ahmadiyya School, Qadian and Maulawi Fazal Deen Sahib was one of them. In 1919, Maulawi Fazal Deen was appointed as the Officer-in-charge of buildings and he also supervised the construction work on Bahishti Maqbara.

Maulawi Fazal Deen Sahib also looked after the Central Library of Qadian which contained thousands of books that had been collected by Hadhrat Khalifa-tul-Masih I(ra). The revered Sheikh Muhammad Ahmad Mazhar, the Amir of Ahmadiyya Communities in the district of Faisalabad also worked in the same capacity. Sayyed Mukhtar Ahmad has reported that Maulawi Fazal Deen as well as Muhammad Ahmad both worked very hard in this particular duty.

In the Kapurthala case, Hadhrat Mufti Muhammad Sadiq Sahib, Maulawi Fazal Deen Sahib and Chaudhry Zafrulla Khan Sahib worked together very devotedly and were greatly appreciated by the Jama'at.

Hadhrat Maulawi Fazal Deen Sahib was indeed from among the most leading scholars of the Ahmadiyya Community. He knew very well the objections, criticisms raised against Ahmadiyyat and was able to respond to these. Whenever some Ahmadi writer wrote a new book, it was thoroughly checked and revised before it went to the press for printing. Quite often, Maulawi Fazal Deen Sahib was given the task of going through the book.

Maulawi Fazal Deen Sahib had also written a number of books about the claims of Bahaullah and on many other religious topics.

In May 1927, over two hundred Muslims had been murdered most mercilessly. Hadhrat Khalifa-tul-Masih II(ra), therefore, organised a deputation, which included Khan Zulfiqar Ali Khan, the elder brother of the famous Ali Brothers, Muhammad Sadiq and Shaukat Ali. The deputation also included Mufti Muhammad Sadiq, Secretary General Affairs of the Ahmadis together with Maulawi Fazal Deen and Bhai Abdur Rahman Qadiani.

Hadhrat Maulawi Fazal Deen Sahib passed away in 1968 at he age of 85 years. He was buried in the Bahishti Maqbara Rabwah.

(56) **Hadhrat Maulawi Sher Ali, B.A.** (1875-1947)

Hadhrat Maulawi Sher Ali was born at Adrahma, a small village in Sargodha District on 24th November 1875. He belonged to the Ranjha clan of the Juts of Sargodha District. His father, Maulawi Niizam-ud-Din, besides being a landlord, was well known for his piety. His mother Gauhar Bibi memorised the Holy Qur'an by heart.

Maulawi Nizam-ud-Din sent his two sons, Abdul Ali and Sher Ali to be educated at Government High School in Bhere. Maulawi Sher Ali Sahib passed his Entrance Examination with credit from the school in 1895. Abdul Ali was sent to Aligarh for higher education and Maulawi Sher Ali Sahib joined the Christian College Lahore where he graduated in 1899. Maulawi Sher Ali Sahib's proficiency in English earned him the admiration of his professors.

Even as he was preparing for his Entrance Examination, Maulawi Sher Ali Sahib was well versed with Ahmadiyyat in the company of his uncles, Maulawi Sher Muhammad and Maulawi Fazal Din and also of Hadhrat Maulana Maulawi Nur-ud-Din of Bhera(ra). During his college life, he came to Qadian in 1897 and was initiated into the Ahmadiyya Movement at the blessed hands of the Promised Messiah(as). While a student, Maulawi Sher Ali Sahib did not enjoy good health. It was feared he might develop tuberculosis but being placed under the careful treatment the excellent physician, Hadhrat Maulawi Nur-ud-Din(ra), he was blessed with the prayers of the Promised Messiah(as), who advised him to drink milk in ample quantity. Soon he began to gain weight and strength.

Maulawi Sher Ali Sahib took charge of the Talimul Islam School in 1899 and again in 1905 when it had been raised to the standard of High School. In 1910, he was appointed Managing Editor of *The Review of Religions*, which edited for a number of years. During the 1930s, he acted as Manager for the Talimul Islam High School in Qadian. He was also entrusted with the onerous duty of translating the Holy Qur'an into English, a duty that he performed extremely diligently to the end of his life. With regards to this task, he undertook a journey to England so that he could have his translation of the Holy Qur'an read by eminent English scholars. He was assisted in his work by Hadhrat Mirza Basher Ahmad M.A. Maulawi Abdur Rahim Dard M.A. and Malik Ghulam Farid M.A. who were his close associates

Hadhrat Maulawi Sahib was a devout and devoted companion of the Promised Messiah(as). He led a very simple and humble life. He would invariably perform his five daily prayers in the mosque and seldom missed his Tahajjud prayer. He had a soft corner in his heart for all his pupils, relatives and friends. In 1924, Hadhrat Khalifatul-Masih II(ra) appointed him Amir of the Ahmadiyya Community of India when he proceeded to England to participate in the Wembley Conference. His Friday sermons were of special interest to the congregation. In the beginning, he lacked fluency but soon overcame this and delivered sermons very clearly.

Maulawi Sher Ali Sahib was like an angle walking on earth. The Promised Messiah(as) said that in one of his visions he saw an angel whose name was 'Sher Ali.'

Maulawi Sher Ali Sahib died at Lahore on 13th November 1947, soon after the sad demise of Sufi Ghulam Muhammad B.A. the Ahmadiyya Missionary to Mauritius. Their bodies were brought together to Rabwah and were buried in the Companions' enclosure of Bahishti Maqbara, Rabwah.

(57) **Mian Chiragh Din of Lahore** (1847-1920)

This family claims descent from the Chughtai Mughals of Turkistan and is one of the old families of Lahore. Mian Qadir Bakhsh, the head of the family, in the days of Maharaja Ranjit Singhs was a man of good influence and respectability. His eldest son, Ilahi Bakhsh, held the portfolio of Wazir under Maharaja Ranjit Singh and was in charge of the construction department. His younger brother, Muhammad Sultan, was a contractor in the early years of British rule in the Punjab. The present railway station of Lahore and the District Court Buildings were constructed under his direct supervision. The family was thus fairly prosperous and influential in the city. Hassan Din was a commander of Maharaja Sher Singh's bodyguard.

Mian Chiragh Din, son of Mian Hassan Din, was born in 1847. He was the first member of the family to be sent to an English school in Lahore. Unfortunately, Chiragh Din Sahib was still in his teens when his father died in Sialkot. All the senior members of the family passed away in the year 1886 and the responsibility of looking after the affairs of the family fell upon the young shoulders of Chiragh Din Sahib. Mian Chiragh Din secured a job in the Chief Engineer's Office (canals) and faithfully served the department for forty-one years with diligence and honesty.

Young and old alike, all had great respect for Chiragh Din Sahib because of his polite manners and character. He developed his friendship with the Promised Messiah(as) in the early years of his life. Chiragh Din Sahib paid a visit to Qadian when the *Barahin-e-Ahmadiyya* was being compiled. He was also invited to the Aqiqa dinner party of Bashir, the first son of the Promised Messiah(as).

Mian Chiragh Din pledged his allegiance to Ahmadiyyat at the hands of Muhammad Saddiq Sahib. When the Promised Messiah(as) issued a general proclamation inviting people to pledge at his hand, Mian Chiragh Din hesitated, not because he had any doubt about the good faith of the claimant, but because he had already pledged at the hands of another person. However, he asked the Promised Messiah(as) if he stood in need of offering his allegiance to him and he replied that when the Messiah had appeared, all previous Bai'ats (pledges) were nullified and that each and every person should pledge at his hand, so Mian Sahib at once offered his allegiance to the Promised Messiah(as).

Chiragh Din Sahib's cousin, Mian Miraj Din, was the first member of the family to offer his allegiance to the Promised Messiah(as). His sons, Mian Abdul Aziz (Mughal) and Hakim Muhammad Hussain (Marham-e-Isa) followed suit and it is to the credit of this Mian family, that all members young and old, women and children joined the fold of Ahmadiyyat and are all well-known for their sincerity and attachment to the Jama'at.

Mian Chiragh Din's house in Lahore was a haven of rest for all Ahmadies who visited Lahore long before the Ahmadiyya Mosque outside the Delhi Gate was constructed. Even the Promised Messiah(as) would prefer staying at his house. At the request of the Promised Messiah(as), Chiragh Din Sahib served the Ahmadiyya Movement in the capacity as an accountant, Sadr Anjuman Ahmadiyya. Hadhrat Khalifatul Masih II(ra) also appointed him a trustee of the Sadr Anjuman.

Only a week after his wife's demise, Mian Chiragh Din Sahib became gravely ill. He was still on his deathbed but was pleased to hear the good news that Dr. Saddiq had been granted permission to enter America as a Muslim Missionary.

Mian Chiragh Din Sahib passed away on 17th May 1920. His body was taken to Qadian for burial at Bahishti Maqbara.

(58) **Hadhrat Mian Muhammad Din of Kharian** (1864-1951)

Hadhrat Mian Muhammad Din was born at Gheeka in 1864. At the age of seven years, he came to Kharian with his father. His father, Mian Nurudin, was advised by an Hindu treasurer that Muhammad Din Sahib should be educated properly as he was very intelligent. Muhammad Din Sahib finished his primary school education at Kharian and undertook his middle school examination from Dinga. He passed the Patwari competition examination with excellent marks. He was appointed as a permanent Patwari at Balani in 1889 where he had a very successful career.

Muhammad Din Sahib had access to some of the books of the Promised Messiah(as) through the sons of Hadhrat Munshi Jalaluddin Sahib. He was very impressed with *Barahin-e-Ahmadiyyah*. In his autobiography, Muhammad Din Sahib said the following about the book: 'It is full of treasure and wisdom of the spiritual life. After reading this book, the excellence and love for the Holy Qur'an penetrated deep into my heart.' He noted a remarkable change in himself after reading *Barahin-e-Ahmadiyya, Aeena Kamalat-e-Islam, Fateh Islam,* and some other books written by the Promised Messiah(as).

In October 1894, Muhammad Din Sahib accepted Ahmadiyyat by signing a written Bai'at and on 5th June 1895, he personally pledged allegiance at the hands of the Promised Messiah(as). Muhammad Din Sahib also joined the system of Wasiyyat. He became Wasil Baqi Nawees at Kharian in 1910

In 1905, Muhammad Din Sahib requested permission to visit Qadian with his family. He received the following reply from Hadhrat Maulawi Karim Sahib: 'This time the Promised Messiah(as) is staying with a few of us in the orchard and there is no provision of accommodation for the ladies. It is possible to get one in the village. If you come alone, you can stay in the orchard and enjoy sittings with Hadhrat Promised Messiah(as)'

Muhammad Din Sahib received many letters addressed to him by Hadhrat Promised Messiah(as). He once mentioned to the Promised Messiah(as) of his lack of knowledge and of being a lone Ahmadi and asked what will be his fate. The Promised Messiah(as) replied: 'The reader of my books will never be defeated.'

As a follow-up to this commandment, Muhammad Din Sahib established a personal library with books of the Promised Messiah(as) and read them all. He had a good command in Arabic and Persian languages. He repeatedly read *Barahin-e-Ahmadiyya* and used to recite Arabic verses of poems. Hadhrat Hafiz Roshan Ali and other religious scholars were fond of his library.

Muhammad Din Sahib once asked

the Promised Messiah(as) about learning the Holy Qur'an. The Promised Messiah(as) replied in Arabic: (Translation): 'Be sincere to Allah with piety, Allah will teach you.' Hence, Muhammad Din Sahib learned Qur'anic knowledge through piety and blessed company of the Promised Messiah(as).

Muhammad Din Sahib was also fond of reading Darsul Qur'an notes prepared by Hadhrat Khalifatul Masih I(ra), and commentary of the Hadhrat Musleh Mau'od(ra).

Hadhrat Musleh Mau'od(ra) said of him: 'Mian Muhammad Din is among the complete devout and dedicated people who are deeply connected with me. He has a son [Sufi Ghulam Muhammad] doing his B.A. degree whom he has dedicated to the service of the religion.'

Muhammad Din Sahib had dedicated his life and migrated to Qadian. He used to collect contributions and Kashmir fund from Jama'ats in District Gujrat. He had a permanent membership of Majlis-e-Shura from 1922 to 1946. He used to prepare budget for Anjuman-e-Ahmadiyya jointly with Mirza Muhammad Ashraf Sahib, the auditor.

The Jama'at at Balani was established through Muhammad Din Sahib and Hadhrat Musleh Mau'od(ra) commissioned him to survey lands of Sind before purchase.

Muhammad Din Sahib used to spend most of his holidays in Qadian and enjoyed blessings from the company of the Promised Messiah(as). He used to take notes of his blessed sayings and lectures. In 1947, he moved to Lahore from Qadian upon the instructions of Hadhrat Musleh Mau'od(ra).

On 15th November 1947, Hadhrat Musleh Mau'od(ra) sent a delegation comprising of Mian Muhammad Din, Bhai Abdul Raheem and Bhai Abdul Rehman (all Companions of the Promised Messiah(as)) to stay in Qadian. He was blessed to have stayed for four years until his death on 2nd November 1951. He was buried in Bahishti Maqbara, Qadian.

His children are Sufi Ghulam Muhammad, Nazir Baitul Maal, Chaudhry Ghulam Murtaza, Wakeel Kanoon and Dr, Ghulam Mustafa.

(59) **Mir Mahdi Hussain Mauj** (1885-1941)

Mir Mahdi Hussain was born in a Shia family in1885 at Sayed Kheri, a village in Patiala State. At the age of only seven years, he completed his first reading of the Holy Qur'an.

At the age of 14, Mahdi Hussain Sahib learnt the art of calligraphy at Ludhiana, which stood him in good stead in practical life. Having been brought up in a Shia family of Sayeds, he developed a natural inclination for Shiaism, but as he advanced in years, he became open-minded and equally benefited from the society of Sunni scholars. But neither Sunni nor Shia satisfied him; he was in search of the Mahdi who could guide him to the right path. By chance, he was able to read some of the books written by the Promised Messiah(as) such as *Surma Chashm Arya* and the Subz Istihar.

Mahdi Hussain Sahib resorted to *Istikhara* prayer for guidance. One night in a vision he was shown a tablet bearing the words 'Victory to Hadhrat Mirza Sahib' which convinced him of the truth of Hadhrat Mirza Sahib's(as) claim to the office of Promised Messiah in 1893. He resigned his post in the postal Department and left for Qadian to place himself in the company of the Promised Messiah(as). By now he had no means of support but was offered a job in the office of the *Al-Badr* publication but this did not allow him to fully enjoy the company of his spiritual master so he gave it up. In those days, there was no ice factory at Qadian or Batala. Ice had to be fetched from Amritsar which was 33 miles from Qadian. Mahdi Hussain Sahib undertook the job with pleasure as it put him in direct touch with the Promised Messiah(as). Soon after, he was entrusted with the several other tasks.

Mahdi Hussain Sahib witnessed many signs and fulfilment of various prophecies of the Promised Messiah(as). For example, the death of Dr. Abdullah Authem of Amritsar, the murder of Pandit Lekh Ram at Lahore on 6th March 1897, the earthquake of Kangra in 1905 and of Quetta in 1934. He was one of those who resigned themselves to the Will of Allah and for whom Allah cares for their personal needs.

After the death of his first wife in Qadian, Mahdi Hussain Sahib married a sister of Hadhrat Hafiz Mukhtar Ahmad of Shahjahanpur. She bore him two sons and a daughter.

Mahdi Hussain Sahib passed away on 31st August 1941. According to his son, Syed Mohammad Baqar, his pious father used to offer his Isha prayers in a lone spot close to the Bahishti Maqbara continously for ten years. At the time of his death the spot where he used to say Isha prayer had become the part of the Bahishti Maqbra and by strange coincidence he was buried at the same spot.

(60) Hadhrat Mir Muhammad Ishaq
(b.1890)

Hadhrat Mir Muhammad Ishaq was born in 1890. His father, Hadhrat Mir Nasir Nawab Sahib, was the father-in-law of the Promised Messiah(as). His elder brother, Dr. Mir Muhammad Ismail, was a well known physician and a very pious person. The Mir brothers were the maternal uncles of Hadhrat Khalifatul Masih II(ra).

Mir Ishaq Sahib was a exemplary lecturer who was well versed in the knowledge of the Holy Qur'an and Ahadith. He was a distinguished teacher of Jamia Ahmadiyya and possessed excellent management abilities to look after Jama'at affairs with which he was entrusted during his lifetime.

Till the end of his life, Mir Ishaq Sahib was Nazir Ziafat and Officer Jalsa Salana. During those days, more than 50,00 people people attended the Jalsa and Mir Ishaq Sahib managed the function very well and personally resolving any complaints that occured.

During the month of Ramadan, Hadhrat Mir Sahib used to deliver 'Dars' of the Holy Qur'an at the Aqsa Mosque after the 'Fajr' prayer which was attended not only by the local residents but also by people living in other parts of the town who came to say their prayers of Maghrib and Isha behind Hadhrat Khalifatul Masih II(ra). If Hadhrat Mir Sahib noticed that they had not eaten, he immediately arranged to prepare food and gathered all the guests in the two rooms of the boarding house. Whilst the food was being prepared, he would start delivering a speech on the life of the Holy Prophet(saw).

Due to his responsibilities, Hadhrat Mir Sahib was always very busy. In addition to being the Headmaster of Jamia Ahmadiyya, Nazir Ziafat and Officer of Jalsa Salana, he was entrusted with many other affairs. If any Nazir was off-duty, he covered their duties himself. Despite his hectic schedules, anybody could freely approach him for any help and guidance.

The year 1939 was a Jubilee Year of Hadhrat Khalifatul Masih II(ra) for his Khilafat and Hadhrat Mirza Bashir Ahmad Sahib was writing his famous book *Silsla Ahmadiyya* (Ahmadiyya Movement) which was regarded as a gift for the Jubilee. Malik Muhammad Abdullah Sahib was working with Hadhrat Mirza Bashir Ahmad Sahib. Malik Sahib was entrusted the task of finding the references, supervision of scribing and printing. Hadhrat Mir Sahib used to help Malik Sahib who often called on him at night which never bothered Hadhrat Mir Sahib in the least.

Hadhrat Mir Sahib possessed many qualities of great calibre. He used to meet everybody very kindly and cheerfully.

(61) **Dr. Mir Muhammed Ismail of Delhi** (1884-1947)

Dr. Mir Muhammad Ismail was from a well-known Sayyed family of Delhi whose members enjoyed influence at the Royal Mughal Court of Delhi. In this family was a well-known person Khwaja Muhammad Nasir. He was a man of spiritual eminence and was given the glad tiding that great spiritual blessings would be granted to him through person of the Imam Mahdi who was to appear later. Mir Nasir Nawab was the great grandson of Khwaja Muhammad Nasir.

Whilst employed in the Canal Department of the Punjab Government in the Gurdaspur District, Khwaja Muhammad Nasir developed a close friendship with Mirza Ghulam Qadir, the Chief of Qadian. Mir Nasir Nawab became an admirer of his younger brother, Mirza Ghulam Ahmad for his piety, devotion and love of Islam and the Holy Prophet(saw).

It 1884, Mir Nasir Nawab was considering the marriage of his young daughter Nusrat Jahan Begum and received a number of letters from men of wealth and power but none was acceptable except that of Hadhrat Mirza Ghulam Ahmad(as) of Qadian who was also one of the people under consideration. He was, accordingly informed of the decision. The Nikah ceremony was performed on 17th November 1884, at Delhiand the two families were thus united and Nusrat Jahan Begum became the mother of a new dynasty who was destined to play a leading role in the renaissance of Islam.

Mir Muhammad Ismail, son of Mir Nasir Nawab Sahib was born on 17th July 1884 and was 16 years younger than his sister Hadhrat Nusrat Jahan Begum Sahiba. The family migrated and settled in Qadian in 189l.

Mir Muhammad Ismail Sahib passed his Intermediate Examination from the Punjabi University in the First Division with credit. He decided to join the Medical College at Lahore. He won a scholarship for RS. 12/- and his father and sister supported him at college till he completed his education in the medical field with distinction. Mir Muhammad Ismail Sahib was a medical student in Kangra in the Himalays when it experienced the immense earthquake that shook North West India on 4th April 1905. Letters were received from Ahmadis about the safety of their own persons and property, but nothing was heard of Mir Muhammad Ismail Sahib for some three or four days. It was natural that his parents and relatives for his safety should have felt anxiety. However, the Promised Messiah(as) received a revelation from God stating: 'Muhammad Ismail, Assistant Surgeon', meaning thereby that the boy was safe and would become an Assistant Surgeon in due time. Mir Muhammad Ismail stood first among the successful candidates in the final examinations and was posted as Assistant Surgeon in 1905. He was promoted to the post of Civil Surgeon in 1928 and retired as such in 1936.

Mir Nasir Nawab Sahib visited Qadian in 1891 and was overwhelmed by seeing the change brought about by the Promised Messiah(as) in his followers in striking contrast with that of non-Ahmadi Muslims. As a result, he subsequently joined the fold of Ahmadiyyat with his wife and children. Mir Muhammad Ismail was then ten years old and having been in the house of the Promised Messiah(as) had frequent opportunities to study the traits of character of his spiritual leader. As he advanced in years. Mir Muhammad Ismail Sahib also advanced in his devotion to the cause of Ahmadiyyat and became passionately devoted to the Promised Messiah(as). His parents thought of marrying him with the daughter of his aunt but Mir Sahib was not willing to do so for personal reasons. Anyhow the matter reached the Promised Messiah(as) who advised Dr. Muhammad Ismail to accept the proposal. Mir Sahib readily consented and the marriage was duly solemnised.

Mir Sahib was an expert surgeon. He had a lucrative practice but it was never his aim to make money from the profession. His desire was to reduce human suffering as far he could. After he retired and settled in Qadian, he treated rich and poor alike and gave free medical advice. He was a doctor, writer, poet and also a Sufi of the first order. He translated all the Persian poems of the Promised Messiah(as) into Urdu. He learnt by heart the 'Khutba-e-Ilhamia' – an Arabic sermon revealed to the Promised Messiah(as) on an Eid day in April 1900. Mir Sahib contributed valuable articles to the daily *Al-Fazl*, Qadian.

Dr. Mir Muhammad Ismail Sahib was a deeply religious man. He had been pondering over the Qur'anic abbreviations (Muqattea'at) and sincerely praying God for a true interpretation of these. One day, like a flash it was revealed to him that all Muqatte'at are none other than verses of the Sura Al-Fatiha, in a shortened form and that every chapter which begins with a certain letters (abbreviation) is explanation of the verse of the al-Fatiha for which that abbreviation stands. He explained many extraordinary attributes of Qur'anic abbreviations and their relationship with verses of Al-Fatiha and the chapters of the Holy Qur'an where the Muqattea'ats appear.

Like his ancestors, Dr. Muhammad Ismail Sahib was also a great poet. The eulogistic poem in praise of the Holy Prophet of Islam(saw) is his masterpiece.

Dr. Mir Mohammad Ismail Sahib breathed his last on 18 July 1947 at the age of 67 years and was buried in a special enclosure of the Bahishti Maqbra, Qadian.

(62) **Hadhrat Mir Nasir Nawab** (1846-1924)

Hadhrat Mir Nasir Nawab Sahib was the son of Mir Nasir Ameer and his mother's name was Raushan Ara Begum. He was born in the year 1846. His father died in 1854 when he was only 8 years old.

There was a general lack of formal education in those days so Nasir Nawab Sahib's uncle, Mir Nasir Hussein, who worked in the irrigation department, gave him some basic tuition and he was able to obtain a post of draftsman and later as an overseer in the same department. Nasir Nawab Sahib began his job at Lahore and later transferred to Sathiali – eight miles North of Qadian.

Hadhrat Masih Mau'od's(ra) elder brother Mirza Ghulam Qadir Sahib used to be a Superintendent of the Treasury and in this capacity, had to travel from Gurdaspur to Qadian on a horseback every week. Nasir Nawab Sahib met him in Tatlay where he was supervising the construction of an irrigation canal and became his close friend. It was on his insistence that he came to stay at his house in Gurdaspur. He often used to say that Mirza Ghulam Qadir's younger brother was a very pious and righteous man.

Nasir Nawab Sahib's wife, Hadhrat Syeda Nusrat Jahan Begum Sahiba was born in 1865. From this marriage, Nasir Nawab Sahib had five children but they all died in childhood. In 1881, he had a son named Hadhrat Mir Muhammad Ismail who lived to be a famous physician. In 1890, Mir Sahib was blessed with a second son, Mir Muhammad Ishaq.

Nasir Nawab Sahib travelled extensively during the course of his employment and at various times he lived at Madhupur, Lahore, Sathiali, Kahnwan, Tatlay, Ambala Cantonment, Patiala, Ludhiana, Ferozepur, and Hoti in Mardan. After retirement, he left Multan and went to Qadian where he spent 29 years of his life in active service .

Initially Nasir Nawab Sahib was under the influence of Maulawi Muhammad Hussein Batalvi, (a very vociferous opponent of the Promised Messiah(as)). As a result of being so closely associated with this Maulawi, Nasir Nawab Sahib had not taken the Bai'at at the hands of the Promised Messiah(as). Eventually in 1892, the Promised Messiah(as) invited Nasir Nawab Sahib to the Annual Gathering of the Jama'at in Qadian. When Nasir Nawab Sahib saw with his own eyes the devotion of the Promised Messiah(as) to the words of Allah and His Beloved Messenger(saw) , he repented from his previous attitude and entered the fold of Ahmadiyyat by taking the Bai'at at the hands of his own son-in-law.

Hadhrat Mir Nasir Nawab Sahib supervised the construction of many of the buildings of the Community, such as those of the Madrasa Ahmadiyya and its boarding house. People held Nasir Nawab Sahib in great esteem and acknowledged his very special status as the father-in-law of the Promised Messiah(as) and the father of Hadhrat Amma Jan (may Allah be pleased with her).

Hadhrat Mir Nasir Nawab Sahib's special status, his relationship with the Promised Messiah(as) and its significance, can be illustrated by a very clear dream of the Promised Messiah(as). He explains:

> 'Mir Nasir Nawab has come with a fruit bearing tree on his hand. When this is given to me, it becomes a large tree and resembles a pomegranate tree which is very healthy and flourishing, full of blossoms and fruit. Its fruit is exquisitely sweet and delicious, but even more surprising was the fact that its blossoms were also sweet in taste. But it was not an ordinary tree, it was unique and its like was never before seen in the world. I was enjoying its fruit and flowers, and all of a sudden I woke up from my sleep.'
> *(Tadhkira, p.544, 2nd. Edition)*

Towards the last days of his life, Nasir Nawab Sahib developed an illness similar to Parkinson's disease but he remained active till his last breath. He passed away on 19th September 1924 and was buried in Bahishti Maqbara, Qadian.

(63) **Hadhrat Mirza Barkat Ali** (1887-1978)

Hadhrat Mirza Barkat Ali was born in October 1887 in Lahore. His father passed away when he was only a few months old. He came with his mother to Qadian. His mother married Hadhrat Bhai Abdur Rehman Sahib thus Mirza Barkat Ali Sahib was brought up under the guardianship of Hadhrat Bhai Abdur Rehman Sahib. Barkat Ali Sahib took his Bai'at in 1900 at the blessed hands of the Promised Messiah(as).

Mirza Barkat Ali Sahib was a witness to the acceptance of prayers of the Promised Messiah(as) through a miraculous recovery of a person known as Abdul Karim who had been bitten by a mad dog and was afflicted with rabies. The doctors had given up on him. However, he recovered fully after the Promised Messiah(as) prayed for him.

Mirza Barkat Ali Sahib was very fond of seeking knowledge. Besides theology his favourite subjects were mathematics, geography and astronomy.

Mirza Barkat Ali Sahib passed his Veterinary Surgeon examination and came to Qadian. He devoted his life and worked in different offices of Sadr Anjuman Ahmadiyya till his retirement in 1943. He also took an active part during the Malkana Movement. He was a very pious person who always gave priority to faith over the worldly affairs. He prayed for others vehemently and kept his nights alive with prayers.

He passed away on 22nd May, 1978.

(64) Maulawi Muhammad Abdullah of Botala (1881-1952)

Maulawi Muhammad Abdullah, son of Muhammad Din, was born on 20th May 1881. He belonged to a Rajput family. Abdullah Sahib passed his Middle School Examination and gained good practical knowledge of Arabic and Persian languages. He also learnt the art of calligraphy, which proved to be an additional source of income for him

Muhammad Abdullah Sahib was employed as Patwari in the canal department of Sawat, Frontier Province and impressed his superior officers with his honesty and diligence. He was introduced to the Ahmadiyya Movement in 1901. He saw in a vision, the two mosques of Qadian – Aqsa and Mubarak mosques as well as the Holy Founder of the Movement before he visited Qadian.

When Muhammad Abdullah Sahib paid his first visit to Qadian, he found to his wonder and amazement, that the Aqsa Mosque was exactly the same as he had seen in his vision. In another dream, he saw the holy city of Madinah. As soon as he entered the holy town, he felt the cool breeze was blowing in the town. It was so pleasing and refreshing that when he looked up he saw a dazzling light which brightened the whole atmosphere of Madinah while beyond there was darkness all around. When he woke up, he at once decided to contact the Promised Messiah(as). He sent a letter to him at Qadian pledging his oath of his allegiance to the Community. Some five years later, he personally visited Qadian and saw the fulfilment of his dreams when he actually saw Aqsa and Mubarak Mosques.

Muhammad Abdullah Sahib retired from service in 1935 and migrated to Qadian the same year and had a house built for himself in the Dar-ul-Barkat area.

Muhammad Abdullah Sahib's pleasure lay in the service of the Community, which he continued to do till the last breath of his life. His eldest son, Hafiz Qudrat-ullah has been serving the community for a long time.

Muhammad Abdullah died on 3 May 1952 and was buried in the Companions' area in the Bahishti Maqbara, Rabwah.

(65) **Maulawi Muhammad Amir Khan** (1846-1950)

Maulawi Amir Khan was born in 1846 at Panja Balla near Peshawar. His father Muhammed Feroze Khan, was a well-known landlord of the area.

Maulawi Muhammad Sahib received his preliminary education at home and from a very young age, he was well versed in Urdu, Arabic and Persian. In about 1860, he migrated to Asam. He also spent a few years in Bhopal where he taught Hadith to Lady Jahan Ara of Bhopal. This was at the time when the Imam Mahdi was awaited with great anxiety. According to his daughter, Mehr-ul-Nisa, a very pious person by the name of Gulab Shah Faqir of Peshawar had declared that the Imam Mahdi had been born. The same person announced again after a lapse of few years that the Mahdi had attained a matured age. Maulawi Sahib was of a young age when he heard these proclamations. Although he had migrated to Asam, he always kept afresh in his mind what he heard from Gulab Shah of Peshawar.

Muhammad Sahib married Ashraful Nisa, the daughter of Munshi Mohammad Hussein who came from a noble family of Bengal.

Muhammad Sahib was very pious and very steadfast in his belief. His belief in the Almighty was exemplary. He was a great helper and exercised great tolerance in all matters.

The claim of the Promised Messiah(as) that he had been appointed by God as Mahdi and Messiah came to the knowledge of Maulawi Sahib. He quickly accepted the proofs given by the Promised Messiah(as) from the Qur'an and Hadith about his advent and truthfulness. He also remembered the saying of Gulab Shah Faqir of Peshawar. So he wrote a letter of initiation (Bai'at) to the Promised Messiah(as). At this time, his elder son, Khan Bahadar Ataul Rehman Khan was of a very young age. This was also the period where opposition to the Promised Messiah(as) was at its peak. Maulawies from Dalroogarh and surrounding areas opposed him and tried to prevent Muhammad Sahib becoming an Ahmadi. However, Muhammad Sahib remained steadfast and concentrated on prayers and Tabligh. He was ultimately declared by these Maulawies as Kafir.

On one occasion, some Maulawis gathered in front of Muhammad Sahib's house and started verbally abusing him and the Promised Messiah(as) and asked him to come out of the house. Muhammad Sahib remained silent for some time but when he could not withstand the abuse any longer, he decided to go out and confront them. His wife tried to stop him as everybody outside were well-equipped. However, Muhammad Sahib went outside and started to recite the Holy Qur'an. The crowd was so ashamed that they all disappeared without uttering a word.

Muhammad Sahib was a wealthy building contractor. He was respected by all due to his ability and noble character. However, local Maulawies continued to oppose him. At one time, a social boycott was declared and Muhammad Sahib was even barred from taking water from the nearby well. It was a time of great test and difficulties. His children sometimes cried for water. An old lady living at the back of their house used to help them. This continued for a long time and finally he had to go to the court. He hired a lawyer called Faiz Noor Ali and won the case against Maulawies. The lawyer asked him to claim for damages but he refused.

Earthquake in Islam in Asam and related incidents

Once the province of Asam was hit by a terrible earthquake. The river, which was running miles away from the village, changed its route and started flowing at a shorter distance from the village. The stream had a high flood and very large and strong buildings were affected. Buildings and large trees vanished. The house of Muhammad Sahib was also in great danger as the stream flowed a few metres away. People left their homes for a safe place but Muhammad Sahib decided to stay. He prayed and cried to Allah for help until the flooded stream adopted a normal flow. Even now the stream is flowing at the same distance of a few metres from the spot.

Muhammad Sahib passed away on the 2nd September 1950. He was buried in the graveyard of Dalroogarh and hundreds of people joined the funeral prayer.

The opponents of Muhammad Sahib still did not stop their bad behaviour at the time of his death. The local judge of Dalroogarh, Mr. Ziaul Rehman Baig announced those who had taken part in the funeral prayer of Mohammad Sahib, and who had been labelled a Kafir, would need to become Muslim by reciting the Kalima. However, the educated elite denounced this declaration. A lawyer by the name of Faiz Noor Ali and a Headmaster, Saful-Din openly declared that Muhammad Sahib was a true Muslim.

A well-known doctor, Mr Ghosh treated Muhammad Sahib on his last day and was immensely impressed by his piety. Muhammad Sahib's eldest son, Ataul Raheem also devoted his life to Ahmadiyyat. His son saw a dream that a clock had stopped suddenly. He interpreted it as the sign of election for the third successor of the Promised Messiah(as). This was all due to the training of Maulawi Muhammad Amir Khan Sahib that even his son had a greater share of wisdom and intelligence.

Maulawi Muhammad Amir Khan Sahib had seven daughters and two sons.

(66) **Mirza Muhammad Ashraf**
(1868-1947)

Muhammad Ashraf Sahib was born in 1868. He was the son of the well-known Maulawi, Jalal-Din Balanvi. Muhammad Ashraf Sahib joined the Ahmadiyya Movement in 1895 and migrated to Qadian in 1906. On the strength of his experience as an accountant in the military department, he was offered a post in the office of the Sadr Anjuman Ahmadiyya Qadian, where he served the department for 25 years. Hadhrat Khalifatul-Masih II(ra) was highly pleased with his work as an accountant.

Muhammad Ashraf Sahib was an eyewitness to the sign of the earthquake and the rain on 28th February1907 as foretold by the Promised Messiah and Mahdi(as).

Muhammad Ashraf Sahib passed away on 14th November 1947.

(67) Maulawi Muhammad Din BA (Alig) (1881-1983)

Maulawi Muhammad Din was born on 4th December 1881 at Lahore. He joined the Rang Mahal High School, Lahore, which was managed by the American Mission authorities. Rang Mahal institution proved to be a cradle where promising youth developed the inherent qualities of their literary attainments. Under the patronage of his American teachers, young Muhammad Din Sahib developed a taste for English literature even in his school days.

Muhammad Din Sahib joined the Islamic College, Lahore, with English, Maths, Science and History. But before he could sit for his Intermediate Examination, he developed a serious disease which did not allow him to continue his studies. It was fortunate that he recovered from the disease but he lost chance to appear in his Intermediate Examination. He secured a job in the Railway Department through the courtesy of a good Hindu neighbour.

Those were the days when the name and fame of Hadhrat Mirza Ghulam Ahmad(as) of Qadian was uppermost in the councils of the Muslim Ulema, the Christian Missionaries and the Arya Samajis of the Punjab. The tragic death of Pandit Lekh Ram in 1897 which occurred in the wake of a grand prophecy of the Promised Messiah and Mahdi(as) of Qadian, drew the attention of Muhammad Din Sahib to the study of Ahmadiyyat. Such a grand sign in this age of materialism, could not fail to lead a straightforward and clear-thinking young man of the calibre of Muhammad Din Sahib to the acceptance of the truth. He at once decided to join the Ahmadiyya Movement amidst bitter opposition and persecution to which the small Community was subjected in those days. He tendered, in writing, his oath of allegiance in 1900 and pledged himself at the blessed hand of his spiritual Master in 1901.

Muhammad Din Sahib resigned his lucrative post in Lahore and bearing his love of the Promised Messiah(as), hastened to Qadian, not having the slightest notion of how he would support himself. But fortune was on his side and no sooner had he arrived in Qadian, he was offered and accepted the post of clerk at a wage of ten rupees per month in the residential school.

Muhammad Din Sahib acted as superintendent, clerk and tutor and worked in collaboration with Sheikh Abdur Rahim Sahib, a renowned teacher. He then thought of completing his education for which he prepared privately. He was helped in the study of mathematics by Maulawi Muhammad Ali M.A, formerly a Professor of Mathematics in the Islamia College, Lahore, and in English by Maulawi Sher Ali. B.A. After passing his Intermediate, he went to Aligarh in 1906 and graduated from there in 1908.

While at Aligarh, he read most of Shakespeare's plays and acquired mastery over the English language. His proficiency of the English language and literature, its idiom and usage, its etymology and grammar, characterise all his original articles as well as his translations from Urdu into English.

While at Aligarh, Muhammad Din Sahib was offered the post of Headmaster at Hyderabad for but he declined the offer and returned to Qadian in 1908. In the same year, he joined the Central Training College Lahore and obtained his diploma in Education. He then joined the Talimul Islam High School, Qadian as assistant Headmaster and took over as Headmaster in 1914. Under his guidance, the school achieved excellent results in the Matriculation Examination. This state of affairs continued till 1918 when he handed over charge to Qazi Muhammad Abdullah B.A, .B.T.

Muhammad Din Sahib worked as editor of *The Review of Religions* till January 1923 when he left for America as a Muslim Missionary. Upon his return, he again worked as Headmaster of Talimul Islam High School, till 1940. He also worked as a Manager, Nusrat Girls High School, Qadian from 1940 to 1947.

After the Partition of India, Maulawi Sahib worked as Nazir (Secretary) Education Department, Sadr Anjuman Ahmadiyya, Rabwah. In 1965, he was asked by Hadhrat Khalifatul Masih III(ru) to take over the charge as Sadr Anjuman-e-Ahmadiyya at the age of 85.

He passed away on the 7th March 1983 at the age of 102 years.

(68) Hadhrat Maulawi Muhammad Hussain (b.1893)

Hadhrat Maulawi Muhammad Hussein Sahib was born in 1893. He was related to a Hindu Rajput family and his ancestor, Gian Singh accepted Islam. He lived in Begowal, Dist. Hoshiarpur but had to move to Batala due to extreme opposition from the non-Muslims. The forefathers of Muhammad Hussein Sahib were involved in timber business in Batala.

Muhammad Hussein Sahib's father was Mian Muhammad Bakhsh. His uncle was the first person in the family to accept Ahmadiyyat.

Muhammad Hussein Sahib is the 77th in the list of 313 Companions of the Promised Messiah(as). He had the honour to be the host of the Promised Messiah(as) on several occasions in Batala.

Muhammad Hussein Sahib's father was an ardent follower of Maulawi Muhammad Hussein Batalvi, an opponent of the Promised Messiah(as). Once Maulawi Muhammad Hussein Batalvi went to court as a witness against the Promised Messiah(as) in the case of an attempted murder of a Christian missionary, Dr. Martin Clark. Muhammad Hussein Sahib's father also went to court to attend the hearing. On seeing the face and personality of the Promised Messiah(as), this developed an honour and respect in his heart for him and he lost all respect for Muhammad Hussein Batalvi. He left Batala and settled in Qadian where he had the opportunity of seeing several heavenly signs there. Muhammad Hussein Sahib, along with his father, also had the opportunity to listen to the 'Khutba Ilhaamia' of the Promised Messiah(as).

Muhammad Hussein Sahib attended school in Qadian but left in 1905 and started as an apprentice blacksmith. One day, he was working in the shop when a maid servant came from the Promised Messiah's(as) house and said: 'Hey Boy, Hadhrat Jee (she used to call the Promised Messiah(as) as such) has lost the keys of his locks. He needs to get some books from the boxes. Could you open them?' Muhammad Hussein Sahib went along with her. The Promised Messiah(as) showed Muhammad Hussein Sahib seven locked boxes and he managed to open all of them. On seeing this, the Promised Messiah(as) said: 'This is wonderful skill, I was wondering how to open them. Can I have new keys made?' Muhammad Hussein Sahib replied that it was possible. The next day he took the keys back. The Promised Messiah(as) thanked him and offered him a rupee coin. Muhammad Hussein Sahib told him that he needed only prayers. The Promised Messiah(as) replied: 'Take the rupee and I promise I will pray for you.' After learning his trade, Maulawi Sahib opened his own blacksmith shop in 1911.

Muhammad Hussein Sahib was initiated into Ahmadiyyat at the hands of the Promised Messiah(as) in 1902. In 1906, he entered Madrissa Ahmadiyya for religious education but soon left to learn more of his trade. After learning his trade, Maulawi Sahib opened his own blacksmith shop in 1911. He however, continued to study religious books from various scholars.

Muhammad Hussein Sahib witnessed the laying of the foundation stone of Minaratul Masih and also witnessed numerous heavenly signs.

A few months before the end of the First World War, Muhammad Hussein Sahib was recruited as a fitter in the British Indian Army and went to Basra and Iran in November 1918. He had the chance to preach to his army colleagues and the local people. Soon afterwards a local Ahmadiyya Jama'at was formed. He also had the opportunity to pray at the tombs of Hadhrat Anas, Hadhrat Zubair, Hadhrat Talha and Hadhrat Hassan Basri. He left the army in 1921.

In 1923, a movement known as 'Shudhi' was started in the Utter Pardesh (UP) province of India to convert poor Muslims into Hindus. Hadhrat Khalifatul Masih II(ra) directed Muhammad Hussein Sahib to go and help in countering this movement. Muhammad Hussein Sahib dedicated himself for this mission and was very successful in keeping thousands of poor and illiterate Muslims steadfast in their faith. Initially Muhammad Hussein Sahib dedicated three months for this purpose but on the directions of Hadhrat Khalifatul Masih II(ra), he became a permanent missionary.

Although Muhammad Hussein Sahib did not have adequate education, he excelled in debating with opponents. He was not only a very good speaker but on account of his mild speech and excellent moral courage, the audience enjoyed listening to him. Muhammad Hussein Sahib used to amuse his friends with his humorous conversation. According to the regulations of Sadr Anjuman Ahmadiyya, Muhammad Hussein Sahib retired as an active missionary in 1954 but because of his experience and success in the field of preaching he was soon re-employed

At the time of the partition of Indian sub-continent in 1947, Muhammad Hussein Sahib was working in Kashmir. After the partition, he was stationed in Jhelum to help Kashmiri refugees. He used this opportunity to also preach but the local people boycotted him several times and he was physically beaten on several occasions. There was also an attempt on his life but he escaped. In spite of all these hardships, his steadfastness and perseverance never wavered. Every adversity and hardship inspired him to speed up his efforts.

Muhammad Hussein Sahib was a pious person and always used to bow before God for his requests. The acceptance of prayer proved a source of blessing for his faith. At the demise of Hadhrat Khalifatul Masih I[(ra)], he saw a vision that Hadhrat Mirza Mahmood Ahmad[(ra)] would be the next Khalifa. At the death of Hadhrat Khalifatul Masih I[(ra)], when Maulawi Muhammad Ali tried to rebel alone with some coronations, Maulawi Muhammad Hussein was one of the first persons to seek protection under Khilafati Thania.

Muhammad Hussein Sahib enjoyed the blessings of prayers of Hadhrat Khalifatul Masih I[(ra)] and lived a long life. At the directions of Hadhrat Khalifatul Masih IV[(ru)], Muhammad Hussein Sahib participated in the opening ceremony of the first Ahmadiyya Mosque in Australia. He came to the Centenary Jubilee Celebrations of the Jama'at in London and visited various Jama'ats in England where he mentioned to the youth the events he witnessed during the blessed period of the Promised Messiah[(as)].

It was a great blessing that despite his age, Muhammad Hussein Sahib had a very clear voice and sharp memory.

Muhammad Hussein Sahib married three times. He had five sons and seven daughters who are actively involved in the Jama'at.

Hadhrat Maulawi Muhammad Hussein died on 19th Jan 1994 in Islamabad, Pakistan at the age of 101.

(69) **Hadhrat Muhammad Ismil** (b.1878)

Muhammad Ismail Sahib was born in a village Manila of District Ambala in 1878 from a noble family. From an early age, he was very punctual in observing prayers. He benefited from the noble company of a pious man Syed Charagh Ali Shah.

Muhammad Ismail Sahib's parents were farmers and were dependent on the earnings from their land. His father died when he was young and his elder brother looked him after. Ismail Sahib was sent to Lahore for his studies. During this stay, he had the opportunity to see the Promised Messiah(as) and listen to one of his lectures that he delivered at Lahore. He also read some books written by the Promised Messiah(as) and took Bai'at in writing.

For long time, Muhammad Ismail Sahib served in the Railway department in the finance section. When he retired in 1929, he migrated to Qadian and settled permanently in Muhalla Darul Barkat where he served as Sadr (president) and also as Imam of his local mosque.

After the partition, Muhammad Ismail Sahib migrated to Lahore and settled in the Dharampura area. He used to teach Holy Qur'an and Namaz (Salat) to children. He was very noble and honest person.

(70) Hadhrat Munshi Muhammad Khan Kapoorthalvi (1861-1904)

Hadhrat Munshi Muhammad Khan was born in 1861. His father's name was Dilawar Khan, whose great grand ancestors had migrated from Afghanistan and settled in Kapoorthala. Hadhrat Munshi Sahib completed his elementary education at Rampur, India and worked in different capacities in various departments of the State Government. He performed his duties with great honesty and dedication .

When Hadhrat Munshi Sahib read *Baraheen-e-Ahmadiyya,* he was spiritually inspired and repeatedly requested for signing his Bai'at but the Promised Messiah(as) did not accept it till he was permitted to do so by Allah. However, when this did happen, Hadhrat Munshi Sahib accepted Bai'at on 23rd March, 1889 at the blessed hands of Hadhrat Promised Messiah(as).

Hadhrat Munshi Sahib was fortunate to be a member of the Promised Messiah's(as) entourage during the debate with Maulawi Nazir Hussain Delhvi. Hadhrat Promised Messiah(as) was impressed by his sincerity and loyalty and had stated about it in his book, *Azalah-e-Aoham*. The Promised Messiah(as) wrote:

> 'Mian Muhammad Khan is employed in Kapoorthala State. He is a thorough gentleman, intelligent and truthful. His love, sincerity and noble intentions towards me are beyond my imagination. I do not entertain any doubt towards his sincerity to me, but fear that he may exceed beyond the limits. He is a true, loyal, obedient, dedicated and straightforward. May Allah be with him. His younger brother Sarwar Ali Khan, has also joined my followers. This young man like his brother is also very sincere and obedient. May Allah be their protector."'

Hadhrat Munshi Sahib was affected by tuberculosis in middle age. Hadhrat Maulana Nur-ud-Din(ra) was sent to Kapoorthala by the Promised Messiah(as) for his treatment, but he could not survive and died at the age of forty-three.

The Promised Messiah(as) was extremely shocked on hearing about his death and after a revelation he prophesied:

'His progeny (descendants) shall be treated kindly.'

And this revelation of the Promised Messiah(as) was indeed fulfilled

Soon after, Hadhrat Munshi Sahib's son, Munshi Abdul Hameed Khan, was appointed as Officer Stable, who subsequently became District Magistrate and retired in the same rank.

(71) **Mirza Muhammad Shafi of Delhi** (1877-1945)

Mirza Muhammad Shafi was born in 1877 and belonged to a respectable family of Delhi. He passed his Primary Standard examination from Jammu where he lived with his maternal uncle and later matriculated from a school in Delhi and joined the Postal Department where he served for 30 years until his retirement. He was selected to head a special Post Office set up in Delhi on the occasion of the Delhi Darbar in 1911 and was awarded a silver medal for performing his duties efficiently.

Shafi Sahib's attention was drawn to the Ahmadiyya Movement in Islam through a devoted Ahmadi of Ballabgarh. The study of some books by the Promised Messiah(as) convinced him of the truth of Ahmadiyyat. In 1901, he joined Ahmadiyyat and his name was mentioned in the *Al-Hakam* newspaper dated 10th June 1901. Muhammad Shafi Sahib visited Qadian in 1903 and met the Promised Messiah(as) and thereafter every year he visited Qadian at Jalsa Salana.

Shafi Sahib was a keen reader of Ahmadiyya literature and contributed to all the journals published by the Community. He was at that time living in Shimla where he was not very happy there so he wrote to the Promised Messiah(as) asking him to pray for his transfer elsewhere. The Promised Messiah(as) directed his Private Secretary, Maulawi Abdul Karim, to write back that he had prayed for him and that God accepts the prayers of His elected one but at the same time He is All Wise and if He so wills, He will do it. The day he received the letter from Qadian, he also received orders of transfer from Shimla as well as his promotion notification.

Mirza Muhammad Shafi migrated to Qadian in 1932. He served the Community in the capacity of auditor and accountant, Sadr Anjuman Ahmadiyya, Qadian for a number of years. He was a very much attached to the family of the Promised Messiah(as).

Muhammad Safi Sahib passed away on 17 January 1945 in Delhi. Hadhrat Khalifatul Masih II(ra) led his Janaza Prayer in Qadian on 19 January and he was buried in Bahishti Maqbra, Qadian.

One of his sons Mirza Ahmad Shafi was a teacher in Talim-ul-Islam High School. He was killed during the riots in 1947. Another son, Mr Manwar Ahmad served as a missionary in USA and passed away in 1948. His wife who passed away in 1951 is buried at Rabwah.

(Extracted from Tarikh-e-Ahmadiyyat Part 10 (copy Printed in Daily Al-Fazl, 24th September 1995.)

(72) Mian Muhammad Yousaf Sahib of Mardan (b.1867)

Muhammad Yousaf Sahib was born at Mardan in the year 1867. He belonged to a famous Rajput Khokhar family of Tehsil Ajnala, District Amritsar.

His father, Mian Ahmad Bakhsh was appointed as Naib Tehsildar in the Frontier Province and served in that capacity at Mardan, Sawabi and Haripur. Mian Ahmad Bakhsh was a very pious person. He arranged construction of Mosques at the above mentioned three places at his own expense.

Muhammad Yousaf Sahib began his elementary education from the studying of the Holy Qur'an at his home. According to Muhammad Yousaf Sahib, he started offering prayers in congregation when he was only 9 years old and till his last days he remained fond of offering his prayers in congregation in the mosque. During his old age, his eyesight became very weak but still regularly attended prayers at the mosque.

Muhammad Yousaf Sahib was extremely fond of learning and gaining knowledge. He passed his middle school examination with distinction at Haripur in the year 1885.

After the demise of his father and at the request of the family members, Muhammad Yousaf Sahib moved to Mardan where Khan Bahadur Muhammad Ibrahim Khan arranged for the family's accommodation. This house was situated near district courts and a Mosque built by his father at his own expense.

In May 1901, the news spread in Mardan that the Railway Station Master of Mardan, Shah Din Chughtai had converted to Qadianiyat and Muhammad Yousaf Sahib wanted to find out more about Ahmadiyyat. Together with some friends they met Babu Shah Din at the Railway Station and explained to him the purpose of their visit. Master Shah Din explained his faith in a beautiful manner. When they were ready to depart, he presented to them a copy of *Baraheen-e-Ahmadiyya* by the Promised Messiah(as) with the condition to return it to him after reading. The other colleagues declined, but Muhammad Yousaf Sahib took the book with him.

That night, he started reading the book and had gone through only six pages when he came to the conclusion that the author could never be a liar and he started reading the book again from the beginning thinking lest the book was being read under satanic influence. After reading those six pages again, his belief about the author became more firm and strong and he repeated the reading of those six pages six times. At that point Muhammad Yousaf Sahib was completely a changed man and made a firm decision join the fold of Ahmadiyyat.

After continuously being engaged in the Tahajjud prayer that night, he wished to personally visit that great personage and see Hadhrat Masih Mau'od(as) himself. He was so spellbound with these thoughts that he could not sleep. Early in the morning, he departed for the railway station and conveyed his intention to Babu Shah din Sahib. He advised him to fully satisfy himself in the matter and not hasten for initiation under the influence of the emotions and complete reading the entire book. Muhammad Yousaf Sahib was well-convinced and he wrote his letter of initiation there and then. He was 34 years old at that time.

With the passage of time, this small Jama'at started increasing in numbers and within six years, the number rose to forty and all of them used to offer their daily prayers, Juma prayers and Eid prayers in the small veranda of the house belonging to Muhammad Yousaf Sahib. Dars-e-Qur'an classes were also held there regularly. A new place for a Mosque was later acquired through the efforts and prayers of the local Jama'at members.

(73) **Sheikh Muhammad Yusaf** (Editor of *Al-Nur*)

Shiekh Muhammad Yusaf was a convert from Sikhism. In June 1906, he came to Qadian, met with Maulana Nur-ud-Din(ra) who introduced him to the Promised Messiah(as). The Sheikh narrated the circumstances under which conversion to Islam was brought about. The Promised Messiah(as) was very much impressed by his narrative and asked Maulana Nur-ud-Din Sahib to arrange for a public lecture. Sheikh Yusaf Sahib delivered his speech in the Mosque on 20th July 1906.

Sheikh Yusaf Sahib was posted as a vernacular teacher in the Talimul Islam High School, Qadian. He started the newspaper *Al-Nur* during the time of Hadhrat Khalifatul Masih(as) which preached Islam to the Sikhs. He also translated the Holy Qur'an into Gurmukhi and Hindi for the benefit of the Sikhs and Hindus and wrote a biography of the Holy Prophet Muhammad(saw) which was read fondly by the Sikhs.

After the partition of India and Pakistan in 1947, Sheikh Yusaf Sahib migrated to Gujranwala with his family. He paid a visit to Rabwah in 1951 and was granted audience with Hadhrat Khalifatul Masih II(ra). On his return home, he was taken ill and passed away on 6th May 1952. His body was taken to Rabwah for burial where Hadhrat Khalifatul Masih(as) led his funeral prayer. He was buried in the Bahishti Maqbara along with the Companions of the Promised Messiah(as).

(74) **Hadhrat Mufti Muhammad Sadiq** (1872-1957)

Hadhrat Mufti Muhammad Sadiq was born in Bhera, India (now Pakistan) in 1872. He was 47th in lineage to Hadhrat 'Uthman Bin Affan(ra), the third Khalifa. Mufti Sahib read the translation of the Holy Qur'an from Hadhrat Hakim Maulawi Nur-ud-Din (Khalifatul Masih I(ra)) at the age of fourteen. He also received education in English, Arabic and Persian and under the direction of the Promised Messiah(as), Mufti Sahib learnt Hebrew as well.

In 1890, Mufti Sahib passed the entrance examination and gained employment in a school in Jammu. He also worked in the office of the Accountant General in Lahore, Pakistan. The Promised Messiah(as) at the house of Nawab Muhammad Ali, initiated him into Ahmadiyyat in 1891. In 1901, Mufti Sahib migrated to Qadian.

During the lifetime of the Promised Messiah(as), Mufti Sahib looked after his mail and was among his foremost helpers. He was editor of the *Badr Weekly* newspaper for a long time and also helped in the publication of *Sadiq* – a weekly for articles on Christianity. He was also the editor of the *Al-Badr* newspaper.

Mufti Sahib was also at one time, the headmaster of Talimul Islam School, Qadian. He also worked as Private Secretary to Hadhrat Khalifatul Masih II(ra) and held the post of Nazir (Director) for external affairs. He was one of the early missionaries to England and the first missionary to America.

Hadhrat Mufti Sahib spent a lot of time preaching and had his own unique style. Once while he was walking in Bombay with a friend they happened to pass by a letter-writer. The friend told Mufti Sahib to preach to the letter-writer. Mufti Sahib then sat beside the letter-writer and asked him to write a letter to the Nizam of Hyderabad Deccan. So he wrote:

> 'According to the prophecy of the Holy Prophet (peace and blessings of Allah be upon him) the Promised Messiah would come and gather all the Muslims under the Muhammadi banner. That Messiah has appeared in Qadian and I invite you (the Nizam) to accept his message.'

The letter was then posted to the Nizam. He then also preached to the letter-writer.

In 1904, Mufti Sahib became ill. His mother went to the Promised Messiah(as) and requested prayers. The Promised Messiah(as) said: 'I always pray for him. You think that Sadiq is your son and very close to you but I can say with certainty that he is dearer to me than he is to you.' On another occasion the Promised Messiah(as) said: 'He (Mufti Sadiq) is a respectable, pious and intelligent young member of the Jama'at and I do not have words to narrate his qualities.'

Mufti Sahib was sent by Hadhrat Khalifatul Masih II(ra) to the United Kingdom in 1917 and in 1920 and later was asked to move to the USA. He started his journey on 26th January 1920 from England and landed in Philadelphia on 15th February 1920.

When Mufti Sahib arrived in America from England, the immigration officer asked him the purpose of his journey. Mufti Sahib replied that he was an Indian Muslim and had come to preach the true faith. The officer replied that he would not be allowed to stay in America. Maulawi Sahib told him he would not go back and was then detained along with some Europeans. Mufti Sahib started preaching in the detention building and by the grace of Allah, fifteen people accepted Ahmadiyyat. When the officials came to know about this, they were concerned and Mufti Sahib was released.

Maulawi Sahib was once invited to give a lecture on Islam by an organisation. After the lecture, a priest asked him how he would be successful all alone while the Christians had sent hundreds of missionaries to India. Maulawi Sahib replied that this was also proof of the truth of Islam that whilst the Christian priests and missionaries had spent millions of rupees in India for more than a century, they could compare it with what he had achieved in two years.

During the First World War 1917, the English Prime Minister made a speech in London in which he stated that Britain had entered the war to defend itself against the Germans. It was essential, therefore, for the nation to fight. During those days, a priest asked Mufti Sahib to mention a quality in Islam which is not found in Christianity. Mufti Sahib in his reply gave the reference of the English Prime Minister's speech and told the priest to ask Jesus Christ(as) that the Germans had attacked the English so what should the English do? According to Christians, Christ(as) had said: 'Do not fight evil. If someone demands a coat from you, give him your shirt also. If you are dragged to a wilderness for a mile, you should go for two miles. If you are slapped on a cheek, turn the other one.' If the English and their allies had followed the teachings of Jesus Christ(as), they should not have fought the Germans. Instead, they ignored the teachings of Jesus Christ(as). On the contrary, the Holy Prophet of Islam(saw) had said: 'Do not attack someone but if you are attacked defend yourselves.' The priest was so much impressed that he acknowledged that this was a better teaching. He rendered faith-inspiring services in the field of Tabligh (preaching).

Mufti Sahib then moved to New

York and by the Grace of Allah, was able to convert many people to Islam. He then went to Detroit to deliver the message of truth particularly to people from Arab countries. In 1921, he moved permanently to Chicago where he purchased a building and set up an Ahmadiyya Mission in U.S.A. He started publishing a quarterly magazine titled *The Muslim Sunrise*.

Mufti Sahib returned to Qadian on 4th December, 1923. He held various assignments at Qadian as Nazir Talim, Headmaster Talim-ul-Islam High School and Private Secretary to Hadhrat Khalifatul Masih II(ra).

Hadhrat Mufti Sadiq Sahib passed away at the age of 85 years on 13th January 1957 and was buried in Bahishti Maqbara at Rabwah, Pakistan.

(75) **Hafiz Sayyad Mukhtar Ahmad of Shahjahanpu**

Hafiz Mukhtar Ahmad belonged to a respectable and learned Sayyad family of Shahjahanpur, India. His father, Hafiz Sayyad Ali Mian was an eminent scholar and a landlord of Utter Pardesh (U.P.).

Mukhtar Ahmad Sahib was remarkably intelligent and had a amazing memory. He learnt the Holy Qur'an by heart while he was still in his teens. Urdu was his mother tongue but he was equally proficient in Persian. From his childhood days, he was inclined towards religion, something that remained with him till the last moment of his life.

While still young, Hafiz Mukhtar Ahmad felt uneasy and concerned at the interpretation of the Qur'anic expression concerning the Holy Prophet(saw) as put forth by various interpreters and Christian critics. and began to seek for more reasonable and decent interpretations of a certain verse. Munshi Muhammad Khan of Kapurthala incidentally sent an incomplete manuscript of the *Aina-e-Kamalat-e-Islam* to Hafiz Mukhtar Ahmad's father at Shahjahanpur which was also read by Hafiz Sahib. He read through the manuscript from beginning to end and was amazed to find a clear, convincing exposition of the verse in question. He became thoroughly convinced that the author of the book, *Aina-e-Kamalat-e-Islam* was a passionate devotee of the Holy Prophet(saw). Since then, he counted himself as one of the followers of the Promised Messiah(as) and formally joined the fold of Ahmadiyyat in 1892.

Hafiz Mukhtar Sahib frequently visited Qadian and stayed for weeks on end in the company of the Promised Messiah(as). In 1896, he had the privilege of attending the historic Religious Conference at Lahore, which was sponsored and convened by a Hindu intellectual.

Hafiz Mukhtar Sahib was the moving spirit of the Ahmadiyya Community of Shahjahanpur in particular and of the Ahmadiyya Community of U.P. He was asked to reside in Qadian for some time, by Hadhrat Khalifatul Masih II(ra), but finally settled there till the partition when he moved to Lahore. Various learned people, Ahmadis and non-Ahmadis and poets frequented his residence. He later moved to Rabwah, where his residence was often the scene of literary discussions on religious and other subjects. His personality may, without exaggeration, be said to be an encyclopaedia of learning, His mastery over the Urdu language was an additional charm, which added to the excellence of his speech and dialectical skill. Poetry was his special subject. He had a great veneration for Amir Minai, his instructor in poetry. Ghazal was his special domain, but he handled many more subjects of his choice. He was a well-read man who had a keen eye on the works of ancient and modern Urdu poets.

One of the many prominent achievements of Hafiz Sahib was his learning of the comparative religions of the world. The deep and intensive study of the books of the Promised Messiah(as) had enriched his knowledge of Christianity and Hinduism. He possessed a great missionary spirit and was never tired of preaching the truth for hours, yet his mode of speaking was never tiring or irksome. Even if he was weak and feeble, an objection on Islam or Ahmadiyyat would bring him into a real missionary spirit and there would remain no signs of weakness and his voice and expression would grow more impressive.

Hafiz Sahib took pains in training young Ahmadiyya missionaries in the art of conducting religious controversies with opponents. He was often asked by the Centre to accompany Ahmadiyya deputations that visited important towns in U.P. Young writers of the Community read out their manuscripts to him for correction before sending them to the press. He took care to see that the manuscript was correct with regard to language, diction and logic.

Hafiz Sahib was a strong advocate of Ahmadiyya Khilafat and served this blessed institution most faithfully throughout his life giving all allegiance to each of the Khalifa in whose time he lived. His love and reverence for all the members of the Promised Messiah's family (peace be on him) was well-known. In general, he had a soft heart for everyone who came in contact with him. His real age is not known with certainty but it is believed that he was over 100 years when he passed away.

(76) Hadhrat Munshi Abdullah Sanauri (1861-1927)

Hadhrat Munshi Abdullah Sahib was born in 1861 and he belonged to Sanaur of Patiala State. His family were well-educated farmers. After achieving appropriate qualifications Munshi Sahib undertook an assignment in the local Revenue office. In 1885, he worked as Patvari in the of village Ghaus Garh of Patiala State.

Munshi Sahib was a very pious person and kept company with religious and spiritual people. His maternal uncle, Maulawi Muhammad Yousaf Sahib introduced him to Hadhrat Maulawi Abdullah Sahib Ghaznavi, a divinely person, who made such an impact on Munshi Sahib with his knowledge, that he took his Bai'at with him – however Munshi Sahib seeked more. Munshi Sahib's uncle was aware of his inner feelings and wanted to send him to 'Ara' in Bihar Province, which was the Centre of Ahl-i-Hadees Sect. During this time, the book *Baraheen-e-Ahmadiyya* by Hadhrat Mirza Ghulam Ahmad(as) reached Khalifa Syed Muhammad Hussain Khan Sahib Bahadur, Prime Minister of Patiala State. The book became very popular amongst people of Patiala. Munshi Abdullah Sahib was told about the book and which mentioned about Promised Messiah's(as) claim and it was suggested that Munshi Sahib should go and meet him personally.

Hadhrat Munshi Sahib travelled to Qadian in 1882. As soon he saw the Promised Messiah(as), his heart was filled with love and affection for him. The Promised Messiah(as) asked his name, to which Munshi Sahib replied, 'Abdullah' and that he was from Sanaur, near Patiala. He stayed with the Promised Messiah(as) for three days. When he returned to Patiala, he could not stay there, so he returned to Qadian. The Promised Messiah(as) asked him why he was there again to which Munshi Sahib replied that he could not bear to leave his company. So he stayed another week or so.

It was Munshi Sahib's desire to leave various mundane affairs and migrate to Qadian permanently to enjoy the company of the Promised Messiah(as). But Hadhrat Aqdas advised him not to leave the job. He used to come to Qadian on and off and Hadhrat Aqdas used to send him on various jobs to Amritsar and Lahore giving him necessary journey's fare.

Munshi Sahib learnt the translation of several chapters of the Holy Qur'an from the Promised Messiah(as) himself. He travelled with the Promised Messiah(as) to Patiala, Ambala, Amritsar, Ludhihana, Hoshiarpur, and Ali Garh etc. On 22nd January 1886, when the Promised Messiah(as) travelled to Hoshiarpur for forty-days seclusion for meditation and prayers, Hadhrat Munshi Sahib, Hadhrat Hafiz Hamid Ali Sahib and Fateh Khan Sahib accompanied him and each was assigned important tasks during his stay there.

On the birth of Mirza Bashir-ud-Din Mahmud Ahmad(ra) on 12th January 1889, the Promised Messiah(as) wrote a personal letter on 15th January, 1889 to Munshi Sahib conveying this good news and also informing him of the ceremony of 'Aquiqa' to be held on a certain day (Friday).

On 23rd March, 1989 at Ludhihana, Munshi Sahib took Bai'at at the hands of the Promised Messiah(as). His name is number four on the list. He was a fortunate person to serve the Promised Messiah(as) on that occasion.

On 10th July 1885, when after Fajr prayer the Promised Messiah(as) was having rest in a room in the Mosque, Hadhrat Munshi Sahib witnessed the great sign of 'Red Spots'. He requested the Promised Messiah(as) that the shirt with 'Red Spots' be given to him. The Promised Messiah(as) granted this with the condition that the shirt should be buried along with him on his death. So, the shirt was buried along with him when he died on Friday 7th October 1927.

(77) **Hadhrat Munshi Ahmad Din, Kakrali** (d1889)

Hadhrat Munshi Ahmad Din Sahib was born in 1889 at Kakrali, a village in Tehsil Kharian, District Gujrat of the Punjab province.

After his primary education, he studied from Hadhrat Mian Muhammad Din Sahib, a very noble teacher and completed his Middle School education and Junior Vernacular (J.V) teacher's course under his supervision. He used to spend most of his time with Hadhrat Mian Muhammad Din who was one of the spiritual fruits from Jehlum of the Promised Messiah(as).

During the Promised Messiah's(as) visit to Jehlum, Mian Muhammad Din Sahib was teaching at Malka and used to read *Al-Hakam* and *Al-Badr* newspapers of the Jama'at. He had pre-determined in his mind before leaving for Jehlum that if the Promised Messiah(as) put his hand on his shoulder, he would accept Ahmadiyyat and submit to him. It so happened that when he arrived at Jehlum, he met a huge assembly of people there and practically found it impossible for him to see the Promised Messiah(as) and to have him touch his shoulder was out of the question. He became very upset of the situation and was in deep thoughts when suddenly the Promised Messiah(as) came out of the crowd and by putting his hand on his shoulder asked him what he was thinking about and what his name was. In this way, Allah Almighty miraculously fulfilled his desire and he immediately submitted to the Promised Messiah(as) by signing Bai'at and joining Nizam-e-Wasiyyat at the same time.

Hadhrat Munshi Ahmad Din Sahib used to spend most of his time in the company of Mian Muhammad Din. In 1928, he was taken ill with a carbuncle, a killer disease. He had read and knew that the Mahdi as prophesied, would cure people from ailments and that with his prayers, the sick would be relieved of their sufferings. Having that in mind he started praying. His prayers were accepted and Allah granted him full recovery from the killer disease. He visited Qadian in 1929 and signed Bai'at at the blessed hand of Hadhrat Khalifatul-Masih II(ra)and at the same time joined the system of Wasiyyat.

After joining Ahmadiyyat, Hadhrat Munshi Sahib lived as a devotee deeply involved and strongly committed to preaching. He bore an outspoken and intelligent personality. He was an intellect bestowed with quick thinking and reasoning faculties. On several occasions, he was assaulted, boycotted and humiliated in the course of his preaching activities. He was transferred from one school to another many times. He was deprived from the right of his property and assets inherited from his father because of his religious beliefs.

Hadhrat Munshi Sahib also loved farming and was content with all he had. He was a staunch Ahmadi who never compromised and feared in saying the truth even in front of worldly leaders.

Hadhrat Munshi Sahib chose teaching as a profession with a missionary spirit and dedication to inculcate and promote the love of education in his own community. Every day, he would bring to school one new child of his Community and that was how he motivated the whole area towards education and literacy. He was highly respected by the people in the areas wherever he served as a teacher. He was also a descendant of the first Muslim who accepted Islam and converted the whole Community to Islam during the rule of Aurang Zaib Alamgir.

Hadhrat Munshi Sahib took Bai'at in 1929 but having spent most of his time with Hadhrat Mian Muhammad Din since 1904, he was always motivated towards Ahmadiyyat. He established Jama'ats in Nigerian, Kalas, Sadhwal Khurd, Bhandgran, Shampur, Banian and Bhahurch. He was responsible for supervision of the first Jama'at at Kakrali. All this was done in the company of Hadhrat Mian Muhammad Din Sahib. Hadhrat Munshi Sahib had occupied the position of Secretary and President of Kakrali Jama'at, respectively till his demise. He taught in Nigeria for 17 years (at the village of Ataullah Shah Bukhari) and Allah enabled him to establish a Jama'at through Mian Muhammad Alam Sahib. He was also assigned the task of preparing the ancestral tree of Ataullah Shah Bukhari by Hadhrat Khalifat-ul-Masih II(ra) which he successfully and jointly completed with the help of the Mian Muhammad Alam.

Hadhrat Munshi Sahib spent his whole life in the service of religion, humanity and his Community. He was very punctual and regular in his daily worship including Tahajjud prayers throughout his life and advocated the same to his children. He regularly participated in all spiritual and financial schemes of the Jama'at and inculcated the same habit among his family.

Hadhrat Munshi Sahib passed away on 12th November, 1964 and was buried at Bahishti Maqbara, Rabwah. In December 1964, the *Al Fazl* published his autobiography.

His only son Mian Ghulam Ahmad is a well-known member of Faisalabad Jama'at while his grandsons Mian Mubarak Ahmad Eyaz, Pakistan, Mian Muzaffar Ahmad Mansoor, Mian Mubashir Ahmad Khalid and Mian Munawar Ahmad Tahir are all devoted servants of Ahmadiyyat and Khilafat.

(80) Hadhrat Munshi Aroora Khan Sahib

Munshi Aroora Khan was one of the earliest Companions of the Promised Messiah(as). He had read the Promised Messiah's book *Baraheen-e-Ahmadiyya* which he acquired through Munshi Abdur Rahman of Kapoorthala. After reading this, he was greatly impressed and concluded that such a book could not be written without the true guidance of God Almighty and that Hadhrat Mirza Ghulam Ahmad(as) was indeed the Imam of the Muslims. He, therefore, went to Qadian and requested him to take his Oath of Initiation. But the Promised Messiah(as) said that, so far, he had not been commanded by God Almighty to take the Oath of Initiation of any person. This was in the year 1889 that the Promised Messiah(as) was commanded take the oaths of Initiation from his followers.

In the book *Seerat-e-Zafar*, a book about Hadhrat Munshi Zafar Sahib of Kapoorthala, it is related that: 'The Promised Messiah announced that God Almighty has commanded him to start taking the Oath of Initiation of those who were very keen and anxious about it. Therefore, my father, Sheikh Zafar Ahmad, Muhammad Khan and Munshi Aroora Khan received a letter from the Promised Messiah(as) which read: "You were very keen to take the Oath of Initiation at my hand. This letter is written to inform you that God Almighty has now granted me permission to accept the Oaths of Initiation of all those who were keen about it.'

As has been mentioned in that letter, all those who had been informed did reach Ludhiana on that date and took the Oath of Initiation at the hands of the Promised Messiah(as). His number of Initiation, as marked on the Register of Initiations is 26. The entry is as given below:

> 'Aroora son of Jeevan, Kapoorthala Judicial Draftsman Kapoorthala Court'
> (History of Ahmadiyyat, vol.2 p.202).'

Munshi Aroora Khan had the honour of being among the first three hundred and thirteen followers who had taken the Oath of Initiation on that day.

In 1914, Mr. Walter who was the Secretary of All India Y.M.C.A, Association came to Qadian with a view to obtain some information regarding the Ahmadiyya Movement in Islam and wished to meet any of the Companions of the Promised Messiah(as) and Munshi Aroora Khan Sahib was introduced to him. After a brief conversation, Mr. Walter asked Aroora Khan Sahib which argument about the truth of the Promised Messiah(as) convinced him most? To this he replied: 'Though he was not a very literate person, yet what impressed most was the personality of the Promised Messiah(as) himself.' Aroora Khan Sahib further added that he never saw a person other than the Promised Messiah(as) who was more honest, trustworthy and had a firm belief in God. As he said these words, he burst into tears feeling nostalgic about the company of the Promised Messiah(as). This event had a profound effect on Mr. Walter so much so that he mentioned this occasion in his book *Ahmadiyya Movement* and commented that 'a person who could produce such followers could not be labeled as an imposter.' (*Tarikh-i-Ahmadiyyat*, vol.5; p.208)

Such was the blessed Aroora Khan Sahib who led a simple and saintly life. These qualities were the product of his association with the Promised Messiah(as) who had ingrained the love of God in the minds of his followers. *(This article was compiled by Nasrullah Khan Nasir, M.A. Shahid).*

(79) **Hadhrat Sheikh Mushtaq Hussain**
(1878-1949)

Hadhrat Sheikh Mushtaq Hussain was born in 1878. He accepted Ahmadiyyat in 1900 after seeing a poster on a wall that said that the Messiah promised for that century has appeared. Having read it, he felt in his heart an attraction towards the Promised Messiah(as) and immediately wrote a letter in which he accepted him.

Sheikh Mushtaq Sahib had the honour to personally meet the Promised Messiah(as) on 15th May 1908, only a few days before the Promised Messiah(as) passed away. It was the occasion when Sheikh Mushtaq Sahib was present when the well-known Muslim political leaders, Sir Fazl-I-Hussain and Hafiz Abdul Kareem also met the Promised Messiah(as).

When the plague spread all over the country in India and people were dying in great numbers, Sheikh Mushtaq Sahib continued preaching Ahmadiyyat – the true Islam. At that time, he used to reside inside Bhaati Gate on the first floor of a house whose ground floor was occupied by some other tenant. Each and every one of them died of the plague and his friends advised him to leave the location and to live somewhere else. However, he told them that the germs of the plague could not do him any harm because he was a true Ahmadi Muslim.

He often gave a copy of the booklet *Kishti-I-Nuh*, written by the Promised Messiah(as) to the residents of that house and advised them to read it carefully and adopt the true faith of Islam.

Sheikh Mushtaq Sahib used to be a clerk in the railway administration. But during the time of Hadhrat Khalifatul-Masih I(ra), he gave up his service and began supplying meat to the British Army at Peshawar. Once, Hafiz Roshan Ali Sahib went to Peshawar and stayed with him at his house. It was here that he learnt of the sad demise of Hadhrat Khalifatul-Masih I(ra). He was the first Ahmadi who sent a telegram from Peshawar of his Oath of Initiation to Hadhrat Khalifatul-Masih II(ra).

Having stayed for sometime at Peshawar he came to reside at Gujranwala. He was always nominated by the Gujranwala Jama'at to represent them in the Advisory Council (Shura) held at Qadian. While he was at Gujranwala, he wrote a number of pamphlets in support of the truth of Ahmadiyyat.

Sheikh Mushtaq Hussain truly loved the Holy Qur'an and he very often used to recite an Urdu verse from one of the poems of the Promised Messiah(as). It translates: 'It is the most true desire of my heart always to kiss the Book that Thou hast revealed: And circuit it round as I deem it to be my Ka'aba.'

He used to get each and every paper that was published by the Ahmadiyya community. and had collected quite a large number of books. He also used to buy many books to give as a free gift to those he preached.

Sheikh Mushtaaq Hussain Sahib was also among the first five thousand Mujahideen of Tahrik Jadid. He passed away on 23rd August 1949.

(80) **Hadhrat Hafiz Nabi Bakhsh** (1860(est)-1942)

Hadhrat Hafiz Nabi Bakhsh Sahib was born in the village Faizullah Chak (which is situated at a distance of 5 miles from Qadian). The exact date of his birth is not known, however, it was probably sometime between 1860-1865. His father, Hakim Karim Bakhsh, was employed in the Canal Department. He was a very pious person and followed the Ahl-e-Hadith School of thought. He was a devoted follower of Islam and the Holy Qur'an and arranged for his son, Hafiz Nabi Bakhsh to learn the Qur'an by heart. After he accomplished this noble task, Hafiz Nabi Bakhsh Sahib was sent to school and later followed in the footsteps of his father by joining the Canal Department. In those days, the Canal Department had earned a bad name for bribery, but he kept himself aloof from such evils and served the department very sincerely and devotedly.

In his young age, Hafiz Sahib availed the opportunity to be in the company of the Promised Messiah(as). He used to travel to Qadian on foot to say his Tahajjud and Fajr prayers. The Promised Messiah(as) once said his prayer in congregation while Hafiz Sahib led the prayer.

Hafiz Sahib sent all his children to Qadian for their education. Around 1906, his son Abdul Rehman, drowned in a deep pond at Qadian and on the very same day, his two daughters were to be married and the bridal processions were expected to come on that day. The parents of the bridegrooms requested for the postponement of the marriage due to this sad demise. However, Hafiz Sahib did not agree to the postponement. He submitted himself to the Will of God very patiently and the marriages were performed as planned in a normal way. When the Promised Messiah(as) came to know about Hafiz Sahib's patience during this ordeal and his submission to the Will of Allah, he specially prayed to Allah to shower His blessings on him.

Hadhrat Hafiz Sahib had four sons and six daughters. However, two of his sons had died at an early age. and the remaining children served the Jama'at devotedly. His son, Hadhrat Hakim Fazlur Rehman Sahib, devoted his life during the Second Khilafat and served in West Africa as a Missionary. He spent about a quarter of a century in Africa alone leaving behind his wife and children.

Mr. Abdul Shakoor of Radio Electric Centre, Multan Cantonment, narrates a personal episode of having witnessed the love and affection of Hadhrat Hafiz Nabi Bakhsh Sahib for Hadhrat Musleh Mau'od(ra) and his complete submissiveness. He says: 'One day my aunt, Mrs. Suraya Begum, wife of Hadhrat Hakim Fazlur Rehman Sahib (Missionary Africa) said to Hadhrat Hafiz Nabi Bakhsh Sahib that

Hakim Sahib has been away from us for the last eight years and now Hadhrat Musleh Mau'od(ra) has issued orders of transfer of certain missionaries, will you please ask Hudhur to call back Hakim Sahib too.'

When Hadhrat Hafiz Sahib heard this plea, his lips started quivering with the ecstasy of solid faithful feelings. For a while, he could not utter a word, but after a long silence, he said: 'I do understand your pain and position, but how often have I told you that I cannot and will not do that because Fazalur Rehman is not my son any more, as I have offered him to Hudhur for the services of faith. Nonetheless, as you are his wife, you can go yourself and request Hudhur. This is your right and I will not be in your way. I am on my last leg, do you wish to spoil my well-earned faith?' He became speechless as he choked with sentiments.

One of his other sons, Malik Habibur Rehman Sahib, served within the education department of Punjab. To one of his daughters, Hajira Begum, was born a son who became a shining star of Ahmadiyyat and became a world-renowned scientist. His name was Dr. Abdus Salam, a Noble Laureate. He was awarded the Noble Prize in honour for his outstanding research in Physics in 1979.

Hadhrat Hafiz Sahib took Bai'at on the 10th March 1890 and his name is registered at No.181. He was the third fortunate amongst his villagers to become an Ahmadi. He died on the 23rd March 1942, and was buried at Bahishti Maqbara, Qadian. Hadhrat Khalifatul Masih II(ra) led his Janaza prayer.

(81) **Chaudhary Nasrullah Khan**
(1863-1926)

The life and character of Chaudhary Nasrullah Khan Sahib is summed up most comprehensively in this short writing of Hadhrat Khalifatul Masih II(ra) who personally wrote the following Memorial Epitaph for Chaudhary Nasrullah Khan Sahib.

'In the name of Allah, the Gracious, the Merciful.
We praise Him and seek His blessings for His Noble Messenger.

Chaudhary Nasrullah Khan took his Oath of Initiation at the hand of the Promised Messiah in the year 1904 at Sialkot, though for many years before the initiation, he believed him to be a great spiritual leader and that he was indeed the Promised Messiah. His wife took the Oath of Initiation prior to her husband.

He was indeed a man of noble nature and advanced spiritually in leaps and bounds. He did learn by heart the whole of the Holy Qur'an at quite an elderly age.

It was because of my suggestion that he gave up his very successful practice as a Pleader and devoted himself to the service of the faith. It was during these days that he performed the Hajj to Makkah.

He had devoted himself very sincerely to the service of the Faith and whatever he did was done most sincerely and in a very capable manner.

I appointed him as the Nazir-e-A'ala and he performed all his duties in a very capable manner. He did indeed perform all his duties in order to achieve the pleasure of Allah the Almighty.

While seeking the pleasure of Allah the Almighty, he always performed his duties most sincerely and to my full satisfaction for which reason my heart is full of love for him. I pray to God Almighty to grant him immeasurable rewards and keep on showering great blessings on him and to grant his children to walk in the footsteps of their beloved father. I also pray most sincerely that God Almighty may grant many more people like the deceased to serve the true faith. Amen.'

Mirza Bashir-ud-Din Mahmud Ahmad – Khalifatul Masih II

Chaudhary Nasrullah Khan passed away on 3rd September 1926 at the age of 63 years.

(82) Hadhrat Nawab Muhammad Abdullah Khan (1896-1961)

Hadhrat Nawab Muhammad Abdullah Khan Sahib was born on 1st January 1896. He was six years old when Hadhrat Nawab Muhammad Ali Khan Sahib moved to Qadian after forsaking the royal life. After arriving in Qadian, Abdullah Khan Sahib was brought up under the direct guidance of the Promised Messiah(as), until he reached twelve and half years of age. In 1915, he passed Matriculation Examination from Talimul Islam High School, Qadian, during the second Khilafat.

On 7th June 1915, Abdullah Khan Sahib married Nawab Amtul Hafiz Begum Sahiba, the daughter of the Promised Messiah(as). She was named as 'Dukher-Keram' in a revelation to the Promised Messiah(as). The marriage was consummated on 22nd February 1917. At that time, he was studying in Government College, Lahore. After marriage he returned to Qadian.

In Qadian, Abdullah Khan Sahib served the Ahmadiyya Jama'at in different capacities. In 1919, he became acting Auditor of Sadr Anjuman Ahmadiyya and later served as Naib Nazir Talif and Isha'at. He also served as Nazir during Tahrik-e-Malkana, and brought back thousands of Muslims who left Islam during 'Tahrik-e-Shuddhi'. He also became the first Nazir-e-Aala after Independence of India and signed as Nazir-e-Aala on documents of purchase of land at Rabwah.

On 8th February 1949, while returning to his home in Rattan Bagh in Lahore, he fell on the ground following a severe heart attack. Hadhrat Musleh Mau'od(ra) and other Ahmadis prayed to Allah Almighty for his recovery fervently and with the Mercy of Allah, he recovered and lived for a further thirteen years.

Abdullah Khan Sahib was dedicated to prayers, especially congregational prayers. He regularly attended the Mosque for each of the five prayers and was often the first person to enter the Mosque that was built near his home.

Abdullah Khan Sahib passed away on 18th September 1961 after another heart attack.

(83) Hadhrat Nawab Muhammad Ali Khan (1870-1945)

Hadhrat Nawab Muhammad Ali Khan was born on 1st January 1870 which was the night between the 28th and 29th of Ramadhan 1286. Hadhrat Nawab Sahib belonged to the Ghauri family which can be traced back to a pious noble man Sheikh Sadr Jahan. The ancestors of Nawab Sahib were responsible for the founding of the principality of Malir Kotlah.

Hadhrat Nawab Sahib's father was Nawab Ghulam Mohammad Sahib. His mother Nawab Begum Sahiba, belonged to the branch of the family named Nusrat Khani.

Hadhrat Nawab Sahib was educated in the Chiefs College that used to be a popular institution for the education of the elite classes of India. His father died when he was about seven years.

Hadhrat Nawab Sahib married three times, twice within his own family and for the third time, he married one of the daughters of the Promised Messiah(as), Hadhrat Sahibzadi Mubarika Begum Sahiba (may Allah be pleased with her) – thus Hadhrat Nawab Sahib had the privilege to become the son-in-law of the Promised Messiah(as). The marriage with Hadhrat Mubarika Begum was solemnised on 17th February 1908 and the Rukhstana ceremony took place on the 4th March 1909.

Hadhrat Nawab Sahib first heard about the Promised Messiah(as) from one of his teachers while he was only three or four years old. His correspondence with the Promised Messiah(as) first began in 1889 and he took Bai'at in November 1890. At first, he kept his Bai'at secret, but in 1891, he made it public and Hadhrat Masih-e-Mau'od(as) included a biographical account of him in his book *Izala-e-Auham*.

In 1892, he attended the Annual Gathering of the Jama'at in Qadian at the invitation of the Promised Messiah(as). When the prophecy of the Holy Prophet(saw) regarding eclipses of the sun and the moon was fulfilled as a sign of the advent of the Messiah, Hadhrat Nawab Sahib was at Qadian.

In 1901, Hadhrat Nawab Sahib moved permanently to Qadian. When Hadhrat Masih Mau'od(ra) established the Madrasa (school) Talim Muslim, Hadhrat Nawab Sahib contributed Rs.1000 towards it. At the time, he was also appointed the director of the school and was given full authority for its administration and expansion.

In a revelation of the Promised Messiah(as), Nawab Sahib was given the title of Hujjatullah (i.e. final argument or sign of Allah). Hadhrat Nawab Sahib also had the distinction that his son Nawab Mohammad Abdullah Khan Sahib was married to Syeda Nawab Amatul Hafiz Begum Sahiba, the daughter of the Promised Messiah(as), and his own daughter Bu Zainab Begum Sahiba was married to

Mirza Sharif Ahmad Sahib, one of the sons of the Promised Messiah(as).

Hadhrat Nawab Sahib also had the honour that Hadhrat Khalifatul Masih I(ra) gave his final Will and testament to him for safe keeping.

Hadhrat Nawab Sahib passed away on 10th February 1945 at Qadian at the age of 75. His funeral prayer was led by Hadhrat Khalifatul Masih II(ra) and he was buried in the special plot in Bahishti Maqbara Qadian, India.

(84) Sheikh Niaz Muhammad of Gujranwala

Sheikh Niaz Muhammad was the son of Sheikh Muhammad Bakhsh, Sub-Inspector Police, Batala, who was a sworn enemy of the Promised Messiah(as). It was he who broke open the locks of trunks in the house of the Promised Messiah(as) at the time of his house search after the murder of Pandit Lekh Ram of Peshawar in 1897. It is strange that Niaz Muhammad Sahib was guided to the truth of the Promised Messiah's(as) claim to be the Mahdi and Masih as given in the Holy Prophet's(saw) traditions. He came to Qadian with a sincere heart and met the Promised Messiah(as).

The short dialogue that took place between the Promised Messiah(as) and Niaz Muhammad Sahib is of interest and is reproduced here:

Sheikh Sahib: *'Hadhrat, I am thoroughly convinced of the truth of your claims to be the Mahdi and Messiah and am prepared to submit my allegiance to you but on one condition.*

The Promised Messiah: *'What is that'?*

Sheikh Sahib: *'Please Sir, pardon my father Muhammad Bakhsh whose attitude had been so hostile towards you.'*

The Promised Messiah: *'Yes, I do so'.*

Sheikh Sahib then pledged at his hand and his sincerity and faith just increased. After his retirement from police service, he settled at Qadian in 1941.

(85) Mian Noor Muhammad Khokhar

Mian Noor Muhammad Khokhar Sahib was a teacher in the Imdaadi Basti, Varyaam Kamlaana, post office, Dab Kalaana, Tahseel Shorkot of Distri Jhang.

The Promised Messiah(as) had mentioned his name as Sign No.141 in his book *Haqeeqat-ul-Wahee*. His younger brother, Noor Ahmad preached the Ahmadiyya faith to him and also gave him a copy of the Holy Qur'an translated by Shah Rafee-ud-Deen and requested him to read it everyday and to keep praying to God Almighty for guidance. This created a great love in his heart for the Promised Messiah(as). He, therefore, went together with Maulawi Muhammad Fazil Ahmadi to Qadian and offered his daily prayers with the Promised Messiah(as) for a few days.

On 15th August 1907, when the Promised Messiah(as) came to say his Asr prayers in the mosque, Muhammad Khokhar Sahib also prayed with him. When the prayers had ended, he stepped forward and requested the Promised Messiah(as) to be kind enough to accept his Oath of Initiation. After the Oath, the Promised Messiah(as) enquired about the state of affairs at Multan and said that most probably the people of that area were not very much opposed to Ahmadiyyat. However, Muhammad Khokhar Sahib replied that the people in that area were also bitterly opposed to Ahmadiyyat. On hearing this, the Promised Messiah(as) said: 'It is indeed quite strange that God Almighty has granted me followers from the places where the people are bitterly opposed to the Ahmadis. Where there is no opposition the number of Ahmadis in that area is also small.' This was later published with some other notes in the newspaper *Al-Hakam* of 24th August 1907.

Muhammad Khokhar Sahib was indeed a very humble person. He was very keen in looking after his poor neighbours. He was very regular in saying his Tahajjud prayers. Whenever he used to talk about the Promised Messiah(as), tears would flow from his eyes. He had deep affection and devotion for the Promised Messiah(as) and prayed vehemently for the progress of Ahmadiyyat as well as for Darveshan (those who were staying at Qadian after the partition of India.)

Muhammad Khokhar Sahib died in the Ganga Ram Hospital, Lahore and was buried in the graveyard of Rabwah. Hadhrat Khalifatul-Masih II(ra) led his funeral prayer.

(86) **Maulawi Obaidullah Bismil** (d.1938)

Maulawi Obaidullah Bismil was the son of Hadhrat Khwaja Mazhar Jamal, a follower of Imam Ali Shah of District Gurdaspur. Young Obaidullah studied the Holy Qur'an from Maulawi Ahmad and Persian lessons with Maulawi Muhammad Hassan. He studied Arabic with Maulawi Ghulam Ali of Qasur who was a staunch advocate of Shiaism. As he advanced in years, he studied medicine with Hakim Murad Ali of Batala who also happened to be a staunch Shia. It is no surprise, therefore, that a simple, young boy of immature views should catch the flame of Shiaism in the constant company of his teachers.

Young Obaidullah made a comparative study of Sunni and Shia views and became a devoted follower of Hadhrat 'Ali(ra). He also wrote a comprehensive book about Hadhrat 'Ali(ra). It was admitted by all at that time that no veteran Shia could write a book better than this. It was highly valued and much appreciated in India as well as in Iran. But the learned author was neither liked by the Shias nor loved by the Sunnis, because he overplayed the traits of Hadhrat 'Ali's(ra) character and was equally eloquent of Abu Bakr(ra) whom the Shias despised. The book however, earned him unparalleled reputation as an authority on Shiaism.

Maulawi Obaidullah rose like a bright star on the firmament of Persian literature. He was a great scholar of Persian and Arabic. The well-known poet Sanjar, poet-laureate of Rampur Darbar said that he could not write better than the author Maulawi Obaidullah.

Maulawi Nur-ud-Din Sahib, Hadhrat Khalifatul Masih I(ra) highly praised Maulawi Obaidullah's literary eminence and scholarly abilities in Persian and the Promised Messiah(as) called him the Firdossi of the age.

Maulawi Obaidullah was a man of simple habits and nature. He was free from sectarian prejudices and was an ardent seeker after truth wherever it lay.

After reading the book *Sirrul Khilafa (Secret of the Caliphate)* written by Hadhrat Mirza Ghulam Ahmad(as), it opened his eyes. He saw in a vision the Hadhrat Imam Hussein telling a man to inform the Promised Messiah(as) that he (Imam Hussein) was there at his disposal. The truth of the Promised Messiah(as) dawned upon him and he hastened to Qadian accompanied by Qureshi Muhammad Hussain of Lahore and came into the fold of Ahmadiyyat.

Maulawi Obaidullah was now at the disposal of his spiritual Master. He worked as Professor of Persian on the staff of Talimul Islam College, Qadian in 1903. He translated the *Tazkiratul-Shahadatain* into Persian and spent the remaining years of his life in the service of the Ahmadiyya Movement and performed many scholarly translations and writings.

Maulawi Obaidullah Bismil Sahib breathed his last on 29th September 1938. He was buried in the Bahishti Maqbara, Qadian.

(87) Hadhrat Sahibzada Pir Manzoor Muhammad (1866-1950)

Pir Manzoor Muhammad was born at Ludhiana (India) in 1866. He was amongst those Companions of the Promised Messiah(as) who took the Covenant Bai'at at a very early stage.

Hadhrat Pir Sahib had made great efforts to become an expert in Urdu calligraphy. His intention was to be of some service to the Promised Messiah(as) in publishing his book in a beautiful format. Most of the first editions of books published by Pir Sahib bear testimony to his great skills in calligraphy.

In 1899, the Promised Messiah(as) issued a poster in which he specifically mentioned services rendered to him by Pir Manzoor Muhammad in the publication of his books. He also mentioned in this poster that it was Allah's special favour to him that a faithful and loyal person like Pir Sahib was available to him even at odd hours of day and night for whatever the duty assigned to him.

Hadhrat Pir Sahib had left his stamp of ingenuity in many other fields too. When he became ill during his work as calligrapher, he obtained permission from the Promised Messiah(as) for teaching his blessed children the technique of reading of the Holy Qur'an. It was during this period that Pir Sahib invented the world famous primer 'The Yassernal Qur'an'.

It was through the medium of this unique primer that hundreds of thousands of people in Asia and Africa were able to read the Qur'an correctly and fluently. So far many editions of this Primer have been printed. In praise of this famous booklet (called Qaidah) the Promised Messiah(as) wrote a Couplet in Urdu.

O Allah, have mercy on him as well who taught (the Holy Qur'an to children).
O Allah reward him adequately in this world and the Hereafter.
O Allah, show the right way of Teaching (the Holy Qur'an).
Holy is He who frustrates my enemies.
(Durre Sameen)

Pir Manzoor Muhammad first met the Promised Messiah(as) in 1884 and later took the Covenant of Bai'at at Ludhiana in 1892. He died at Rabwah in June 1950 and was buried in Bahishti Maqbara. Hadhrat Pir Sahib was the son of Sufi Ahmad Jan of Ludhiana and brother-in-law of Hadhrat Maulana Hakim Nur-ud-Din – Khalifatul-Masih I(ra).

(88) Sahibzada Pir Sirajul Haq Sahib Nomani

Hadhrat Sahibzada Pir Sirajul Haq Sahib Nomani came from the village of Sarsawa of District Saharanpur. He was pious and blessed person and an early Companion of Hadhrat Promised Messiah(as). He belonged to a keeper of a saint's tomb and himself was a great Pir (Saint) and had hundreds of followers.

Siraj Haq Sahib migrated to Qadian and settled there permanently. He took Bai'at at the hands of the Promised Messiah(as) on 23rd December 1889. Hadhrat Promised Messiah(as) decided to send him on a long journey for some religious missions.

Sirajal Haq Sahib was blessed to spend a lot of time in the company of the Promised Messiah(as). He used to write copies of the Promised Messiah's(as) writings and was responsible for the correspondence on his behalf. He was also devoted to other literary duties.

Sirajul Haq Sahib accompanied Hadhrat Aqdas at his Ludhiana visit and was also present during the Al-Haq debate with Maulawi Muhammad Hussain of Batala. Hadhrat Sahibzada Sahib had the opportunity to write down the details of events during the journeys while accompanying the Promised Messiah(as) which were later published in his two-volume compilation titled *Tazkaratul Mahdi*.

On the instructions of the Promised Messiah(as), Siraj Haq Sahib sent the message of truth to various other religious scholars and keepers of saint's tombs. The very first person was Maulawi Rashid Ahmad Gangovi who was a great scholar and a religious authority. He was also his brother-in-law. He wrote letters to prominent keepers of tombs like Mian Allah Bakhsh Taunsvi Sanghri and Shah Nazamuddin Barelvi Niazi. Sajjada Nasheen Sanghri gave no reply but the Promised Messiah(as) received an answer from Barelvi in which Shah Nizamuddin Barelvi expressed his inability to face the debate or the dialogue. He wrote that this was the job of Maulawis or scholars.

Hadhrat Sahibzada Pir Sirajul Haq Sahib was a great scholar and a pious man gifted with true visions and dreams. This was the basic reason, which helped him to accept the message of Ahmadiyyat.

(89) **Hadhrat Maulawi Abdul Qadir Khan**

(1840-1920)

Hadhrat Maulawi Abdul Qadir Khan, son of Maulawi Muhammad Musa of Ludhiana belonged to a very respectable family. He was born in 1840 in the Rajput dynasty and became a well-respected and reputable preacher of Ahmadiyyat. His father was also a pious preacher of the Hanafi Sect in Islam and was well known in the surrounding areas became of his morals and spirituality. His family resided in land Panjara, Tehsil Khana Distt. Ludhiana, but due to different upheaval in the country, the family was refused into other parts of Punjab Province, Lahore Amritsar and Ferozpur. During his lifetime, he married four times and had 10 children.

Maulawi Abdul Qadir Sahib and his father were closely attached to the Promised Messiah(as). They considered the Promised Messiah(as) to be the Chosen One by Allah. Hadhrat Sheikh Yaqooh Ali Irfani in his book *Hayat-e-Ahmad*, has also explained the fact that even after the publication of Part 3 of his famous book, *Barahin-e-Ahmadiyya,* whilst the holy character of the Promised Messiah(as) was evident to many people, the Promised Messiah(as) preferred to remain in solitude.

The town of Ludhiana was becoming a nucleus for the devotees of Hadhrat Promised Messiah(as). All these devotees were waiting anxiously for a 'call' from the Promised Messiah(as) and were ready to travel to Qadian for Bai'at at short notice. Maulana Dost Muhammad Sahib Shahid has also mentioned in his book, *Tarikh-e-Ahmadiyyat,* that since these devotees were very closely attached to the Promised Messiah(as), they requested him to visit Ludhiana. The Promised Messiah(as) accepted this and travelled to Ludhiana in the beginning of 1884. The railway station was full of people wishing to welcome him on his arrival including Maulawi Abdul Qadir Sahib and his father.

It is further narrated that it was at the time of Asr prayer when the Promised Messiah(as) arrived. He performed ablution but did 'Massah' on his socks. Some people enquired from the Promised Messiah(as) if that was allowed, he replied 'yes'.

Maulawi Muhammad Musa requested the Promised Messiah(as) to lead the prayer, but he declined and allowed Maulawi Abdul Qadir Sahib to do so. In fact, Maulawi Abdul Qadir Sahib had the honour to lead all the prayers with the exception of the morning prayer during the Promised Messiah's(as) stay in Ludhiana. Many visited the Promised Messiah(as) in Ludhiana and when he would go for a walk, many accompanied him.

Hadhrat Mirza Bashir-ud-Din Ahmad(ra) elaborated this in his book, *Seeratul Mehdi*, that the Promised

Messiah[as] said his prayers behind others including Maulawi Nur-ur-Din Sahib[ra], Hadhrat Maulawi Abdul Karim Sialkoti, Hadhrat Hakim Fazal Din Sahib, Pir Siraj-ul-Haq Nomani Sahib, Maulawi Abdul Qadir Sahib, Maulawi Sarwar Shah Sahib, Maulawi Muhammad Ahsan Amrohi Sahib and Pir Iftikhar Ahmad Sahib.

The daughter of Maulawi Abdul Qadir, Ustani Safia Begum who was a very pious and famous learned teacher within the Jama'at, once narrated that when her grandfather Maulawi Moosa Sahib met the Promised Messiah[as] for the first time, he was so over whelmed by his facial appearance, that he abruptly addressed Promised Messiah[as] in Punjabi which meant: 'I find the prophetic sublime glaze on your face, Hudhur, please accept my allegiance.' The Promised Messiah[as] replied in Punjabi that he was not commanded to take Bai'at. Moosa Sahib died before the Promised Messiah's[as] claim but he left a will for his progeny that Hadhrat Mirza Sahib[as] was the Promised Messiah and Mahdi of the age and that in no way should they ignore him.

The Promised Messiah[as] allowed Maulawi Abdul Qadir Sahib to accept allegiance from people on his behalf. Dr. Hashmatullah Khan Sahib of Patiala initiated Bai'at when he was only sixteen at the hands of Maulawi Abdul Qadir Sahib along with five other members of his family as authorised by the Promised Messiah[as]. He was also among the first 313 Companions of the Promised Messiah[as] and his name appears at No. 41 in the list. He also attended the first Jalsa Salana in 1891. Hadhrat Promised Messiah[as] also mentioned about the firm faith and financial sacrifices of Maulawi Abdul Qadir Sahib in his book, *Azala Auham*.

Maulawi Sahib migrated to Qadian around 1895. The incident of his wife joining the fold of Ahmadiyyat is worth mentioning here. One day she was at home with her children and suddenly they heard the continuous sound of something falling outside. They came out and saw fresh berry fruits falling from now where and also someone calling her name 'Safia, Safia.' She went to the house of the Promised Messiah[as] to report the incident to Hadhrat Ammanjan, the wife of the Promised Messiah[as]. Upon hearing the phenomenon, Hadhrat Ammanjan said to her that this was not a good sign and that she should immediately return home. When she came back she saw that the children were still busy in fruit-picking and then suddenly with a big bang the roof of the children's room fell. She then knew that Allah, the Almighty had saved her and the children from catastrophe and soon after this she accepted Ahmadiyyat.

Hadhrat Maulawi Abdul Qadir remained involved in the teaching the Holy Qur'an, giving sermons and explaining about Islam throughout his life. He was also a Hafiz Qur'an and would lead Taraveeh prayers during Ramadan.

He had a very close personal relationship with Hadhrat Khalifatul Masih I(ra) and II(ra). Hadhrat Musleh Mau'od(ra) paid a visit to his house when he became ill to enquire of his health. He passed away on 31st December 1920 in Qadian and was buried in a special enclosure reserved for the Companions of the Promised Messiah(as).

(90) **Mir Qasim Ali, Qadian** (d.1942)

Mir Qasim Ali joined the fold of Ahmadiyya Movement in July 1902. He had extensive knowledge of contemporary religions especially Christianity and Hinduism and was from among the great spiritual talents of Qadian.

Mir Qasim Sahib was an excellent debater, well known for his eloquence and arguments. While at Delhi, he successfully edited the *Al-Haq* and another monthly publication. When he finally settled at Qadian in 1920, he started *Al-Farooq* which served the cause of Ahmadiyyat and proved very effective against the bitter and venomous criticism of some Muslim publications from Lahore and Amritsar.

His mighty pen produced a number of publications which proved to be a valuable contribution to the Ahmadiyya literature. Perhaps the masterpiece of his literary attainments was the compilation and publication in chronological order of all the Ishtiharat (announcements or circulars) of the Promised Messiah(as) from beginning to end in ten volumes. As a result of his long stay in Delhi, Mir Qasim Sahib acquired a taste for Urdu literature and poetry, which he profitably used in his lectures and writings.

Mir Sahib was a fine gentleman, with polite speech and pleasant manners. He took a keen interest in the up-bringing of his near relatives and orphans of the Community. One day, as he was coming out of the Noor mosque at Qadian after Maghrib prayers, he slipped from the steps of the Mosque and fell on his side. Two of his ribs were fractured. At the beginning, Mir Qasim Sahib did not take it seriously but the pain increased as the time went by his illness took a serious turn and he passed away in April 1942. Hadhrat Khalifatul Masih II(ra) led his funeral prayer and he was buried in the Bahishti Maqbara at Qadian along with the other Companions of the Promised Messiah(as).

(91) **Hadhrat Babu Qasimudin** (1893-1986)

Babu Qasimudin Sahib was born in 1893 in Sialkot, Pakistan. He had the honour to be initiated into Ahmadiyyat at the hands of the Promised Messiah(as). He worked for a long time at the office of the Deputy Commissioner, Sialkot. During his employment, he demonstrated such honesty and. trustworthiness that people remembered for a long a time after he has left.

Babu Qasimudin Sahib spent most of his time dedicated to services for the Community. He was a kind, honest, sincere and very pious. He had a true and dedicated love and respect for the Promised Messiah(as) and Khilafat. After the establishment of Tahrik Jadid, Babu Qasimudin Sahib contributed half his salary to this institution. He also had the honour for being the Amir of Jama'at Ahmadiyya, Sialkot for 28 years. He passed away on 11th October 1986.

(92) **Qazi Muhammad Abdullah** (1986-1972)

Hadhrat Qazi Muhammad Abdullah was the younger son of Hadhrat Qazi Zia-ud-deen. He was born on 9th November 1986 at Qazi Kot in the district of Gujranwala. The Promised Messiah(as) wrote a letter to him in 1901 and advised him to come and settle permanently in Qadian.

Muhammad Abdullah Sahib had not completed 3 years as a student when his father passed away. The Promised Messiah(as) was not at Qadian at that time but when he learnt about the demise of Qazi Zia-ud-deen, he wrote a letter to the officer in-charge of the community kitchen that his supply of daily food should be continued.

After obtaining his B.A. degree, Muhammad Abdullah Sahib also qualified as a trained teacher. In 1907, he approached the Promised Messiah(as) and offered his services to preach Ahmadiyyat for the rest of his life. In 1915, Hadhrat Khalifatul-Masih II(ra) asked him to go to London as a missionary to preach Islam. On 28th August 1915, the newspaper *Al-Hakam*, published the news: 'One more preacher of Islam has sailed for London.' That fortunate young man was Qazi Muhammad Abdullah, B.A., B.T.

At the time of his departure to London, Hadhrat Khalifatul Masih(ra) gave him the following instructions: -

> 'I hand you over to the care of God Almighty who will look after you. He is the God who is One and Alone. He Who has no son nor any wife. He alone will look after you and shall be your guide, your Protector and your teacher. May He be your Protector and look after you always. Ameen, Ameen'

Chaudhri Fateh Muhammad Sayaal Sahib was at that time, in-charge of the mission and Muhammad Abdullah Sahib started to work as his assistant which he did for 4 years.He was indeed a zealous worker in preaching Islam and was always foremost of the preachers of Islam. The London Mosque was purchased only a short time before his arrival though the old address of Melrose Road, SW18, London was still used by him for postal service.

On 30th November 1919, Muhammad Abdullah Sahib delivered a speech in which he told the audience how Islam was being preached in London. He said:

> 'All my friends and associates know very well that I used to live a very quiet life here among all of you and never had the opportunity of making a speech. It was our beloved leader and Imam who commanded me to come and preach Islam in London. I was indeed greatly worried of such a great responsibility and I prayed to

my God Almighty to grant me His help and guidance in my work. It was put into my mind that when help comes from God Almighty no one can ever defeat that person.

As the result of the above-mentioned glad tidings, I found that in England I had to stand against a number of Christian scholars and though none of them accepted me but I was always self-assured and knew that none of those high priests could really contradict me. We must, therefore, praise Him Who is the most Supreme."
(Al-Fazl, 4th December, 1919)

Hadhrat Qazi Muhammad Abdullah was appointed the officer-in-charge of the Annual Gathering after the demise of Hadhrat Mir Muhammad Ishaaq Sahib at Qadian and later at Rabwah also he was in-charge of the Annual Gathering for a number of years.

The name of Qazi Muhammad Abdullah Sahib is also included among the first 313 Companions of the Promised Messiah(as) along with his elder brother Hadhrat Qazi Abdul Raheem and his father Qazi Zia-ud-deen.

Qazi Sahib passed away on 27th September 1972 at Rabwah and his funeral prayers were led by Hadhrat Khalifa-tul Masih III(ru) who was also present in the graveyard when he was buried in the area reserved for the Companions of the Promised Messiah(as) at Bahishti Maqbara, Rabwah. Hadhrat Khalifa-tul Masih III(ru) also instructed that Qazi Sahib's wife must not be asked to vacate the house where she was residing.

(93) **Qazi Sayyed Ameer Hussain of Bhera**

Qazi Ameer Hussain was one of the older Companions of the Promised Messiah(as). He joined the fold of Ahmadiyyat in 1893 when the great controversy between Christianity and Islam was in progress at Amritsar. Qazi Ameer Hussain belonged to a Sayed family of Bhera in the Shahpur (now Sargodha) District of the Punjab. His father was a prosperous dealer in horses. Young Ameer Hussain first took interest in his father's trade, but suddenly lost all interest and devoted himself to the acquisition of knowledge. After finishing his studies with his local teachers he undertook a long journey to Saharanpur in the United Provinces, where he specialised in the knowledge of the Hadith. From Saharanpur, he proceeded to Delhi and later to some other towns in the U.P. where he completed the course of his studies. He then returned to his native town of Bhera where he met with Maulawi Haji Hakim Nur-ud-Din, a great luminary of the Punjab. The acquaintance between the two soon developed into friendship and then into kinship when the latter gave the hand of his niece in marriage to Qazi Ameer Hussain.

Around 1893-94, Qazi Ameer Hussain was working in an institution in Amritsar. His association with the Ahmadiyya Movement was a signal for persecution, which he braved with courage and determination.

While still at Amritsar, Qazi Sahib received a letter from Maulawi Mohammad Ali M.A inviting him to come over to Qadian to take up the duties of the teacher of Theology in the Talim-ul-Islam High School at Qadian, to which he replied that he was prepared to accept the post provided the invitation had the approval of the Promised Messiah(as) or of Maulawi Nur-ud-Din(ra). He eventually accepted the post and arrived in Qadian where he was put in charge of the Theology class, which served as a nucleus of the present Jamia Ahmadiyya, the Missionary College at Rabwah. He served as theology teacher in the Madrasa-i-Ahmadiyya headed by Sheikh Abdul Rahman Misri. Sheikh Sahib was a pupil of Qazi Sahib but so far as discipline was concerned, Qazi Sahib gave the best of his cooperation to the Headmaster of the School. He retired around 1925 but continued giving lessons in *Bukhari* and *Muslim* in the Masjid Mubarak at Qadian.

Qazi Ameer Hussain had his own views concerning the interpretation of some verses of the Holy Qur'an. He freely discussed these verses with Maulana-Nur-ud-Din Sahib(ra) but so great was his respect for the Khilafat that he stopped all discussions with him when the latter was chosen Head of the Ahmadiyya Community in 1908.

Similarly Qazi Sahib did not first

believe in the fatherless birth of Jesus Christ(as) but then he learnt that the Promised Messiah(as) so believed, he retired from his own view and took the line of his spiritual master. As a trustee of the Sadr Anjuman Ahmadiyya, Qadian and member of the Majlis-e-Shura, he always gave his opinion frankly and freely.

In the early part of 1930, Qazi Sahib fell seriously ill and his health was causing anxiety. It was feared that he would not live long. Hadhrat Khalifatul Masih II(ra) on his return from Shimla to Qadian went straight to see Qazi Sahib and seated himself on the bedstead by his feet. Qazi Sahib tried to sit up and was helped in doing so by Hadhrat Khalifatul Masih himself.

He breathed his last on 24th August, 1930 and was buried in the Bahishti Maqbara, Qadian the following day.

(Reproduced with thanks from *In the company of the Promised Messiah*, by Ch. Ali Muhammad BA. BT).

(94) **Qazi Mohammad Yusuf of Peshawar** (1883)

Qazi Muhammad Yusuf, son of Qazi Muhammad Saddique, was born at Hoti, Mardan District in 1883. He claimed to have descended from Hadhrat 'Umar Farooq, the Second Caliph after the Holy Prophet Muhammad(saw). His forefathers migrated from Madinah to India in search of employment and finally settled at Hoti in the Frontier Province in the time of Muhammad Shah, the Mughal Emperor of India. Ahmad Shah Abdali, King of Kabul, conferred upon Muhammad Qabil, Qazi Muhammad Yusuf's great grandfather, the office of Chief Justice.

Muhammad Yusuf Sahib's mother was a pious and a well-educated lady and taught him the Holy Qur'an. His father gave him lessons in Persian. Muhammad Yusuf Sahib was a bright student. He joined the Mission High School, Peshawar and passed his Primary stage with credit from the school. He learnt the Bible from his missionary teachers and won a number of prizes due to his academic abilities. He then joined the Islamia High School in Peshawar where he passed his Matriculation Examination in 1906.

While still a student at the Islamia High School, his English teacher Maulawi Khadim Hussain of Bhera introduced Muhammad Yusuf Sahib to the Ahmadiyya Movement. He later wrote a letter of allegiance to the Promised Messiah(as) at Qadian which was acknowledged in *Al-Hakam*, 28th February, 1902. He attended the Annual Conference of December 1902 and pledged his allegiance at the hands of the Promised Messiah(as).

Muhammad Yusuf Sahib's visited Qadian every year and was able to derive blessings in the company of the Promised Messiah(as). Muhammad Yusuf Sahib had a passionate zeal for the propagation of Islam and held open debates with Christians, Arya Samajists and the non-Ahmadi Ulema and was instrumental in bringing a large number of people into the fold of Ahmadiyyat. Maulawi Muhammad Yaqub Khan, editor of *The Light* was one of the fruits that he brought. On the strength of his sincerity and zeal for the Ahmadiyya Movement, Muhammad Yusuf Sahib was elected as the Amir of the Ahmadiyya Communities in the Frontier Province. He wrote number of treatises in Pashto in defence of Islam and the Ahmadiyya Movement and presented a set of his Pashto books to Khalifatul Masih I(ra) at Qadian in 1912 for which he was thanked and received Hudhur's prayers.

In March 1914, some of the influential Ahmadies of Lahore revolted against Khalifatul Masih II(ra). All the Ahmadies of Peshawar joined the Lahori Sect with the sole exception of Muhammad Yusuf Sahib. However, through prayers and incessant efforts, he convinced many to return. Maulawi Ghulam Hassan Khan also re-joined his old compatriots at Qadian. Master Faqir Ullah followed suit.

Muhammad Yusuf Sahib survived a brutal assault on 9th June 1935 in the Qassa Khwani Bazar of Peshawar. The culprit was imprisoned in another case for nine years. Through his sincere efforts, Ahmadiyya mosques with private quarters were erected at Peshawar, Mardan, Abbotabad, Kohat and Dere Ismail Khan. He dauntlessly preached Ahmadiyyat to the Afghan Chiefs and rulers of States and to his own English Officers in the Frontier.

Qazi Muhammad Yusuf Sahib was a man of letters. He was well versed in Persian, Urdu and Pashto literature and authored more than a hundred books and pamphlets in these languages. He also wrote in Urdu about the history of the spread of Ahmadiyyat in the Frontier Province.

(95) **Alhaj Maulawi Qudratullah Sanori** (1882-1968)

Hadhrat Maulawi Qudratullah Sanori was born at Sanor, Patiala State, India, in 1882. He accepted Ahmadiyyat in 1897, first through letter and then personally went to Qadian and was blessed with Bai'at at the hands of the Promised Messiah(as) in 1898.

Maulawi Sanori Sahib was the first person in his immediate family to accept Ahmadiyyat. As a result, his mother Karam-un-Nisa Begum joined the fold of Ahmadiyyat with the permission of her husband. She was a pious and good mannered lady. She was also a Moosi.

Maulawi Sanori Sahib's grandfather was about 100 years old when he also accepted Ahmadiyyat through a letter wriitten to the Promised Messiah(as).

Maulawi Sanori Sahib's father, Maulawi Muhammad Musa, born in 1842, was a very pious and learned person. He preached to Qudratullah Sahib about the Promised Messiah(as)'s claim and when he felt satisfied and convinced, Qudratullah Sahib also accepted Ahmadiyyat. His father died in 1927 at Sanor and his body was brought to Qadian and buried in Bahishti Maqbara, Qadian.

Maulawi Qudratullah Sahib was a well-known Companion of the Promised Messiah(as) and was extremely dedicated to the cause of Ahmadiyyat. He was a fearless preacher of Islam and a very inspired person. He had many true visions, which fulfilled in time.

During the time of the Promised Messiah(as) and later as well, he used to go regularly to Qadian and stay there as much as possible for him to benefit from the spiritual atmosphere.

In 1951, he was appointed by Hadhrat Mirza Bashir-ud-Din Mahmood Ahmad(ra) to collate and compile *Riwayat* (sayings and incidents) of the Promised Messiah(as) from his 'Sahibs'. An announcement about this was also published in *Al-Fazl*, 5th December 1915. and Qudratullah Sahib later published a book *Seerat-e-Ahmad* on the subject.

Maulawi Qudratullah Sahib was married to Rahim un Nisa Begum. This was arranged through consultations and blessings of the Promised Messiah(as). From this marriage, he had no children. He was very anxious and tried his level best for medical treatment from well-known doctors and hakims. In this context, he also consulted Dr. Abdul Hakeen, Assistant Surgeon, at Patiala who was very much opposed to Ahmadiyyat. After examining Maulawi Sahib's wife, he declared very confidently that she cannot bear a child throughout her life and cannot even conceive. Dr. Abdul Hakeen then challenged that if Hadhrat Mirza Ghulam Ahmad(as) is true in his claim as the Promised Messiah, then he should pray for Rahimun Nisa Begum to be able to bear a child.

Hadhrat Maulawi Sahib then sent his wife along with her father, Karim Bakhsh Sahib to Qadian where she met the Promised Messiah(as) and humbly requested the Promised Messiah(as) to pray for her that she should have some children. At that time the Promised Messiah(as) was strolling in his house. He prayed to Allah Almighty and then told her she had no illness. 'The doctors are wrong', he said: 'Go and tell your husband that you will have so many children that you will not be able to look after all of them.'

By the grace of Allah, fourteen children were born and the prophecy was fulfilled magnificently. Five children died in different ages, but four sons and five daughters had long lives and their progeny has flourished all over the world and serving the cause of Ahmadiyyat to the best of their capacities.

Hadhrat Maulawi Qudratullah Sanori served in Sind for 20 years as an Estates Manager for Jama'at's land and properties at Ahmadabad, Nasirabad, Mahmoodabad and Mubarakabad. Hadhrat Musleh Muhammad had mentioned about his sincere services and his vehement prayers in some of his sermons and letters.

Due to his old age, Qudratullah Sahib decided to reside in Rabwah and constructed a house on land purchased by his son Masood Ahmad. He served as President of that area, Darul Nasar for many years.

As the population of Rabwah increased, there was a need for a mosque. With the permission of Hadhrat Khalifatul Masih III(ru), he paid a substantial amount from his own resources and asked other members of his family to contribute as well. For this cause, he also travelled to different cities of Pakistan to gather enough funds for construction of the Mosque and a small garden with it. When the Mosque was constructed, Hadhrat Khalifatul Masih III(ru) named it as the Iqbal Mosque.

Maulawi Qudratullah Sahib was very regular in saying 'Tahajjud' prayers from his young age until his last breath. He was very particular in the daily reading and understanding of the Holy Qur'an. He encouraged all family members to observe the five daily prayers, to study Hadith, books and other literature of Jama'at Ahmadiyya. Allah had bestowed Maulawi Qudratullah Sahib During his lifetime he had published his autobiography. *Tajalliat-e-Qudrat* for the benefit of future generations.

His special favour of accepting his prayers and many Jama'at members and members of the family of Promised Messiah(as) used to request him for prayers.

Maulawi Qudratullah Sahib had opportunity to perform Hajj twice. First in 1958 along with his wife and again in 1967. Once, during his stay he had the blessing of seeing a vision of the Holy Prophet(saw). After his second Hajj in 1967, he visited England and collected substantial funds for the Fazl-e-Umar Foundation.

On 30th July 1967 Hadhrat Khalifatul Masih III(ru) laid the foundation stone for the building of Mahmood Hall and offices in London. At this occasion, Hadhrat Khalifatul Masih III(ru) invited Hadhrat Chaudhry Muhammad Zafrulla Khan Sahib and Maulawi Qudratullah Sanori sahib to participate in laying the foundation.

After few month's illness on 18th November 1968, he passed away in Karachi, Pakistan and his body was brought to Rabwah. Hadhrat Khalifatul Masih III(ru), led the funeral prayer in which thousands of Ahmadis participated. He was buried at Bahishti Maqbara Rabwah.

(96) **Hadhrat Maulawi Raheemullah of Lahore**

Hadhrat Maulawi Raheemullah Sahib was a very unassuming and quiet man who was steeped in the love of the Holy Qur'an and the Hadith. He travelled extensively in search of the truth which eventually led him to Akhoond Sahib Sawat, who was a famous Sajjada. Nasheen Maulawi Sahib went to him in order to take the Bai'at and requested that his Bai'at be accepted. Akhoond Sahib advised Maulawi Raheemullah Sahib to always keep Akhund Sahib's picture in his mind. On hearing this, he left him saying that this was tantamount to associating partners with God or shirk.

Maulawi Raheemullah Sahib had a great love and affection for the Promised Messiah(as). He used to lead the prayers in a Mosque opposite the Waterworks in Lahore (Pakistan). He was a man of inspiration and was granted visions by God. Maulawi Sahib states: 'I sought divine guidance with regards to the claims of the Promised Messiah(as) by means of Istikhara [a special formal prayer in which divine guidance and help is sought in matters of importance]. I saw a hand carriage descending from sky. From this, I concluded that Messiah had descended from the heavens. As I lifted the curtain and looked inside, I saw the Promised Messiah(as) seated therein and then I took the Bai'at.' Hadhrat Maulawi Sahib was among the first 313 Companions of the Promised Messiah(as).

As far as is known of his family life, Maulawi Raheemullah Sahib had four wives, but nothing is known of his children. He lived mostly in the confines of the mosque. Despite financial hardships, he never used to seek any aid from anyone and did not let his situation become known to others. He was an extremely patient and steadfast person.

(97) **Hadhrat Raisuddin Khan (d.1921)**

Hadhrat Raisuddin Khan was the second person from Bangladesh who had the good fortune to become an Ahmadi. He came from the village Nagar Gaon in district Kishorgan.

When he was employed as a Post Master in Myanmar (Burma), he came into contact with two Ahmadis from the Punjab. Raisuddin Khan Sahib was friendly towards these two even though other people were hostile towards them. As a result of his sincere enquiries into the claims of the Promised Messiah and Imam Mahdi(as), Raisuddin Sahib accepted Ahmadiyyat. He travelled to Qadian in 1906 and took the Bai'at at the hands of the Promised Messiah(as) himself.

Hadhrat Raisuddin Khan Sahib narrated the incident of his clothes getting partly wet while he was travelling on a horseback towards Qadian at a place where he had to pass through water. The Promised Messiah(as) on seeing his wet clothes, was extremely perturbed and repeatedly asked him whether he had hurt himself while travelling on horseback. This display of genuine anxiety for the safety and good health of a visitor made an unforgettable impression on the mind of Raisuddin Khan Sahib about the greatness of the Promised Messiah(as).

Hadhrat Raisuddin Khan actively engaged in preaching Ahmadiyyat and continued to do right until his death in 1921.

(98) **Hadhrat Hafiz Roshun Ali** (b.1883)

Hadhrat Hafiz Roshun Ali Sahib was born in 1883 or 1884. He memorised the Holy Qur'an during his childhood and under the guidance of his teacher Hafiz Ghulam Russeal Sahib Vazirabadi.

In 1900, Roshun Ali Sahib became a student of Hadhrat Maulana Nur-ud-Din Sahib(ra). Roshun Ali sahib had the use of only one eye, which was also weak, but he learnt a great deal simply by listening. He was a very clever and knowledgeable and became recognised among the great scholars of the Jama'at. Roshun Ali Sahib also helped produce many other famous scholars in the Jama'at.

Roshun Ali Sahib memorised a large number of references and thousands of Arabic verses. His voice was very attractive and full of affection. He was humorous and well spoken. He delivered many speeches and held hundreds of debates. His speeches became very popular in Syria. Many times he delivered Dars of the Holy Qur'an, particularly in the month of Ramadan.

Hadhrat Khalifatul-Masih II(ra) used to keep him in his company as a scholar while on a journey and Hafiz Roshun Ali Sahib had the honour of accompanying Hudhur when he visited Europe for the first time. He was very pious and a devotee of Islam and his last will was 'My pupils should always keep preaching'.

Hadhrat Roshun Ali Sahib passed away on 23rd June 1929. On his death, Hadhrat Khalifatul-Masih II(ra) said: 'Hafiz Sahib was the second Maulawi Abdul Karim. Every Ahmadi should look him upon him with great respect and honour. He has done a great service to Islam and his name will not be forgotten as long as this holy mission remains in this world. His death is a great shock to our mission and Islam'.

(99) **Hadhrat Sayyed Munshi Sadiq Hussain Mukhtar** (1857-1949)

Hadhrat Munshi Sayyed Sadiq Hussain Mukhtar, son of Hakeem Sayyed Waarith Ali joined Ahmadiyyat on 11th April 1889 when he was a leading lawyer in his district as well as the whole of the United Provinces of India. He was a great scholar of Urdu, Persian and Arabic. At an early age, he loved to learn and acquire a high grade of efficiency in oriental languages.

Hadhrat Hussain Sahib edited a monthly magazine which contained articles and poems. He also used to attend meetings where a number of poets used to recite their own verses. These meetings were highly regarded and even Nawab Faseeh-ul-Mulk Daagh and the famous poet, Ameer Meenaaee of Lucknow used to send their work to be recited at these meetings and published in the magazine.

Hadhrat Hussain Sahib was indeed like a pillar of Ahmadiyyat at Ataava, Agra, Kaanpur and the other districts of the United Provinces. He was a man who people trusted and often appointed him as their mediator and arbitrator. Scores of people accepted Ahmadiyyat because of his pious character and preaching.

The Anjuman-e-Himaayat Islam had opened a Middle school at Ataava and they used to hold Annual Meetings at which the divines and leaders used to make speeches. Once during a meeting, a discussion was held between the Muslims and the Arya Samaaj. The Muslims elected Hadhrat Hussain Sahib as their President.

Hadhrat Hussain Sahib spent a great deal of his life writing books about the truth of Ahmadiyyat and also preaching. His articles were often published in the monthly magazines such as *Tashheez-ul-Azhan*, *Review of Religions* and the *Daily Al-Fazl*.

Hadhrat Hussain Sahib studied in detail, the views of the Shia sect. Once he faced a very well known scholar of Shias and a written discussion took place between the two. But the Shia scholar Mullah stopped after having written only ten pages.

Hadhrat Hussain Sahib also had a small library of his own in which he had collected quite a few books. Besides the monthly paper, *Subhu Saadiq* and the newspaper, *Izhaar-ul-Haq*, he had written many other books. Some of these were: *Saadiq Kalimaat*, *Izaala-tush-Shakook* (the book contradicting the faith of the Arya Samaaj), *Al-Haq-Delhi*, *Tasdeeq-i-Kalaam-i-Rabbaani* (contradicting the Arya Samaaj), *Mathnavee Piyaam-i-Saadiq*, *Tableeghi Khatoot* and *Samsaam-ul-Haq* (contradicting the views of the Shia – This was a written debate between the Shia and the Sunni in Ataavah), *Tarkeeb-i-Band-Saadiq* (Poem) and *The Tomb of Jesus*.

He passed away on 6th October 1949 at the age of 92 years.

(100) **Sahibzada Mirza Mubarak Ahmad** (1899-1907)

Mirza Mubarak Ahmad was the youngest son of the Promised Messiah(as). He was born on 14th June, 1899. His Aqiqa was fixed on Sunday 25th of June but owing to rain during the night, the morning prayer was performed earlier than usual. After the prayers, everyone in the vicinity of the mosque went to bed again and slept late after sunrise. The Promised Messiah(as) sent for Munshi Nabi Bakhsh of Batala (incharge of ceremonial arrangements) and asked him if everything was well in hand. Nabi Bakbsh was in a fix. Nothing had been done so far. The Promised Messiah(as) thought of the inconvenience of the guests who had been invited for the occasion. But then he suddenly remembered his 14 year old vision in which he was told that he would have a fifth son whose Aqiqa would be performed on Monday. Accordingly the Aqiqa was postponed for a day and was performed on the following day, which was Monday.

Even before Mubarak Ahmad Sahib's birth, the Promised Messiah(as) received a revelation: 'I come down from God and will go back to Him'. In addition to this, there are other visions and revelations in which the Promised Messiah(as) was clearly told that the boy would die young. In the second week of September 1907, Mubarak Ahmad Sahib became ill and his disease caused anxiety. Maulana Hakim Nur-ud-Din(ra) attended him and did his utmost to cure him but to no avail. The boy breathed his last on the morning of 16th September, 1907.

The Promised Messiah(as) bore the loss of his dear son with great dignity and patience. He sat down to write letters to his friends living outside of Qadian that Mubarak Ahmad sahib had died in accordance with the revelation and that he was resigned to the will of God. The boy was buried in the Bahishti Maqbara on the same day.

(Reproduced, with thanks from *In the company of the Promised Messiah*, by Ch. Ali Muhammad, BA, BT.)

(101) **Sardar Abdur Rahman (Mehr Singh)** (1872-1952)

Sardar Abdur Rahman Sahib was born in 1872 at Domeli, State of Kapurthala to a Sikh family and was the youngest of four sons.

Rahman Sahib did not feel at ease with the customs of Sikh and Hindus and their way of life and happened to read *Rasoom-e-Hind* in his school-days. This book mentioned the advent of the Mahdi besides the brief sketch of other faiths prevalent in India. Sardar Abdur Rahman Sahib prayed earnestly to God, requesting for him to be one of the Companions of the Promised Messiah(as). It was this book and his sincere supplications that brought Sardar Abdur Rahman to the ultimate acceptance of Ahmadiyyat.

Rahman Sahib left his home secretly in search of truth at the age of 13 years, leaving his parents and the family in extreme pain and distress. He came across Maulawi Khuda Bakhsh Sahib of Jalandhar who brought him to Qadian in 1890. There he accepted Ahmadiyyat at the hand of the Promised Messiah(as) and became one his early 313 Companions.

The Promised Messiah(as) sent him to Hadhrat Alhaj Maulawi Nur-ud-din Sahib at Jammu, and then at Bhera. He subsequently obtained his B.A and B.T degrees.

Rahman Sahib taught at the Talimul Islam High School in Qadian and then at Madrasa Ahmadiyya. He had the great honour to be the special coach of the children of the Promised Messiah(as) and stayed at Al-Daar (the House of the Promised Messiah(as)) upon his instruction. He used to say in Urdu: 'I have the honour of staying at the house of the Promised Messiah(as)'. The Promised Messiah(as) appointed him the In-charge of security of his house.

Rahman Sahib possessed a few manuscript papers of the book *Kashti-e-Nuh* and some pieces of the clothing of the Promised Messiah(as).

Rahman Sahib was a great preacher. He used to preach to Captain M. W. Douglas during the hearings of a legal case of attempted murder filed by Dr. Martin Clark against the Promised Messiah(as). Later when Captain Douglas was transferred to Andaman as Commissioner, Sardar Abdur Rahman was called there to be the Head teacher of Govt. High School at Port Blair. As a result of his efforts in Andaman, several teachers and people from other professions accepted Ahmadiyyat and a local Jama'at was established.

Rahman Sahib always had religious discussions with followers of other faiths. His preaching and discussions were well known to the Chief Commissioner of Andaman and the Commissioner M. W. Douglas once commented: 'Mr. Abdur Rahman was a zealot to the point of madness.' Hadhrat Khalifatul Masih II(ra) once said: 'If I can get people like Sardar Abdur Rahman I can conquer India.' Due to his piety and nearness to God, Rahman Sahib was provided in abundance for whatever he wished for.

Rahman Sahib wrote around 35 books on various topics, delivered hundreds of lectures on Islamic teachings in India, Sir Lanka and Andaman. He was also imprisoned because he published a pamphlet about the Ahmadiyya claim that stated Hadhrat Baba Guru Nanak Sahib was in fact a Muslim.

Rahman Sahib was one of the members of the first consultative body appointed by Hadhrat Musleh Mau'od(ra) in 1922.

Sardar Rahman Sahib died on 4th June 1952, leaving behind 13 children. He was buried in Bahishti Maqbarah in Rabwah Pakistan.

(102) **Hadhrat Sayed Sardar Ahmad** (1885-1974)

Hadhrat Sayed Sardar Ahmad was born at Lahore in the year 1885. Sardar Ahmad Sahib belonged to Sayyed Abdullah Shah as one of his ancestors who came from Bukhara. He migrated from Gujrat to Dehli and later on to Lahore. King Jahagir allotted him land for the family that was later bought by the Railways of India. However this family is settled at Shah Maskeen and own about hundred acres of agriculture land.

Sardar Ahmad Sahib passed his Matriculation examination when he was fifteen years old. He was employed in the Railway Department and later as a head clerk in the water and irrigation department. He was also well-known Hakeem.

In 1900, during his work holidays, Sardar Ahmad Sahib visited Qadian to see the Promised Messiah(as) who was so renowned for his services to Islam and claims of Messiahship. He came to the Mubarak Mosque at Qadian and soon after his arrival, the Promised Messiah(as) also came and his eyes were focused on him. He also reciprocated and saw the Promised Messiah(as). This situation created such a wonderful emotional and spiritual charge that gave Sardar Ahmad Sahib a sense of peace and contentment within the presence of the Promised Messiah(as) that he became convinced of the truth of his claim. Sardar Sahib joined the fold of Ahmadiyyat the same evening and left Qadian after two days. His mother and the rest of his family never knew about his visit to Qadian.

After Bai'at, Sardar Ahmad Sahib was a totally changed person. His practice and actions showed a complete spiritual advancement. When his mother, grandmother and relatives came to know about his initiation, they strongly opposed his decision. As he was knowledgeable in the Qur'an and Hadith, the opposition had little effect on him and he was able to convince his mother of the truth of Ahmadiyyat and she too joined the Jama'at and remained a loyal member till her death in 1970 in Lahore.

Sardar Ahmad Sahib was a great preacher and defender of Ahmadiyyat. While preaching, he was beaten up several times and persecuted in different ways. He never tolerated any insulting language against the Promised Messiah(as). The Promised Messiah(as) advised him to visit Qadian regularly with prolonged stays where the Promised Messiah(as) always treated him with special affection and love. This was a great honour for him.

Sardar Ahmad Sahib was blessed with three sons, Noor Muhammad, Mukhtar Ahmad and Sultan Muhammad Shahid of T.I College Rabwah and two daughters Amtul Hafeez-Amtul Rashid and Zubdedah Begum.

Sarwar Ahmad Sahib was a great

devotee to Islam and Ahmadiyyat. Once Sheik Abdul Qadir Sahib attended a Conference in Maskeen Shah and from there he left for Sharqpur, 8 miles away to attend another meeting. Sarwar Ahmad Sahib accompanied him (he was 83 years old at that time) and reached the destination walking together with Sheik Sahib. This shows his respect for guests and devotion for Ahmadiyya activities. He passed away in June 1974 at the age of ninety.

(103) **Hadhrat Maulana Syed Muhammad Sarwar Shah**

Hadhrat Maulana Syed Mohammad Sarwar Shah Sahib was the eldest son of Hadhrat Syed Muhammad Hassan Shah Sahib. He was from among the descendants of Hadhrat Syed Abdul Qadir Jilani. Hadhrat Maulana Sarwar Shah Sahib was the Khatib (one who delivers the sermons usually at congregational prayers) of the main Jamia Mosque at Abbottabad (now in Pakistan). He was employed as a teacher at the Madrasa (religious school) of the mosque.

During this period, Maulana Sarwar Sahib experienced five visions one after the other. As a result of these visions, he became inclined towards Ahmadiyyat and subsequently convinced of its truth. He expressed his desire to enter the fold of Ahmadiyyat to Babu Ghulam Mohiyyuddin, his Ahmadi friend based in Abbottabad. who advised him not to take the Bai'at (oath of Allegiance) immediately, as the people of the area were not familiar with Ahmadiyyat and would become very hostile. Maulana Sarwar Sahib did not agree with this advice and felt it was time to write to the Promised Messiah(as). He wrote:

> 'There is no doubt that my proclamation of Ahmadiyyat will be met with great opposition by the people and I will be relieved of my employment. However, rather than being fired, I would prefer to tender my resignation from this job and then declare my faith. Ahmadi friends have advised me to delay my remit for two or three months, but I feel that now that God has manifested the truth for me, I should take the Bai'at.'

The Promised Messiah(as) replied through his revered disciple, Hadhrat Maulawi Abdul Karim Sahib (may Allah be pleased with him):

> 'The advice of the brother Ahmadi is not correct. Because one's own soul has a greater claim on oneself than on others, therefore you should proclaim the Ba'iat immediately. Furthermore, the idea of resigning from the job is not right. The verdict of the Shariat is to remain standing where God has placed one. If in contrast to this one rejects whatever provision God has provided, then God will say that since you rejected my bounty, therefore now you provide for yourself. If however one is forced out of ones provision for the sake of God ,then He is sufficient for His servant.'

Maulana Sarwar Sahib received this letter in the mosque after Zuhr prayer. After having read it, he immediately stood up and declared: 'I have received the letter of acceptance of my Ba'iat from Qadian and from this day I am an Ahmadi.' After this, there was uproar and opposition throughout the town. Maulana Sarwar Sahib was relieved of his duties by the employing authority after which he decided to leave and settle in Qadian. In the meantime, he received a letter from Padri Ziauddin of Peshawar. In this letter, the Padri had informed Maulana Sarwar Sahib of an opening at an Arabic school in the Christian Missionary College in the North West Frontier Province and that the Chief Officer of the Missions, Padri Day had asked him for a suitable person. Padri Ziauddin wrote that because of his old acquaintance, he had recommended Maulana Sarwar Sahib for the said post and that Padri Day had agreed to the appointment. He therefore asked Maulana Sarwar Sahib to reach Peshawar as soon as possible to assume his new duties. Maulana Sarwar Sahib complied with this request and was appointed Professor of Arabic at Edward College Peshawar on a monthly salary of 180 Rupees as against Rs. 25 that he was earning before. He spent two and a half years at Peshawar before migrating to Qadian in 1901 on the instructions of the Promised Messiah(as).

In 1902, Maulana Sarwar Sahib was sent by Promised Messiah(as) along with Maulana Abdullah Sahib to hold a debate in a small village of Mudd where there was severe opposition to Ahmadiyyat. Both of these disciples conducted a successful debate with Maulawi Sanaullah Sahib of Amritsar.

On their return, they reported the successful proceedings to the Promised Messiah(as) who composed an epic poem in fluent Arabic and named it 'Aijaz e Ahmadi' (Miracle of Ahmed). In this poem, he mentions the names Hadhrat Maulawi Sarwar Shah Sahib and Hadhrat Mian Muhammad Yousuf Sahib in the following couplets:

> 'And Sanaullah was chosen from amongst his people while we were represented by Sarwar (i.e. Maulana Sarwar Shah sahib) – The place of the debate was like an arena in which on one side the Wolf yelled while on the other side the Lion roared.'

In the second couplet, the Promised Messiah(as) has referred to Maulana Sarwar Sahib as the Lion.

Maulana Sarwar Sahib served as Superintendent and Headmaster of Madrasa-e-Ahmadiyya and Principal of Jamia Ahmadiyya. He was appointed Mufti of the Jama'at and also had the honour to be the teacher of Hadhrat Musleh Mau'od(ra). During the absence or illness of Hadhrat Musleh Mau'od(ra), Maulana Sarwar Sahib used to officiate as Imam, Khatib and as the local Amir. He was also an excellent commentator of the Holy Qur'an. His commentary of the Holy Qur'an was serialised in the journal, *Talim ul Islam*, during the lifetime of the Promised Messiah(as).

Throughout his life, Maulana Sarwar Sahib was very strict in the observance of the daily prayers in congregation. He used to be in the first row, immediately behind the Imam, of Masjid Mubarak in each prayer and would also attend Majlis-e Irfan of Hadhrat Musleh Mau'od(ra) without fail.

Once, while delivering a sermon in the Aqsa Mosque in Qadian, Maulana Sarwar Sahib, speaking with great emotion declared: 'Listen carefully and reflect – By God, the gist of whatever I have learnt in the service of the Promised Messiah(as) is that congregational prayer is obligatory and that without a valid reason individual prayer is not accepted.'

Maulana Sarwar Sahib had a phenomenal memory and even in his old age, he had a vivid recollection of his childhood days. He used to be a very loving teacher and used to advise his students to study those lessons before hand which were going to be taught next.

Maulana Sarwar Sahib passed away in June 1947. On this occasion Hadhrat Khalifatul Masih II(ra) made the following remarks:

'In those days (i.e. during the early days in the life of the Promised Messiah(as)) there was no one who had a philosophical and logical intellect. God then guided Maulawi Sahib Muhammad Sarwar Shah Sahib and he believed in the Promised Messiah(as). After that he was appointed Professor at Peshawar but after a while the love of Qadian prevailed and he moved to Qadian and took the Bai'at at the hand of the Promised Messiah(as). The Promised Messiah(as) said to Maulawi Sahib: "You should remain here (in Qadian)," and so he remained there. Some people stressed the fact that Maulawi Sahib's position as a Professor in a college could be useful to the Movement and could be a source of preaching, so Hadhrat Sahib permitted him to return, but shortly after that Maulawi Sahib returned with the permission of the Promised Messiah(as) and settled permanently in Qadian. During the lifetime of the Promised Messiah(as), his Debate of Mudd is well known, at that time Maulawi Sahib used to teach in Madrasa Ahmadiyya. He left his Professorship at Peshawar to become a Schoolmaster, for a paltry sum of Rs.15.00 per month. I also used to study at school in those days and for a while he also taught me. The supervision of such a learned scholar was invaluable for the young scholars of the Jama'at, who were looked after by him....Our Jama'at can only become a dominant intellectual force if we have such brilliant scholars (as

Maulawi Sahib). So I pray to God Almighty that he may never let us be humiliated in any company and may our scholars progress both intellectually and in practice and may they dominate the world.'

(Daily Al-Fazl 13th. June 1947.) (Monthly Ansarullah Rabwah, Vol 22, Number 12 December 1981).

This article has been extracted from a speech given by Maulana Chiragh Din Sahib, Murabbi of the Ahmadiyyah Muslim Association in the Ansarullah's Ijtimah held in 1980.

(104) **Hadhrat Chaudhary Sharif Advocate** (1894-1966)

Chaudhary Muhammad Sharif had the privilege to become a companion of the Promised Messiah(as) in 1906 when he was initiated into Ahmadiyyat at the age of 12 at the hands of the Promised Messiah(as). Since his childhood, Chaudhary Muhammad Sharif believed in truth and reality. Due to this feeling, he joined Ahmadiyyat even before his father, Chaudhary Nawab Din. Ahmadiyyat was introduced into the family by Chaudhary Sharif Sahib's uncle, Chaudhary Muhammad Hussain.

Chaudhary Sahib was a kind and sincere person. He belonged to a prosperous family and always gave preference to Jama'at duties. When Hadhrat Khalifatul Masih II(ra) visited London to attend the Wembley Conference, Chaudhary Sahib accompanied the entourage at his own expenses. Apart from being a good-natured person, Chaudhary Sahib had a charismatic appearance. A lot of poor people used to come to him for assistance and he did his best to see that the authorities could hear their voice.

Chaudhary Sahib was the Amir of Montgomery (Sahiwal) for a long time. He spent most of his time reading the literature of the Jama'at and was a regular speaker at the Annual Ansarullah Conference. One could not believe by his habits and leading a life strictly according to the tenets of Islam that by profession, he was a lawyer. The lawyers Association of Montgomery had great regard and respect for him.

Chaudhary Sahib passed away on 7th November 1966 at the age of 72. Hadhrat Khalifatul Masih III(ru) led his funeral prayer on 8th November 1966 and he was buried in the special enclosure reserved for the Companions of the Promised Messiah(as). Chaudhary Sahib left behind four daughters and three sons.

(105) **Hafiz Sufi Ghulam Muhammad, B.A.**

Sufi Ghulam Muhammad's father, Wali Muhammad of Lyallpur district, passed away when Sufi Sahib was a young boy. Chaudhari Rustum Ali Khan, a kind hearted man and a devotee of the Promised Messiah(as), took the boy under his care and sent him to Qadian for studies where Sufi Sahib passed his Entrance Examination and later joined the Talim-ul-Islam College, Qadian and passed his F.A. Examination. He then joined the Aligarh College in 1907.

Sufi Ghulam Sahib was an eyewitness to the sign of the earthquake and rain occurrence on 28th February 1907 as predicted by the Promised Messiah(as). In the morning, the sky was clear and there was apparently no sign of clouds. However, a severe earthquake shock was felt about midday followed by a shower of rain.

On his return to Qadian, Sufi Ghulam Sahib was posted in the Accountant's Office but was soon transferred to the T.I. High School Qadian as an Arabic and Theology teacher. He was deeply devoted to the study of the Holy Qur'an, which he recited melodiously following the style of Maulawi Abdul Karim of Sialkot. He could point out any reference of a verse of the Holy Qur'an from the style of the verse in question as every Sura (chapter) has a style of its own, Sufi Ghulam Muhammad argued.

The style of the diction of the Holy Qur'an is such as makes it easy to be memorised in a short time. Hadhrat Khalifatul-Masih II(ra) in his *Introduction to the Holy Qur'an* refers to three members of the Ahmadiyya Community who learnt the Holy Qur'an by heart in the later part of their lives in a very short period of time. These were:

(1) Sufi Ghulam Muhammad.
(2) Chaudhri Nasrullah Khan pleader.
(3) Dr. Badr-ud-Din, M.B.B.S.

The Promised Messiah(as) proposed the marriage of Sufi Ghulam Sahib with the young widowed daughter of Maulawi Shadi Khan of Sialkot and himself fixed the sum of Rs. 500 as the dowry. She bore him four sons and a daughter.

Hadhrat Khalifatul-Masih(ra) sent Sufi Sahib as an Ahmadiyya Missionary of Islam to Mauritius where he remained for 12 years. During this period, the foundations of the Movement were firmly laid in the Island. In a court case over the Ahmadiyya Mosque, Sufi Ghulam Sahib, very effectively, pleaded the cause of the Movement.

After a brilliant record of missionary work in Mauritius, Sufi Ghulam Sahib returned to Qadian. He led prayers in the Dur-ur-Rahmat Mosque till the partition of the country when he migrated to Lahore where he breathed his last on 12th October, 1947. His body was brought to Rabwah where he was buried in the Bahishti Maqbara.

(108) **Sufi Nabi Bakhsh of Lahore (1863-1944)**

Sufi Nabi Bakhsh was born at Sarai Alamgir, Gujrat District in the 1863 and received his education in Rawalpindi. He passed his Middle School Examination from the American Mission High School in 1881 and his Entrance (Metric) Examination in 1883.

Sufi Bakhsh Sahib of Lahore was a Surai Bansi Rajput of Kashmir. His grandfather, Raja Fateh Singh embraced Islam of his own free will and called himself Raja Fateh Khan. His father Samund Singh was named Samad Khan.

It is related that a week after Sufi Bakhsh Sahib's birth, his mother took him to a spiritual leader at Rohtas District, Jhelum and asked him to give a suitable Muslim name to the boy. The holy man looked at the boy and said that he would witness the advent and time of a prophet and named him Nabi Bakhsh. In 1886, when the fame of Hadhrat Mirza Ghulam Ahmad(as) of Qadian also reached the ears of Sufi Nabi Bakhsh, he paid his first visit to Qadian. He offered his evening prayer with Hadhrat Promised Messiah(as) and had a talk with him. He developed closer contact with the Reformer of the age and received invitation from the Promised Messiah(as) to attend the Ahmadiyya Conference in the last week of December 1891. Sufi Nabi Bakhsh formally joined the Ahmadiyya Movement the same year.

Sufi Bakhsh Sahib often talked boldly and fearlessly to his Bible teacher who spoke against Islam in the classroom. When Sufi Bakhsh Sahib passed his Examination with credit, his headmaster did not recommend him for a stipend at the college, depriving him a chance to receive higher education. However, Sufi Bakhsh Sahib contented himself with a job at the office of the Kalka-Simla Railway. When Sufi Bakhsh Sahib was a railway employee in Lahore, he also worked as honorary manager of the Anjuman Himayat-e-Islam, Book Depots Lahore, (from 1889 to 1892).

Pandit Lekh Ram, a leader of the Arya Samaj and author of the *Takzib Barahin-e-Ahmadiyya* was an arch-enemy of Islam and of the Holy Prophet (peace and blessings of Allah be upon him). He lived in Lahore inside the Shah Alami Gate and Sufi Bakhsh Sahib often had discussions with him at his house. When Pandit Lekh Ram was murdered on 6th March 1897, by an unknown assailant in accordance with a prophecy of the Promised Messiah(as), the police on suspicion arrested Sufi Bakhsh Sahib. But he was released after the statement of a Bengali Superintendent of the Statistical Branch that Sufi Bakhsh Sahib had been working in the office at the time of Lekh Ram's murder.

When the foundations of the

Minara-tul-Masih at Qadian were being raised, Sufi Bakhsh Sahib contributed a sum of Rs.100 towards the construction fund. For some time, he was Amir Jama'at Ahmadiyya, Shimla.

Sufi Bakhsh Sahib passed away in 1944 at Qadian and was buried in Bahishti Maqbara.

(Reproduced with thanks from, 'In the company of the Promised Messiah(as)'. by Ch. Ali Muhammad, BA. B.T.)

(107) **Maulawi Sayyed Mehdi Hussain** (d.1904)

Nawab Imadul Muluk Sayyed Mehdi Hussain was a very pious person from Lukhnow (India). He was a Barrister-at-Law. He served as Home Secretary and Chief Justice of Hyderabad State. Nawab Sahib was the trustee of Alligarh College and was a great scholar of ancient and modern History. He was a very respectful person amongst Muslim scholars of his age.

When he heard the story of Bishop Lefroy in the newspaper *Pioneer* of Allahabad that how the Promised Messiah(as) defeated this Christian Missionary, he was attracted towards the personality of Hadhrat Promised Messiah(as) and wished to meet him. He reached the conclusion that a person who invited his opponents on such matters, which do not usually happen, and many intelligent and knowledgeable persons come into his fold, must be a great personality by all means. He also read a book about his life written by Maulawi Abdul Karim Sahib. In the meantime, he met with Hadhrat Dr. Khalifa Rashiduddin Sahib, who was an Assistant Surgeon there. He later on presented himself to the Promised Messiah(as) at Qadian on 26 December 1901. He heard from the Promised Messiah(as: 'I am appointed to bring the victory of Islam on all other religions.' On hearing the Promised Messiah's instructions, his mind cleared from all doubts.

Hadhrat Pir Sirajul Haq Sahib narrated that Syed Abdullah Sahib Bughdadi asked Nawab Sahib, his impressions of the Promised Messiah(as). He answered in Arabic that the Promised Messiah(as) has a resemblance of Prophets and there is no doubt that his work is also like Prophets. Nawab Sahib left Qadian soon as he had to attend the All India Muhammadan Educational Conference.

After he left Qadian, his loyalty with the Jama'at was on the increase. He always participated in the National Movements. He had great love of the Promised Messiah(as) and *Al-Hakam*. He had a great desire to visit Qadian, and several times sought the opportunity he could not do so. He died on 13th January 1904 at Lukhnow.

(108) **Hafiz Muhammad Ibrahim** (d.1948)

Hafiz Muhammad Ibrahim, son of Nadir Ali, joined the Ahmadiyya Movement in 1899 through the missionary efforts of Sayyed Bahawal Shah. Hafiz Ibrahim belonged to Makhowal, a village near the River Suttlej where it enter the plains.

His father, Nadir Ali sent him three times to visit Qadian but every time he missed the opportunity. One day he had a vision in which he saw the Holy Prophet Muhammad (peace and blessings be upon him). Hafiz Muhammad Ibrahim asked the Holy Prophet(saw) about the truth of the claim to Mahdiship of Hadhrat Mirza Ghulam Ahmad of Qadian. The Holy Prophet(saw) confirmed the truth of his claim. Hafiz Ibrahim again asked the Holy Prophet(saw) to declare on oath that Mirza Sahib(as) was right in his claim of Mahdi and Messiah. The Holy Prophet(saw) replied that he needed no swearing as he was The Amin (Honest) on earth and in the heavens.

The following morning Hafiz Sahib wrote a letter of allegiance to the Promised Messiah(as) at Qadian (1899) and the following year he visited Qadian and settled there permanently.

Hafiz Muhammad Ibrahim in his early years had a severe attack of smallpox as a result of which he lost his eyesight. He lost all chances of receiving education but he learnt the Holy Qur'an by heart with translation and commentary. He had a strong memory and he remembered thoroughly well whatever he heard.

Hadhrat Khalifatul Masih II(ra) appointed Hafiz Sahib Imam of the Mosque Dar-ul-Fazal. He regularly and diligently performed his duty till the partition of India in 1947. He migrated to Pakistan and settled in Gujranwala. He died there on March 29, 1948 but his body could not be brought to Rabwah for burial in the Bahishti Maqbara.

Hafiz Muhammad Ibrahim related a number of anecdotes from the life of the Promised Messiah and Mahdi (Peace be upon him), which are contained in the pages of the *Al-Hakam*, 1935. Once Hafiz Sahib saw a vision that the Promised Messiah(as) had a close resemblance with Imam Muhammad Baqar of the Shia group of Muslims. He related his dream to the Promised Messiah(as) himself who remarked that Baqar means one who tills the land to sow seeds in it. Baqar, in Arabic, means the cow that ploughs the land. We also plough the land (land of heart) for sowing seeds in it, just as Imam Baqar did.

Hafiz Muhammad Ibrahim had no means of income. He received a meagre amount of stipend from the Sadr Anjuman-e-Ahmadiyya, Qadian. But he contributed something, however small it might be, towards the propagation fund.

(109) **Hadhrat Sayyed Willayet Shah** (d.1948)

Hadhrat Sayyed Willayet Shah Sahib was born in 1890 and joined the fold of Ahmadiyyat in 1903. He was a very devoted Companion of the Promised Messiah(as) and had dedicated his life for the Jama'at. He was a Moosi as well. He died at the age of seventy-three and was buried in the Bahishti Maqbara in Rabwah. He left behind a son Sayyed Mohammad Amin Shah who is serving as a local Missionary. Sayyed Mooin Shah is one of his grandsons and Dr. Sultan Mehmood Sahib – (Professor in T.I-College Rabwah) is one of his nephews.

Willayet Sahib had great love for the Holy Prophet(saw) and the Promised Messiah(as) and was an obedient follower of Khilafat. He had a very convincing way of talking and always helped the poor and needy. His piety was so well recognised that even the government officials would ask him to mediate in disputes.

Shah Maskeen was well known place for worship of the Great Saints. Every year the followers of those saints held the gathering, which was attended by thousand of their followers. They used to exercise many objectionable actions, which were opposed by Willayet Sahib.

Once a Maulawi of the area ordered the people for a complete boycott. The shopkeepers stopped selling to Ahmadies, people always mocked at him and he was expelled by force from the mosque. He faced all these problems with steadfastness until many people of Shah Maskeen became Ahmadies within a few years. His character, piety and zeal for preaching was blessed with sweet fruits.

In 1939, Willayet Sahib dedicated himself for Tabligh for one month. He preached effectively in district Gurdaspur and earned a Certificate from the Headquarters. He actively took part in Tahrik-a-Jadid and made contributions on behalf of the Holy Prophet(saw) and Promised Messiah(as). Willayet Sahib took his son to Qadian in 1946 and offered him to Hadhrat Khalifatul Masih II(as) who had asked the Ahmadies to dedicate themselves far the noble job of local preaching.

In 1947, many Ahmadies had migrated to Lahore due to partition and Hudhur instructed local Ahmadies to help them to settle. Hadhrat Willayet Sahib obeyed the orders and he settled nearly 114 people at Shah Maskeen. Some of them settled permanently and acquired land while others left for better places when an opportunity came. His hard work, dedication to duty, piety, character and good habits made him a popular and successful worker for any duty that he was assigned. His officers always praised him for his tireless efforts.

Once an opponent had a religion

debate with Ahmadies. One of the conditions the Maulawi put forward was that Hadith would be given preference over Qur'an. Willayet Sahib immediately declined to accept this and stated that Qur'an shall be accepted superior to Hadith as it represented the Word of Allah. This debate was cancelled. This shows his firm faith in God and respect for religion principals.

Once he had to visit a Jama'at and he asked his son to take him to the station on his bicycle. When they were a few miles away from the station, his son said that the time for the departure of the train has already passed. Willayet Sahib told him that he was going on God's mission so keep on going. On arrival at the station they were informed that the train had been running late by an hour. This is a simple example of his confidence in Allah.

Hadhrat Willayet Shah Sahib was simple and pious person. He always tried to excel others in goodness. Being a true follower of Islam he tried his best to defend his faith and severed humanity in the best possible manner with kindness and love for others.

One day before his death, he announced in the presence of some people that he believed in the finality of Hadhrat Prophet Muhammed(saw) and that Hadhrat Mirza Ghlam Ahmad(as) was the true Mahdi and Messiah of Allah. He said: 'I am a Muslim and believe the creed (Kalima) of Islam.'

(110) **Hadhrat Doctor Wilayat Shah (1886-1965)**

Dr. Wilayat Shah was born on 11 December 1886 in Miranpindi, District Sialkot, Pakistan. After learning to read the Holy Qur'an in his village mosque and receiving elementary education in a neighbouring rural school, he joined the American Mission High School in Sialkot Town, from where he matriculated in first division in 1903.

Dr Shah Sahib had heard from his father that Mirza Ghulam Ahmad Sahib[(as)] of Qadian claimed to be the Imam Mahdi. So he considered his stay in Sialkot a suitable opportunity to investigate about his claim. Because the Promised Messiah's opponents had spread strange stories about him, it was inconceivable that Dr Shah Sahib would embrace Ahmadiyyat. However, Allah of His grace and Mercy created some favourable circumstances that helped Shah Sahib in his quest for the truth.

It so happened that one day he was standing in the forecourt of his living room when he noticed a procession carrying bodies of victims who died of plague for cremation or burial. He thought that he might also fall a victim to the plague and thought what answer he could give if he were asked on the day of Judgement about his proficiency on reciting the Holy Qur'an since he had neglected the regular reading of it after early childhood. He now wondered where he should go to revise his reading of the Holy Qur'an. He soon learnt that the only place in the whole town where 'Dars' of the Holy Qur'an was given was in the house of Mir Hamid Shah Sahib, an Ahmadi dignitary.

After listening for a few days to the recitation of the text and the commentary as given by Mir Sahib, all his doubts and misgivings about Ahmadiyyat were dispelled. So, in 1899 he was fully convinced of the truth of Hadhrat Mirza Sahib's claim of Messiah and Mahdi. A postcard was sent on his behalf of his allegiances addressed to Hadhrat Promised Messiah[(as)]. Soon his Bai'at was accepted.

For his employment, the Postal Administration invited Shah Sahib to Baluchistan. Pending the availability of a permanent post, he took up a teaching job in Barkhan. There he stayed in the house of Dr. Sayyed Saadat Ali, in-charge of the local dispensary who was also from Sialkot. At his persistent persuasion, Shah Sahib finally decided to be trained as a doctor and in 1906 he left for Lahore in order to join the Medical School there.

Principal Perry told him that though admission to the civilian class was closed, he would grant him admission to the military class. Within those months of his having started medical studies, students of the third year class started a strike in protest against some complaints, and pressed the newcomers to join them in the strike. Thereupon, accompanied by Sheikh Abdul Hakeem, a fellow Ahmadi student, Shah Sahib went to Qadian in order to seek the Promised Messiah's(as) instructions. The Promised Messiah(as) said to them that he regarded strike as a rebellion and directed them straightaway to go back to their school and resume their studies, which they did.

Shah Sahib successfully completed his Sub-Assistant Surgeon's course in 1910, and after spells of duty in the Medical Department of the Army, consecutively in Abbotabad, Chitral, and Sialkot, he was directed to go to Kenya. He served at Kisumu, Kericho, Fost Hall, Nyeri, Nakuru, Nairobi, Malindi, and Kajiado in various positions and was promoted to the rank of Assistant Surgeon in 1940. He retired from government service in July 1945 on pension. His work in his certificate of service was commended as excellent.

In September 1945, he went on pilgrimage to Makkah, and also visited the tomb of the Holy Prophet(saw) of Islam in Madinah.

Dr. Shah Sahib married Ameer Begum, daughter of Peer Rasul Shah in 1908 and was blessed with five boys and three daughters. People would ask him how he would raise such a large family and educate them properly. He would reply that he had great trust in God, The Provider.

Because he had gone to East Africa in the early days of the British rule, the educational facilities for children of expatriate staff were non-existent, particularly in those remote places where he was generally posted. So he coached all his sons and daughters himself at home up to the primary education level, and then got them formally admitted to the T.I. High School, Qadian, as boarders. After passing their matriculation examinations, they went to colleges elsewhere in India to complete their higher education. Their parents had the satisfaction and joy of seeing all of them become suitably educated to fairly high grades in their respective fields, some of them serving in responsible positions at the same time in the branch Jama'ats of the Ahmadiyya Community. After retiring from service, Dr Shah Sahib decided to settle in Nairobi and started his private practice there.

Except for his mother who pledged her allegiance to Ahmadiyyat on the hand of Hadhrat Khalifatul Masih II(ra) and then remained steadfast until her death in 1924, his remaining close relatives did not join the fold of Ahmadiyya for fear of kinsman.

After the death of his mother, Dr Shah Sahib stopped visiting his ancestral village, but he extended due hospitality to those who cared to visit him in Qadian, where he had built two houses and used to spend his vacation leave. During his stay there, he treated the needy people of Qadian free of charge.

Dr Shah Sahib was a sincere person who meticulously fulfilled all the requirements of a good Ahmadi, including the saying of Tahajjud prayers and took part in all schemes announced by Hadhrat Khalifatul Masih.

He led a very disciplined life and observed fixed hours for all the routines. That was one of the secrets of his long life. Although he could afford transport of his own, he found it more purposeful to walk. Following his retirement, and for the sake of exercise, he would dig up bricks with which the compound of his house was paved and he would then re-lay them carefully. This was in conformity with the Persian adage: 'Do not sit idle; if you have nothing else to do, un-stitch your clothes and then stitch them again'.

Dr Shah Sahib paid all his dues and subscriptions punctually never falling into arrears. He was a Moosi and gradually raised the rate of his subscription from 1/10th to 1/4th of his income, and the estate he would leave behind. He used to donate money to such individuals and organisations as were engaged in religious or charitable works and to those who approached him for help.

In mid November 1965, Dr. Shah Sahib had a second and more severe attack of paralysis, and had to be admitted to hospital. But in spite of three days of intensive treatment, he passed away on the 25th November 1965. He was buried in the exclusive section of the Ahmadiyya Cemetery in Nairobi, reserved for Moosis. A commemorative plaque was put up for him in the Bahishti Maqbara Qadian.

(111) **Sheikh Yaqub Ali Turab, Irfani** (1875-1957)

Sheikh Yaqub Ali Turab, editor of the publication, *Al-Hakam*, in Qadian was one of the most well-known and leading personalities of the Ahmadiyya Community. He was a pioneer historian, speaker, writer and author. The Promised Messiah(as) once remarked that *Al-Hakam* and *Badr* (two weekly papers of the Ahmadiyya Movement) were his two arms which had done yeoman's service for the cause of the movement.

Sheikh Yaqub Ali Turab (afterwards Irfani) Sahib was born in 1875 at Jadla, a village in the Jullundhar district of the Punjab. Yaqub Ali made his first acquaintance with Maulawi Mohammad Ibrahim of Baqapur who was also a fellow learner of Urdu and Persian with him at Ludhiana.

The Promised Messiah(as) once visited Ludhihana under a divine call to invite people to pledge at his hand and lead pure and holy lives in strict conformity with the directives of the Qur'an and Hadith. Sheikh Yaqub Ali also heard the Divine call and young as he was, decided to join the Movement. Ever since Ali Sahib dedicated his life for the sake of Islam, he decided to take to journalism as his profession and as a means to serve the Movement and the country. The cardinal point of the policy of the *Al-Hakam* had been the propagation of Islam as enunciated by Hadhrat Mirza Ghulam Ahmad of Qadian, the Promised Messiah(as) and Mahdi. The first issue was published on October 8, 1897 from Amritsar. The annual subscription was RS.6.

The editor decided to shift its publication from Qadian so that the diary of the Promised Messiah(as) could be regularly and systematically published in the columns of the *Al-Hakam* for the benefits of its readers. The first number of the second volume of *Al-Hakam* was, therefore published from Qadian on February 20, 1898. As for his literary attainments, it is suffice to say that he was the author of no less than fifteen books including:

1. *The Haqiqat-e-Namaz* – about philosophy of worship

2. *The Maktubat-Ahmadiyya , vol. 1, 2, 3, 4, 5.* – Some letters of the Promised Messiah(as).

3. *The Hayat-un-Nabi vol. I, 2.*– about early life of the Promised Messiah(as).

4. *Hayat-i-Ahmad vol.1, 2.*– Biography of the Promised Messiah(as).

5. *The Visions and Revelations of the Promised Messiah(as).*
6. *The Hayat-e-Nasir*

7. *The Tafsir-ul-Qur'an* – specifically

answering the objection of abrogation of verses.

Sheikh Irfani's adventurous spirit urged him to undertake a tour of the Arab lands. The occasions came when he was invited by Hadhrat Khalifa-tul-Masih II(ra) to accompany him to the Wembley Conference, London in 1924. Sheikh Sahib availed himself of this opportunity. In the following year (1925), he again, set out on his journey to Egypt and Europe. His experiences are recorded in a book, *Mushahidat-e-Irfani*.

After Ali Turhab Sahib's return from the West, family circumstances took a serious turn and Mr. Irfani was obliged to spend the rest of his life in Hyderabad State. There he proved to be a great asset to the Ahmadiyya Community of Secunderabad. He developed close friendship with Seth Abdullah, Allah Din of Secunderabad who was brought into the fold of Ahmadiyyat by him.

After the partition of India, Sheikh Irfani paid a visit to Rabwah, new Headquarters of the Ahmadiyya Movement in Pakistan in 1954. He died in Secunderabad on December 5, 1957 and was buried in the Bahishti Maqbara, Qadian.

(112) **Hadhrat Munshi Zafar Ahmad**

Hadhrat Munshi Zafar Ahmad belonged to the Jama'at of Kapoorthala. His father's name was Mushtaq Ahmad alias Mohammad Ibrahim who belonged to a Small town of Budhana in the District of Muzaffar Nagar in the United Provinces of India. One of his uncles, Hafiz Ahmadullah, was a Tehsildar (Revenue Officer) in the town of Sultanpur of Kapoorthala state. He had no child of his own. Therefore, he adopted Munshi Zafar Muhammad as his son and had great regard and love for him. At the age of 20 he got a job of a Scribe in one of the Kapoonhala courts and was very happy with his new appointment.

Munshi Zafar Ahmad obtained his early education in Urdu, Persian and studied some other books in local madrasa. The word 'Munshi' was attached to his name because he could read and write. In fact he was a very learned man.

After the completion of his education, Munshi Sahib once went to the Court of a Tehsildar where someone presented a script in ornamental style. No one in the court was able to decipher that script. As Munshi Sahib had completed his education quite recently, he deciphered it without any difficulty. Everyone, including the Tesildar was very much impressed with his skill and knowledge.

Haji Waliullah was the Sessions Judge at Kapoorthala and Munshi Sahib used to read to him, *Baraheen-e-Ahmadiyya*, the pioneer and celebrated work of the Promised Messiah(as). The reading of this book generated Munshi Sahib, a deep love for the Promised Messiah(as).

On one occasion, when the Promised Messiah(as) went to Jallendhar, Munshi Sahib stayed with Munshi Sahib. During one of his addresses there, Munshi Sahib says that he thought saints and pious people could read the inner thoughts of a person. To test this he thought in his mind 'what is the remedy if one cannot concentrate in Salat's'. Munshi Sahib said that on hearing this, the Promised Messiah(as) turned towards him and said a few sentences that precisely answered his inner question. Munshi Sahib was very much amazed and impressed and pleased. He became firm that Hadhrat Mirza Sahib(as) was really a saint.

These loving affections grew deeper. Munshi Sahib requested the Promised Messiah(as) a number of times for accepting his Bai'at, but he replied that he had not yet been permitted, but the Promised Messiah(as) advised him to keep in constant touch and visit him often. As a result of this, Munshi Sahib regularly visited Qadian with his friends, Mohammad Khan and Munshi Aooray Khan. At the end of 1888, the Promised Messiah(as) announced that people could pledge allegiance as he had received permission. Munshi

Sahib pledged his Bai'at at the hand of the Promised Messiah(as) on the first day of Initiation on 23 March 1889.

Munshi Sahib had intense love for the Holy Qur'an and the Holy Prophet(saw). Often his eyes were full of emotion when he talked about the Holy Prophet(saw). During Ramadan, Munshi Sahib prepared notes of the part of the Holy Qur'an to be recited during Taraveeh prayers which he repeated afterward and gave a detailed account of what was mentioned in that part and other scholarly points for those who had come for Taraveeh prayers.

Munshi Sahib was so much fond of visiting Qadian and remaining in the company of the Promised Messiah(as) that he had requested the Promised Messiah(as) to travel with him on journeys. Therefore the Promised Messiah(as) allowed Munshi Sahib to accompany him whenever he was going outside Qadian. When requested, Munshi Sahib used to take leave from the court and reached Qadian without any delay. This was the reason that Munshi Sahib was with the Promised Messiah(as) on most of his journeys. Once the Promised Messiah(as) said: 'that as Jama'at Kapurthala has been with me in this world, they will remain with me in the hereafter also'.

Munshi Sahib was a highly intelligent person and could sense complex situations quickly. In the case of Karam Deen, Munshi Sahib appeared in the court as a defence witness. After the cross examination, the judge asked Munshi Sahib: 'Can you Sacrifice your life and property for Mirza Sahib?' Munshi Sahib immediately sensed the purport of the question. If he replied in the affirmative, the judge could set aside his evidence by declaring it prejudiced. Munshi Sahib promptly replied: 'I have pledged allegiance to safeguard my own life and property'. The judge was deeply impressed by the way of his reply. It meant the same, but objectionable aspect was removed with this intelligent answer.

Once the Promised Messiah(as) was staying at Ludhiana and fortunately Munshi Sahib was also there with him. The Promised Messiah(as) needed sixty rupees for the printing of a leaflet, which he did not have at that time. Promised Messiah(as) said to Munshi Sahib, 'Munshi Sahib, we urgently need sixty rupees. Can Jama'at Kapurthala arrange for this amount?' Munshi Sahib did not say that he will go and try or he does not know until he enquires from the friends there. He promptly said: 'Yes, they will provide the required amount'. Saying this, he right away left for Kapurthala and did not tell the brothers there about it. He went to his wife and her about the urgently needed money.

The faithful wife brought her jewellery and asked her husband if it would raise enough funds the Promised Messiah(as) needed. He sold that jewelery and brought the amount and placed the money at the feet of his beloved master. The Promised Messiah(as) felt very pleased that the amount was available at the right time. Even at that time, Munshi Sahib did not tell the Promised Messiah(as) that it was his wife's jewellery which he had sold for this purpose. That is why Promised Messiah(as) remained under the impression that the money was provided by Jama'at Kapurthala.

After sometime, Munshi Arooray Khan visited the Promised Messiah(as) and on seeing him, the Promised Messiah(as) expressed his appreciation for Kapurthala Jama'at for providing the money at the right time. Munshi Aroora Sahib was very much surprised to hear about it and said that he knew nothing about it. On return to Kapurthala, he asked Munshi Zafar Ahmad why he did not tell them about it. He replied that since it was no a big amount, he sold some ornaments of his wife and presented the amount to the Promised Messiah(as). But Munshi Arooray Khan was not at all happy with the answer and remained crossed with him for many months.

Munshi Munshi Sahib was with the Promised Messiah(as)on the occasion of the debate with Abdullah Atham in 1893. It was he who took the dictation from the Promised Messiah(as) of the papers of the debate as he had a beautiful handwriting and was a fast writer too.

Sheikh Mohammad Ahmad Mazhar was one of his illustrious sons who became one of the star lawyers of Pakistan and a devoted and dedicated member of the Jama'at. He remained Ameer Jama'at Ahmadiyya Faisal Abad Pakistan for over 30 years. He carried out research on the linguistic discovery by the Promised Messiah(as) that Arabic is the mother of all the languages and traced the origin of many languages to Arabic.

(113) **Sir Muhammad Zafrullah Khan** (1893-1985)

Choudhry Sahib was born on 6th February 1893. He was called to the bar by Lincoln's Inn after having obtained a first class Honours' degree in law from King's College, London. He was elected to the Punjab Legislative Council in 1926 and served until 1935 when he was appointed a member of the Governor General's Executive Council till 1941. He then opted to go to the Bench of the Supreme Court of India where he gained the reputation of being the dissenting Judge.

Choudhry Khan Sahib resigned on the eve of Partition and was appointed Foreign Minister of Pakistan by Quaid-e-Azam Jinnab. He held this post with great distinction until 1954 when he was elected a judge of the World Court. He was Vice President of the Court for some years. President Ayub Khan appointed him Permanent Representative of Pakistan at the United Nations and as a special mark of honour, he was elected President of the 1962/63 session of the General Assembly. His presidency was unique in three respects in as much as all the meetings started punctually, no point of orders were ever raised during the entire session and the Assembly completed the agenda for the session in time. In 1964, he returned to the International Court of Justice and retired in 1973. He was President of the Court during the last three years of his tenure. This was, perhaps, the fulfilment of his mother's dream in which it was revealed to her that Zafrulla Khan, son of Nasrulla Khan, will be chief Justice.'

Choudhry Khan Sahib was a gifted and eloquent speaker with an enormous wit. He always presented his case in a lucid and masterful manner. He never lost an appeal during the time that he practised as a lawyer in Lahore High Court. He was chosen by Mr. Jinnah to represent the Muslim League before the Boundary Commission on the Partition of India. His presentation earned him the personal accolade of Mr. Jinnah.

While Foreign Minister, he established Pakistan's reputation in the international field and presented the Kashmir case at the Security Council with his customary eloquence, which endeared him to the Pakistan public. His exposition on the Palestine cause was a godsend for the Arab nations, which earned him their respect and affection to the extent that Jordan, Syria and Egypt bestowed on him their highest civil awards. He worked tirelessly towards the independence of countries under the yoke of colonialism and was instrumental in bringing about the independence of Libya, Morocco, Somalia, and Indonesia etc. King Hasan of Morocco described him as the greatest Muslim of this century.

Choudhry Zafrullah Khan Sahib was blessed with remarkable parents. His father memorised the Holy Qur'an at the age of fifty. His mother who was a deeply religious woman was guided and blessed by Almighty God through dreams. Choudhry Sahib had great love, respect, and obedience towards his parents. He wrote a book about her mother entitled *My Mother* which is a great source of inspiration to all children.

Choudhry Zafrullah Khan exercised extreme exactitude in all spheres of life. He never wasted time, words or money. He was extremely generous and assisted a large number of students whose parents could not afford their education. He always lavishly donated towards appeals launched by the Supreme Heads to the Ahmadiyya. Movement.

He was endowed with a keen intellect and a photographic memory. He was able to describe his first meeting with the Promised Messiah(as) when he was only a young boy very vividly in its minute details. His command of English was perfect and to a great extent he employed his scholarly faculties in writing about Islam and the truth of Ahmadiyyat. He translated the Holy Qur'an into English and wrote many books and articles giving a brilliant exposition of different aspects of Islam.

He spent all his life in public service but regarded the time after his retirement as his happiest. He devoted all his time to the service of Islam. He vas a real servant of God, and happiest when participating in functions of the Ahmadiyya Community. His sermons and speeches were a great source of inspiration, full of wisdom and guidance for the community. He was a true exemplar of what Ahmadiyyat; the true Islam wants us to be like. Once a non-Ahmadi person asked him: 'What would I gain if I become Ahmadi?' Choudhry Sahib replied: 'You would become like me'. This was his high status that he could quote his own self as an example of a true Ahmadi. He was indeed an embodiment of Islamic teachings.

Ch. Zafrulla Khan was truly one of the internationally known figures of the Muslim sub-continent. He had been a trusted lieutenant of the Quaid-i-Azam and it was not strange then that soon after the creation of Pakistan, the Quaid-i-Azam had entrusted him with the task of introducing the new country to the outside world. He performed the onerous responsibilities of the Ambassador-at-large for some time before being sworn in as the country's first Foreign Minister. Much that he was able to chart of the pathway of Pakistan's foreign policy is still being pursued. For all intents and purposes, he could be termed as the architect of Pakistan's foreign policy.

So long Chaudhry Sahib's voice kept on rising from the United Nations' platforms it was listened to with rapt attention and it was-and still is difficult to ignore the biting logic of his arguments, his flair for turn of phrases and highly learned diction which assimilated the best of multifarious disciplines he had come to imbibe in his person. It was perhaps in deference to his international status that he was elected President of the UN General Assembly in 1962-63. In 1954, he became a Judge of the International Court of Justice in which capacity he served till 1961. He was also the vice President of the World Court from 1958 to 1961 and then its President from 1972-73. For the last twelve years he was living as a recluse, devoting most of his time to meditation. He has left to posterity two autobiographies – one in English and the other in Urdu, which throw ample light on his career. Numerous books and article have been written by him including a book about his life by Bashir A Rafiq, Ex-Imam of the London Mosque.

Choudhry Muhammad Zafrulla Khan passed away in Lahore, Pakistan, on the 1st September 1985. He was ninety-two. He was a Companion of the Promised Messiah(as) – the Holy Founder of the Ahmadiyya Movement in Islam. His death has been widely mourned in many countries and the kind of press he has got only proves that he was respected throughout the world. He was buried in Bahishti Maqbara, Rabwah, Pakistan in special enclosure for the Companions of the Promised Messiah(as).

(114) **Hadhrat Muhammad Zahoor Khan**
(1893-1982)

Hadhrat Muhammad Zahoor Sahib went to see Hadhrat Promised Masih(as) with his father in 1905 and remained a staunch and devoted Ahmadi Muslim. He served Ahmadiyyat throughout his life devotedly although he had to face a lot of opposition. He had the blessings to be alive during the four Khilafats.

Hadhrat Muhammad Zahoor Khan Sahib was born in Patala in 1893. He accepted Ahmadiyyat at the age of 12 in 1905, at the hands of Hadhrat Masih Mau'od(as).

He was a Moosi and led a very simple life. He moved to Qadian in 1939 and lived near the Masjid Mubarak. He often stayed in the Mosque doing Zikr-e-Illahi. He used to sit for Itekaf in Ramadan in the local mosque.

Hadhrat Muhammad Zahoor Khan Sahib had an exceptional memory. He was a great lover of the Holy Qur'an and had good recital voice.

In 1947, Zahoor Khan Sahib came to Pakistan and stayed in Lahore and then he moved to Rabwah and brought a house in Ahmad Nagr. He became in-charge of Ahmad Nagr Mosque. He used to teach children the Holy Qur'an and was also in Saff-e-Awwal of Tahrik-e-Jadid.

In 1982, at the age of 89, he had a bad fall and seriously injured his hip and passed away. Hadhrat Mirza Tahir Ahmad(ru), Khalifa-tul-Masih IV said his funeral prayer. He is buried in Bahishti Maqbara in Rabwah

(115) **Qazi Zahoor-Ud-Din Akmal of Goleki** (1881-1966)

Qazi Zahoor-ud-Din was the son of Maulawi Imamud-Din of Goleki, District Gujrat. He was born on March 25 1881 at Goleki in the Hashmite family of Pirzadas. Maulawi Imam-ud-Din Sahib taught his son well in the intricacies of religious philosophy, Islamic principles and practices.

Akmal Sahib was a renowned Urdu poet who contributed his poems to the Urdu dailies and weeklies of the time. He was a proficient journalist well acquainted with his profession and from 1905 onwards he edited various periodicals and newspapers started by the Ahmadiyya Community at Qadian.

In 1913, Hadhrat Sahibzada Mirza Bashir-ud-Din Ahmad(ra) started the *Al-Fazl* of which he was the editor and Qazi Akmal Sahib was responsible for successfully running the paper under his managerial supervision.

Long before the *Al-Fazl* was started, Qazi Akmal Sahib had been the Manager of *Al-Badr* and assisted Hadhrat Mufti Muhammad Sadiq as managing editor. Sahibzada Hadhrat Mirza Bashir-ud-Din Mahmud Ahmad also used his services for the *Tashhiz-ul-Azhan* in 1906.

Qazi Akmal Sahib's poems had been collected into a book called the *Naghma-e-Akmal*. He was the author of a number of works in Urdu. Some of these are: *The Zahoor-ul-Masih*, *The Zahoor-ul-Mehdi* and the *Alwah-ul-Huda*.

Qazi Akmal Sahib had a charming personality. His office room was the meeting-place of friends who visited him from morning till evening. After the partition of Indo-Pakistan, Akmal Sahib migrated to Lahore where he spent some years and later moved to Rabwah, the new Headquarters of the Ahmadiyya Community.

Qazi Akmal Sahib passed away on September 27, 1966 and was buried in the special enclosure reserved for the companions of the Promised Messiah(as) of the Bahishti Maqbara, Rabwah.

(116) **Syed Zainul Abideen Vali-Ullah Shah**
(1989-1967)

Shah Sahib was born on 13 March 1989 in Riaya. He lived with his parents up to the age of 14 when in 1903, his father sent him to Qadian for his education. It was at the age of 14 that Shah Sahib accepted Ahmadiyyat and availed the pious company of the Promised Messiah(as) until 1908.

In 1908, after passing his matriculation examination, Shah Sahib gained admission in Government College Lahore to study F.Sc. according to the wishes of his father. But Hadhrat Khalifatul Masih I(ra) said that he should become his pupil. In accordance with the these instructions, he learnt Arabic, its grammar and literature from Hadhrat Hafiz Rowshun Ali Sahib and Hadhrat Maulawi Muhammad Ismail Sahib Hilalpuri. He also benefited from the commentary (Dars) of Hudhur.

On 26 July 1913, on the instructions of Sahibzada Hadhrat Mirza Bashiruddin Mahmood Ahmad sahib(ra), Khan Sahib and another person set off for Egypt in order to preach and gain Arabic knowledge. Due to various reasons, he could not stay long in Cairo and went to Beirut and then to Halb. He passed his Arabic literature exam in Baitul Muqqaddas.

Khan Sahib obtained his education from highly qualified teachers. Among his teachers were Al-Sheikh Hashmul Sharif of Beirut, Alama Al-Sheikh Bashir Al-Gharabi of Halab (a member of Turkish Parliament) and Al-Sheikh Salehul Rafie Al Trablsi. Shah sahib related: 'I remember every moment of the time when these teachers used to teach me in dark nights, torrential rains, severe cold and sometime even when I felt very sleepy. Many a time they stayed with me till midnight. These teachers used to teach me without any reward because they use to say that they can see some goodness in me.'

His teacher Al-Sheikh Salehul Rafi had a great regard and affection for Shah Sahib. In fact he accepted Ahmadiyyat through Shah Sahib's preaching. He had a photo of Shah Sahib in his house on which he wrote: 'A pupil from the pupils of Hadhrat Mahdi (peace be upon him) who came from India to learn Arabic.'

Many people accepted Ahmadiyyat due to Khan Sahib's preaching. They included a family in Syria and Ameer Jama'at Ahmadiyya Syria. His appointment as a lecturer in a college provided him an opportunity to establish friendship and relationship with highly educated society. He also established very good relations with Mufti-a-Azam and Philistine Ameenul Hussini. Whenever Mufti-a-Azam visited Pakistan, Shah Sahib used to go (under the instructions of Hadhrat Khalifatul Masih II(ra)) to meet him. Mufti-a-Azam also used to give him a lot of respect and affection.

Shah sahib came first in a competition on 'Art of education and teaching' arranged by the Ministry of Education Istanbul. He was awarded a medal and a £50 prize. Then he became vice principal of Sultania College where he was also responsible for teaching of religious knowledge and philosophy. When Shah Sahib used to give the commentary of some difficult portions of the Holy Qur'an, many of his Arabic friends and teachers used to ask him where he learn the meanings. Shah Sahib used to say: 'I have learnt it from Al-Sheikh Nooruddin i.e. Hadhrat Maulawi Nuruddin Khalifatul Masih I(ra).'

In 1919, after the First World War, Shah Sahib returned to India. Initially he was temporarily appointed as Nazir Amoor-e-Ama (while Sahibzada Bashir Ahmad sahib was on holidays). During the period 1920 to 1954 he held positions of Nazir Dawah and Preaching, Nazir Amoore Ama & Kharja, Nazir Education and Training, Temporary Nazir Ala and Additional Nazir Ala. After retiring in 1954, he remained as Nazir Amoore Kharja. During the Indo-Pak partition he had the honour of being kept in prison for the sake of Allah, from 14th September 1947 till May 1948.

In 1924, Hadhrat Khalifatul Masih II(ra) went to Europe to participate in the Wembley Conference. Hudhur nominated Shah sahib along with others as a member of the Majlis Shura. Hudhur praised Shah Sahib in his Friday sermon on 11th July as follows: 'Although Syed Vali-ullah Shah Sahib, who works in Nazarat, is young and have lived in foreign countries where the way of governments is not Islamic but he is very obedient. Anytime he is asked to do something he accepts it without any hesitation.'

Hadhrat Khalifatul Masih II(ra) stayed a few days in Damascus during his visit to Europe in 1924. God accepted his prayers and so many people were inclined towards him that from morning till midnight people used to stand outside the hotel. Most of them showed great respect and love.

After returning from London, Hudhur selected Shah Sahib and Hadhrat Maulawi Jalalud-Deen Sahib Shams as Mujahiddeen and himself came to see them off. The preaching in Arab world was not easy.

A report of Hadhrat Maulana Jalaluddin Sahib Shams describes difficulties encountered in preaching during the war in Syria. In November l925, a religious sect declared independence with the result that the French government bombarded and destroyed Damascus. In April 1926, an Ahmadiyya Jama'at was formed by the Grace of Allah. The preaching was done through writing letters, speeches, and meeting people and through magazines and books with great hardships.

Hadhrat Shah Sahib returned to Qadian on 10 May 1926. He met Hadhrat Khalifatul Masih II(ra) in

Mubarak Mosque and mentioned the details of his preaching and other circumstances. On 17 May, students of Talimul Islam High School invited Shah sahib on a tea party where in his speech, Shah sahib talked about his experiences in Syria and the difficulties in preaching there. Hudhur lead the silent prayer afterwards.

Hadhrat Khalifatul Masih II(ra), praising the missionary work by the two Mujahideens said that Shah sahib had to face such difficulties in the way of preaching about which he never imagined. He had some friends in Syria and so he hoped that with their help he would perform a great task with excellent success. But when he arrived there, the war had started. If just two persons fight with each other, the shops would close and work halted. In view of the difficulties encountered, our Damascus missionaries work is worth of praise. They continued their work of preaching and did not waste their time due to the dangers. In spite of the situation getting very dangerous, they did not say or complained that we were sent for preaching not for fighting in a war and that we should be called back. This is their faithfulness and love for religion and Ahmadiyyat. So preaching in such circumstances is even more courageous and both our missionaries are worthy of praise. The work that they have done could not have been done by many people.

Shah sahib died on 16th May 1967 at the age of 78. Hadhrat Khalifatul Masih III(ru) led the funerals prayer in the ground of Bahishti Maqbara Rabwah and also gave shoulder to the coffin. After burial, Hudhur also prayed on his grave. Many residents from Rabwah and outside attended the funeral. Shah sahib had five daughters and two sons.

Shah sahib remained dedicated throughout his life to the service of Islam and Ahmadiyyat. God gave him the courage and strength to provide excellent service to Jama'at Ahmadiyya in the way of preaching, training and education.

Shah sahib was a very pious person and God accepted his prayers. Many a time, he was given guidance and glad tidings by God. He performed Tahajjud (night prayer) regularly. He loved reciting the Holy Qur'an and had a good knowledge of the books of Hadhrat Masih-e-Maud(as). With the blessings of Hadhrat Masih-e-Maud(as) and the special mention of both Hadhrat Khalifatul Masih I(ra) and II(ra) he was an excellent Arabic translator and writer. He translated *The Philosophy of the Teachings of Islam*, *Kishti Noaha* and *Message of Ahmadiyyat*. Shah sahib wrote a very good book on: *The life and death of Jesus* and a copy of this book was given to Prime Minister of Syria Alsyed Mohsin Albrazi.

(117) **Qazi Zia-Ud-Deen** (1843-1904)

Qazi Zia-ud-Deen was born in 1843 at QaziKot Gujrnwala after the birth of his eleven sisters. God Almighty revealed to his father, Qazi Ghulam Ahmad, that a son shall be born to him who shall be named 'Zia-ud-Deen'.

From his very young age Deen Sahib kept company with very pious people. When he heard that the Promised Messiah(as) had already appeared, he went to see at him in Qadian in the February 1885.

Qazi Zia-ud-Deen took the oath of Initiation in 1889 at the age of forty-six. Both his sons, Hadhrat Qazi Abdul Raheem Bhatti and Qazi Muhammad Abdullah Bhatti are also included in those who were blessed to be among the first 313 Companions of the Promised Messiah(as).

Qazi Zia-ud-Deen used to accompany the Promised Messiah(as) whenever he had to attend his court cases. He was a learned man in Arabic and Persian languages and was considered to be a scholar in the Traditions, in Islamic Law and jurisprudence. He was also a good physician.

Qazi Zia-ud-Deen was very fond of preaching. There were 21 persons from his district who had the good fortune to have their names included in the list containing 313 companions of Promised Messiah(as) and from these 21 people, eleven embraced Ahmadiyyat as a result of his preaching.

In 1901 Qazi Zia-ud-Deen migrated to Qadian from his hometown. The Promised Messiah(as) had himself written to him to come and live at Qadian near him. He gladly obeyed this personal command and he never thought of going back to his own town. There he started the work of binding the books of the Promised Messiah(as).

Qazi Zia-ud-Deen began the habit of offering his Tahajjud prayers at a very young age. He was a man of humble and simple nature.

On 15th May, 1904 when Qazi Zia-ud-Deen passed away at the age of nearly 61 years, God Almighty revealed to the Promised Messiah the message: 'That poor has passed'.

Qazi Zia-ud-Deen was buried in the Muslim graveyard of Qadian and Hadhrat Maulawi Abdul Kareem Sahib led the Janazah Prayer. But when the Promised Messiah(as) came back to Qadian from Gurdaspur, he again offered a funeral prayer for him.

Deen Sahib's grandson, Qazi Abdus Salaam, the writer of this rendering, once wrote to Hadhrat Khalifa-tul-Masih II(ra) that at the time when his grandfather died, the Bahishti Maqbarah had not come into being. If the said Bahishti Maqbarah had been in existence before his grandfather died he would most certainly have arranged for his burial in that graveyard. He requested Hudhur that permission be granted for a remembrance stone to be erected in the Bahishti Maqbara. Accordingly in the year 1953 Hadhrat Maulawi Abdul Rahmann Jutt Sahib erected the said stone.

(118) **Khan Sahib Zulifiqar Ali Khan of Rampur (U.P.)** (d.1866)

Zulifiqar Ali Khan Gauhar, elder brother of the veteran political leaders of India, known as the Ali Brothers, was born in 1866 at Rampur in the U.P. After passing his Matriculation, he joined the Aligarh College and imbibed the spirit of a true nationalist and Aligarhian. He was a born orator and was well known for making extempore speeches.

After leaving the College, Khan Sahib took service in British India. He served as Naib-Tahsildar at Etah, Etawah and Mainpuri in U.P. He rose to be a courtier of the Rampur Durbar and a favourite of His Highness the Nawab of Rampur. He was also a renowned poet of Urdu. A selection of his poems was prepared by Maulawi Abdul Malik Khan, a worthy son of the worthy father.

The Editor of the *Riaz-ul-Akhbar*, Gorakhpur, U.P., published in 1888 a letter of Hadhrat Mirza Ghulam Ahmad(as), the Promised Messiah and Mahdi to Alexander Russel Webb, the American consul at Manila, Philippines, which attracted the attention of Maulawi Zulifiqar Ali Khan Gauhar. Then the publication of the Promised Messiah's(as) work, the *Izala-i-Auham* in 1900 convinced him that the author was a Divinely appointed Messenger whose advent was timely. He at once wrote a letter to the Promised Messiah(as) at Qadian and later visited Qadian in 1903. At Batala, Khan Sahib learnt that the Promised Messiah(as) was at Gurdaspur in connection with a civil suit-filed by Maulawi Karam Din. He proceeded straight to Gurdaspur and met the Promised Messiah(as) there. The Promised Messiah's(as) stay was prolonged by the hostile attitude of the magistrate who happened to be an Arya Samajist.

During the course of his stay at Gurdaspur, the Promised Messiah(as) received a deputation of Benares Muslims with Abdur Razzaq and Abdur Rashid Bakhshi as members. The Promised Messiah(as) explained his viewpoint to the deputation for three days, with the result that the deputation was convinced of the truth of the claim. They took leave of the Promised Messiah(as) and departed for home. During the course of their journey they had the opportunity and freedom to ponder over the affair and draw their own conclusions. But they were all agreed on the point that they must tender their oath of allegiance to the Divine Reformer before they reached their destination. Maulawi Allah Bakhsh mailed a post-card from the railway station, Lucknow, to the address of the Promised Messiah(as) at Qadian together with their Joint oath of allegiance to him.

According to Khan Sahib, on one

occasion, food was served to all the guests at Gurdaspur but nothing was left for the Promised Messiah(as) who desired to have something to eat before going to attend the court. The manager, Maulawi Sayyed Muhammad Sarwar Shah was at his wit's ends. In all haste, he procured a cup of milk, three pieces of toast and some sugar. The Promised Messiah(as) quietly ate the softer parts of two pieces of toast with sugar and left for the court.

Khan Sahib Zulfiqar Ali Khan migrated to Qadian in 1920 where he was given charge of Amoor-e-Ama (public affairs). In 1924, Hadhrat Khalifatul-Masih II(ra) undertook a voyage to England to represent Islam at the Wembley Conference. Khan Zulfiqar Ali Khan Sahib was a prominent member of the entourage that accompanied him to England. Before the partition of India, a Prominent member of the Indian National Congress inquired of Khan Sahib why he did not serve the cause of the liberation of India like his younger brothers (the Ali Brothers). Khan Sahib, curtly, but courteously retorted that the whole world is in the grip of Satan and that the spiritual liberation of the world was more important than the political liberation of India.

Khan Sahib migrated to Lahore after the partition of India and died on 26 February 1954 at the age of 88. His body was brought to Rabwah to be entombed in the Bahishti Maqbara.

(Referenced from: Kalam-e-Gohar By (Ex) Professor Habib Ullah Khan Sahib).

NOTES